Faith that Heals:
Stories of God's Love

Faith that Heals:
Stories of God's Love

Collected and edited by
H. Jane Teas, Ph.D. and
Melinda Holland, M.S.
with Tara Georgianna Jackson

H. Jane Teas, Ph.D.

Produced by SC McAC, Inc. (http://www.scmcac.org) in collaboration with the South Carolina Cancer Center, University of South Carolina, Columbia, South Carolina, USA.

The work described in this book was supported by Cooperative Agreement Number U48/CCU409664: SIP 6-00 from the Centers for Disease Control and Prevention. The contents of this book are solely the responsibility of the authors and do not necessarily represent the official views of the Centers for Disease Control and Prevention.

This book was printed in the United States of America.

To order additional copies of this book, contact:
Xlibris Corporation
1-888-795-4274
www.Xlibris.com
Orders@Xlibris.com
43168

Contents

To my mother, Polly Houston,
who encouraged, inspired, and challenged me
along every step of this faith and healing journey.

Introduction

"They who wait upon the Lord shall mount up with wings as eagles;
they shall run, and not be weary."
Isaiah 40:31

It is not often that God is the subject of a U.S. government research project. However, I have always been fascinated by complementary and alternative medicine, especially by the intersection of belief and health. Long before there was medicine, people turned to God for healing, finding comfort in their faith. When I heard about a major research grant to study complementary and alternative medicine with curative intent, I wrote a proposal outlining how I would study faith and healing. In retrospect, the whole idea of putting God and healing into a tidy box, providing references and indexing people's ideas about God and His actions, seems unthinkable. God and healing are just too vast a concept to fit into any report. Yet, in the beginning, it seemed more straightforward.

The Centers for Disease Control funded this study in 2001 to explore healing and faith. Dr. Deborah A. Jones at the CDC initiated the call for this proposal, Dr. Barbara Ainsworth monitored our progress through the Prevention Research Center at the University of South Carolina, and I received the grant to collect information on what constituted being healed by faith. This study was supported by a cooperative agreement between the United States Centers for Disease Control and Prevention and the Prevention Research Center of the Arnold School of Public Health at the University of South Carolina.

At first I convened a biweekly dinner and conversation forum and created a project team to do the work. At our opening dinner, where members of the academic and faith community gathered to discuss complementary and alternative medicine, Andrew Cousins appeared. I asked him why he was there, and he said that he felt like he should be there. I reorganized the project to include him as our anthropologist, and he trained others in how to do interviews. Soon after, while searching for books on faith and healing in a Christian bookstore, I met Georgianna Jackson. She told me of her personal interest in recording healing stories. I invited her to the dinners, and Georgianna talked about her spiritual trepidation in sharing her interests with us. She prayed about it, and determined that it was all right to share her stories and her personal contacts. At first she was our "gatekeeper," helping us identify people, and then later she became one of our interviewers, concentrating on her family and contacts in Green Sea, South Carolina, a rural farming area near the coast.

Puja Verma, our project director, was a consummate organizer, and with her devout Hindu beliefs, she reminded us that God speaks not only to Christians. Sue Heiney, the head of psychosocial oncology at our hospital, loved stories, especially about healing, so we included Sue in our study. Sue is originally from Pickens, an Upstate mountainous region of South Carolina. People in the Upstate have a long tradition of doing for themselves and making do with what they have. Sue interviewed some of the older members of her community about folk practices like "taking out the fire" and other Scripture-based healing resources.

Ethnicity is an important factor in South Carolina, where a third of the people are of African descent. To make sure we were including African American testimonies, we asked Vivian Moore, a member of the African Methodist Episcopal church, to work with us. Using her own personal networks and those of her church, Vivian further expanded our network of people who had healing testimonies to share.

In our project discussions and dinner forums, I tried intellectually to pin down issues of faith and healing, all in the absence of any real experience of having been healed by faith. After a few months, the project moved on to the work of interviewing people who had been healed by God. For the next three years, we listened to people who were willing to share their stories. The project profoundly affected each of our lives, in some cases leading from disbelief to belief, in others to a greater appreciation of existing personal faith.

I was also invited to attend the Greater Columbia Minister's Fellowship Breakfast meetings. Once a month for the last 23 years, ministers have met at a local restaurant for prayer and fellowship. The meetings were led by Glenn Anderson, a Southern Baptist who had been unexpectedly "slain in the spirit" more than twenty years earlier. He reached out to small non-denominational church pastors, both African American and white, and made them feel welcome. The breakfast always ended by standing in a circle, praying in tongues, laying on of hands for members with healing needs, singing, and prophecizing. These specifics of worship were unfamiliar for me, but were treated with both respect and unconcern by others, and so these gifts of the Spirit quickly seemed completely normal and conventional. However, not all the people who told us of having being healed by God experienced this within church-based activities of prayer and anointing or as a result of even belonging to a church. Some had a direct understanding of God that was both personal and private.

Nestled in the heart of the Bible Belt, Columbia, South Carolina has over 800 churches to serve its 100,000 people. More than 70% of South Carolinians belong to a faith organization. Charismatic Christians, those who believe in the gifts of the Spirit, including being healed by faith, predominate. Religion is part of people's lives in a way that is both real and mundane. In the hospital hallways and elevators, it is not uncommon to overhear people talking about God and praying for healing. God seems part of the everyday fabric of life here, and faith miracles are part of the people's social consciousness.

With all of human history before us, and all the beliefs and variations on beliefs of people living today, we had to set limits on what we could hope to explore in depth. Because five of the interviewers had been raised in Christian traditions, we had some personal familiarity with the Bible and stories of Biblical healing and decided to limit our study to Christians living near us in Columbia and/or their friends. But even within those definitions, we found differences of opinion and experience. Expanding on a quotation by William Blake, the 18th century poet, "To see a world in a grain of sand," a friend of mine once added, you must first see the grain of sand. And in the grain of Christian Columbia, South Carolina sand, we indeed found a world of healing testimonies as diverse as any landscape we had ever imagined. Here we present the highlights of our journey, the dramas of everyday Christian life as it is practiced in just one small area of the world at the turn of the millennium.

We began with the assumption that people would use faith as a coping mechanism, making the pain and suffering of illness tolerable by seeking divine comfort. We assumed that we knew what using faith to heal would be like. As we listened to people, however, our preconceptions seemed inadequate to describe divine healing. It was more than a cuddly comfort mechanism for believers, more than the psychosomatic result of following prepared visualization texts or meditatively living in the moment. It seemed that God had been nearly lost in the secular equation of what we thought happened when a person used faith to heal. In contrast, in the stories we heard, God is active, sometimes appearing unexpectedly, sometimes healing in timeless ways almost identical to those described in the Bible. Sometimes God serves as a comforter in times of trouble. Sometimes God is at the beck and call of a petitioner responding to desperate pleas, to shameful reproaches, or to someone who bargains for healing in return for faithful service. A strong sense of grace, that elusive quality of mercy, pervades the tales.

Our interviewees vary in socio-economic status from people who grew up without electricity to the very privileged, including one man who had been given his first Porsche before he even had a driver's license. Our subjects ranged from people in their twenties to people in their eighties. Although we had thought we would primarily find healing stories among people in non-denominational Charismatic churches, we learned that faith and healing also includes parishioners of the well-known mainstream churches (Southern Baptist, Baptist, Lutheran, Catholic, Quaker, Methodist and Episcopal).

We were not interested in proving or disproving a person's claim to healing. For individuals who told us their stories, the proof of healing was in how the person lived life, the changes in quality and sometimes length of life, and the change in perceived suffering. The issue of documenting miracles is further complicated by the fact that non-medical people think of their suffering in terms of pain, bleeding from sores, fatigue, and stiffness, and not in terms of medically circumscribed conditions like heart disease, cancer, or diabetes. There is a grey area between suffering and conventional medicine; for example, chronic pain clinics utilize conventional medicine, but they rarely eradicate suffering. In a similar but opposite way, faith may take away suffering but have no measurable clinical effects. Certainly for those with clear resolution of health conditions like cancer or a withered limb, medical verification would be possible. However, we simply chose to take the stories at face value and believe that for the interviewees, the healings were completely real.

Normally in academics, researchers collect stories, look for themes, and then create a new academic story about what other people have said. However, as I listened to these stories, I was unwilling to use only my voice in describing how others had been healed. I felt it was more important for individual stories to be told with all the richness of different vibrant voices, and I felt led to share the specific individual stories, using people's own words as they describe their experiences of the fullness and diversity of God.

In August 2002, Dr. Katherine Ott, a curator at the Smithsonian Museum of American History, invited me to donate all the transcripts to their permanent research collection, where the testimonies would be preserved for posterity. In a hundred years or so, some scholar will discover this intimate picture of Christian spiritual life at the turn of the millennium. However, I also wanted people to have access to them now.

Copy-editing the 1,465 single-spaced pages of transcripts had rendered me temporarily saturated and numb to the meanings of the words. So when Mindy Holland appeared in my South Carolina office to do temporary secretarial work late in the fall of 2004, I was astounded to hear her describe spell-checking the transcripts as inspirational. Mindy, a Lutheran lay minister from Seattle, was working in the secular world while her husband completed his final year of seminary training in South Carolina. Mindy's enthusiasm validated my initial impressions of the stories as worthy and extraordinary. We worked together, along with my mother, Polly Houston, to choose the most interesting and insightful 45 stories from the original 107. The choice of stories depended on the vividness of the words used by the teller and how unique the specific story was compared to others in our collection. Keeping the speaker's words and meanings theologically intact, like Michelangelo freeing the delicate angel from the marble slab, Mindy released the stories from the transcripts.

God emerges as a personality, with wholeness and a plan for each person's life. There is direction and movement, along with excitement in discovering God in the midst of adversity, giving glory to God and delight to the people who have been healed. Some people have been blessed with the gift of healing others, and their accounts give further insight into how God works miracles. For most, openness to God and belief that God can heal was a prerequisite for healing. For all except one person, the healing was intentional, either on the part of the healer or the person specifically seeking healing. The exception was a man praying for his father's recovery during a healing service, who instead was healed himself.

What have we learned from the stories? God heals, but in His time and in ways of His choosing. We wait upon the Lord, like Sarah waiting for her first-born child, and we must be patient. These stories tell of God's actions, how He has healed the rich and the poor, the educated and the uneducated. God is beyond any box of definitions, any restraints of rules . . . and in the end, there is only God.

Our stories give testimony to a supreme presence and power of God; but not as passive, hidden in people's souls or sitting aloof on a throne in heaven. God in these stories is active, transforming the ordinary wounds of sickness and adversity to well-being and joy, using visions, dreams, and whispers heard in heart. Like an eagle soaring above everyday cares, God lifts the burden of pain and suffering, giving rise to the gliding flight of the spirit.

Jane Teas, Ph.D.

Co-Editor's Note

Christ drew me into this project at a time when I was longing to do the work of ministry. I was "on leave from call" as a Diaconal Minister of the Evangelical Lutheran Church in America and newly married. I knew that I would be spending just one year in Columbia, South Carolina, while my husband completed his seminary study, so I sought temporary employment through the University of South Carolina. My third clerical assignment enrolled me as support staff for Dr. Jane Teas. Initially I helped her with detailed proofreading of interview transcripts from her "Faith that Heals" collection being prepared for the Smithsonian.

Several weeks later, Jane shared with me that she hoped to gather the strongest stories from the project and combine them into a book. As a former English major, I was intrigued by the thought of setting free the gems of inspiration shining at the core of each interview. The healing stories you are about to read remain in their tellers' own words, transformed from rambling interviews to succinct accounts through some judicious editing and reorganizing. Throughout the project, I have sought to set my Lutheran bias aside, wanting each narrative to stay true to its teller's experience of God and to that individual's practices of faith and prayer. It has been a privilege to encounter such ecumenical and vibrant testimonies of the Lord's power to heal and transform lives. These stories have by turns challenged, surprised, and uplifted me as each teller speaks from the heart with courage and with joy.

The first chapter, *Visions*, presents accounts of how God breaks through into daily life with clear words and images. These five stories hold in common a sense of wonder and gratitude. Lightning strikes, its form so brilliant that we blink. *Receiving Prayer* offers portraits of how those who suffer from illness find their lives embraced and healed through the intercession of others. These stories bathe us in a bright light, the sun emerging through storm clouds. At times, however, healing is not dramatic or immediate; it provides, instead, a foundation of peace and joy in the midst of suffering, as in the accounts shared in *Psalm 23*. Each prayer becomes a candle that lights the way to healing.

For some, the act of prayer is accompanied by anointing with oil, as described in the New Testament's book of James. *Prayer and Anointing* includes four such healing stories, piercing the darkness of injury and illness like oil lamps on a winter's night. In *Folk Healing* we learn about "talking out the fire," in which the use of Scripture, coupled with a deep faith in the Lord's power to heal, brings surprising results. The tellers are prisms, directing God's light to those in need, holding nothing back for themselves. The *Healers* collection presents the rich diversity of healing practitioners, ranging from those called into formal ministry to medical doctors to everyday folks with a heart for prayer. Our stories take us from hospital rooms to worship services in South America; whatever the setting, we see the light of the Lord reflected like sunbeams on a dancing stream.

Then the sky explodes in fireworks, pinwheels of light and sound, sparks flying right over our heads. We read of *Casting Out Demons*, of this mysterious spiritual realm that western culture has put aside as an idle tale. These individuals speak in grounded, undaunted faith in the Name of Jesus Christ to set others free. And finally, our journey ends with *Amazing Faith*. With boldness and determination, by means of their prayers, these tellers invite the Lord to shine without measure into their lives, a day without sunset, a star that never dies.

As I near the end of this project, I recognize that this work has been a ministry: a means of bringing the good news of God's healing touch to those who long to hear. It has also ministered to me, showing me the Light of the World in greater fullness and delight. It is my prayer that those who entrusted us with their stories will find that we have been faithful in their transmission, quality, and intent.

May you, as readers, be met with healing and hope as the Light of God illumines these stories and reaches out to warm our hearts and spirits.

Melinda Holland, M.Div.
SDG

Chapter 1

VISIONS

" . . . I will pour out my spirit on all flesh;
your sons and your daughters shall prophesy,
your old men shall dream dreams,
and your young men shall see visions . . .
in those days I will pour out my spirit."

Joel 2:28-29 excerpts

Be Still and Know that
I Am God–Molly Ritter

In 1992, I had my fourth child, and after I had him, there was a two-month period when I started experiencing a lot of different problems that we thought were related to having the baby. I started running low grade fevers and having night sweats. I had a lot of back pain, but we thought that was from the epidural. I went to see a specialist, and he thought I had a herniated disc. He had me go for an MRI, and the results were going to come in a week. In the meantime, I found a lump in my breast that was about the size of a golf ball, and it had not been there the week before. That really scared us. I ended up going to the emergency room that night. It was about three in the morning; Frank stayed home with the children, and I went down by myself.

We have a friend who is an emergency room doctor, and he was down there. He said, "Molly, there are a lot of different things that we need to talk about." So I spent three hours with him. I told him that I had already gone to an orthopedic surgeon and that they had taken an MRI. He said, "Is there anything that has been unusual?" I said, "I found a lump in my breast two days ago." He left the room and called the other doctor. When he came back in he said, as a friend and a professional doctor, "Molly, it looks like we are dealing with some form of cancer. Spots were found up and down your spine." When someone tells you that, you are in shock; you can't believe it. But in some way, there was a little bit of a relief because this had been going on for months, and we did not know why. All of a sudden, the pieces to the puzzle were starting to fall into place.

I will never forget leaving that night. I was driving home, and it was raining and dark, and I thought, "I am faced with going home and telling my husband this." I turned on the radio to a Christian station, and there was a program that talked about how the Lord surrounds us and keeps a shield about us. In my life God has allowed me to see His sovereignty, that He does bring good out of bad. I had that security in my heart, and I had also walked with the Lord long enough in relationship with Him that I trusted him; but still there was that shock: cancer.

I told my husband, Frank, and we did not even have time to process it. I started on the fast track that week, doing all these different tests, like a bone marrow biopsy, and they did surgery on the lump on my breast. That is when they found out that it was non-Hodgkin's lymphoma. They said it was very aggressive; having a child had thrown me into a hormonal change which made it go wild. In October, while I was meeting with my oncologist for the first time, he received a phone call from the CAT scan department; they had found seven tumors in my liver. It all had metastasized: I had a tumor in my chin, one in my chest, and one in my arm. They were up and down my spine. He said, "If we don't deal with this aggressively with high doses of chemotherapy, you will not be alive by December because of how fast it is moving." So he laid out the protocol for me and said, "You will be a candidate for a bone marrow transplant afterward. We will try to get you in remission." At that point, they gave me a 40% chance of long-term survival, so I was to start the next week.

The Lord went before me. I had many people praying, people from different nations and countries whom we had known through missions. Everyone was praying, "Lord, would You allow this woman to live?" I knew that He wanted me to live each day in the grace that He gave. I was really searching the Scriptures and asking the Lord for a word from Him. The Lord said, "Molly, it's okay to be afraid. As you walk through this, I want you to remember My past faithfulness in your life. I want you to use this as a faith builder to remember how I have already walked you this far in your life, and I never let you down. I want you to acknowledge your dependence on Me." Throughout this we never had the stand of "I am fighting cancer," because it was not me fighting it. God had the ultimate say. My only goal was to keep my eyes on the Lord and let Him direct my path and give me wisdom as we went along.

The night before I went in the hospital for the chemotherapy, I got up in the middle of the night. It was about three o'clock in the morning, and I was standing at my window looking out. It was a full moon, and it was beautiful outside. I remember contemplating what I was getting ready to go through and not knowing. I said, "Lord, this doesn't seem like a good thing, cancer, but I am going to choose to thank You for what You are going to do through this," and I began to thank the Lord as an act of my will, as a choice to thank Him for what He was going to do and how He was going to sustain me. As I did that, I felt like it was the Spirit of God in me, and I began to thank Him and praise Him. All I could say in my heart and in my mouth was, "Holy, holy, holy is the Lord God Almighty, who was and is and is to come." I really sensed the Lord's presence at that time in my life. An incredible sense of peace, contentment, and joy enveloped me, and I knew that He was strengthening me.

I started getting chemotherapy; my protocol was two months of exactly the same thing, which required two or three weeks of isolation. I struggled daily in the hospital, having to work moment by moment because every single day something different physically was happening to me. I had a tape player in my room, and I constantly had tapes of the Word being played; that kept my focus and brought me peace. Through the whole thing I never lost a sense of deep confidence, that deep, deep in my heart He was in control, and I could trust Him.

Three weeks after I was in chemotherapy, I came home from isolation. I was lying in the bed, and I was feeling really bad and discouraged about the future. I closed my eyes, was lying there and talking to the Lord, and I became aware that a presence came into my room. I had never experienced a presence like this. I knew it was the Lord, but I could not even open my eyes. I was enveloped in light, light not even like the sun; it was so pure and white. It was almost like the peace and the joy and the presence were so strong that I felt I could not stand it. I knew it was God choosing to manifest Himself like that in my life. He knew my heart; He knew I was discouraged, and He knew what He was going to do. It was like He placed His hands on me. I never saw anything—it wasn't like I saw a vision or I saw God—but I was aware that He came over to me. All He said was, "Be still and know that I am God." It almost felt like an elephant was on me, but it was so incredible and wonderful. I remember thinking in my mind, "If this is heaven, this is incredible." I will never forget it fading. It was like the light started fading. I remember thinking, "I don't ever want to leave this place; I just want to stay here." And then it left, and I was lying there, but my faith was so strengthened. The Lord said, "It's okay. It is going to be okay; trust Me."

I came out of the hospital in time for Christmas. That Christmas was wonderful; I was regaining a little bit of strength. We were hopeful for remission. We had seen periodically that I was responding; the tumors were shrinking, so the doctor was very hopeful and confident that I was going to go into remission. I had to wait six weeks for the results. Finally in January we got a call from the oncologist. I had not gone into remission. We knew that was not a good sign. He said we definitely needed to move toward the bone marrow transplant.

I had had a month and a half where I started feeling better, but then all of a sudden old things started coming back. I knew there was still cancer in my body; all the little symptoms started to come back again. The oncologist said, "I have to tell you that you have a 30% mortality rate going through the treatment itself." They had only given me a 20% long-term survival rate anyway, so I started weighing my choices. I really struggled; I did not know if I wanted to go through that. Finally, I decided I did not want to do it. Everybody thought I was crazy. I was becoming very fearful and very stressed. All those emotions were starting to rule in my heart, but I wanted to do what the Lord wanted. I knew that He knew the end result, and I did not want to fight against that.

We had heard from a lot of people, and I was very confused. One weekend I said to my husband, "We need to get away, just me and you. I need to pray." All I wanted to do was spend time with the Lord, and Frank did too, and we happened to get a two-room suite. My husband was in the other room, and I began to pour out my heart to the Lord and read the Scriptures. He sent me one particular verse that says, "Unless a grain of wheat falls to the ground and dies, it dies alone, but if it dies, it comes back and bears much fruit." What the Lord was telling me in my heart was, "Molly, are you willing to die to do what you feel is best? Do you trust Me? Will you trust Me that I know what I am doing? Will you die to do this and continue on?" From that point on, I had such a peace. He gave me the sense that I was to continue in that, so we began on the fast track again.

This was the end of February, and the doctor said, "We need to do a biopsy on this place on your back." So I had the surgery. We had a pathologist who was a friend of ours, and when she came out she said, "Molly, I was in there, and as that needle went in, we knew we had hit cancer because it was soft instead of bone. We looked under the microscope, and we confirmed it was the lymphoma." The bone marrow specialist came back as I was recovering, and he said, "Because you still have cancer in your body, you are going to have to go home and go through another round of chemotherapy to get this down." Otherwise, the bone marrow transplant was not going to work.

In the middle of that week, I received a call from the pathology department, to give me my final report. They said, "The report came back negative." I was stunned. She said, "We feel like we have hit on the periphery of the tumor because there are still some suspicious cells. We need you to come back next week; we're going to have to do more extensive surgery." I did not know what the Lord was going to do, but we were still praying for a healing. I felt emotionally like I was coming to the end, but I was still hanging on and trusting and trying to walk each day. When I went back the next week, the doctor told me, "I'm going to make a two-inch incision on your lower back. There is a spot there that we see on the scan, and I'm going to go in and look. If I don't see anything there, I'm going to have to go up to T9, which is on the upper part of your back. That's going to mean a six-inch incision."

The night before the procedure, Frank and I prayed before we went to bed: "Lord, give me the strength to go through this again. Let me see Your hand in this because I'm not excited about going through the surgery and obviously a little nervous." Then I woke up in the middle of the night. When I woke up, it wasn't like I heard an audible sound, but in my heart I felt like what I was hearing from the Lord was, "Enough is enough. I am going to do a great thing." I was half-asleep, but I was awake. I began, as an act of my will, to thank the Lord for what He was going to do. I remember Him in my heart saying, "I'm going to do a great thing." In my mind, He was going to help me through that surgery because I was struggling with going through it again. But as I was lying there and was talking to the Lord, that same verse came back in my mind: "Holy, Holy, Holy is the Lord God Almighty, who was and is and is to come." I could not stop saying that; it was like the Lord was in my heart. I began to feel His presence in such a strong way. I remember thinking, "Frank is over there snoring; he has no idea what's going on, and I am over here feeling like I am so surrounded in the presence of the Lord with such peace and joy in my heart."

The next morning, when we woke up early to go to the hospital, I did not choose to tell my mom and Frank, but Frank said later, "Your countenance was different." I was moving real quick, trying to get ready, and I feel like the Lord just strengthened me to have enough faith to go through the surgery. I trusted the Lord, whatever the "great thing" was, that He knew what was best. I didn't want to get my hopes up, and I didn't want to say anything. I took it in the back of my mind, wondering what this great thing was. My fear was gone, as well as the anxiousness and the worry of going through the surgery; that's what I chose to think about. It ended up being six hours of surgery, and I knew when I woke up in the recovery room that they had gone up to my upper back because I could feel it.

I remember lying there and consciously choosing, "Okay, Lord, You call us in Your Word to give thanks for everything; I choose to thank You for whatever You are doing. I know You have it in control, and Your grace has been sufficient through every day. I trust You with that." Frank came in, and Mom was waiting for him; she wanted him to say it. He came over and took my hand, and he had tears in his eyes. He said, "Molly, you're not going to believe it, but there was no cancer there at all! Whatever was there was completely gone, and the bone that had deteriorated was completely new. There were new bone cells that they saw." I began to cry, and I had my hands over my face. I said, "I knew it, I knew it! I have to tell you what God did last night," and I began to tell them.

Was I thrilled that the cancer was gone? Yes. But because I had lived in it for months I could not process: oh, it's gone; good, let's move on. Instead, my mind was thinking, if I could have crawled off that bed and lain prostrate on the floor before God, I would have because what I felt was so humble. I felt such humility and so overwhelmed that the cancer was gone; but what overwhelmed me more was the sufficiency and the grace of God through hard times. He saw me through, never let me down, and never let me stay in despair long. That is what I was feeling, so humble before the Lord and so grateful.

Then the orthopedic surgeon came in. I had known that he was not a believer, that he was not a Christian. He came in with his scrubs on; he pushed them back, and he was just shaking his head. That's all he was doing, and he said, "Molly, there's nothing there. It was there, and then it was gone. There is new bone, and I can't explain it. It's just one of those things." I was there for another week or two, recovering from the surgery, and I will never forget coming home. All I could do is choose to believe what God had done because it was just gone. I knew that the Lord had healed me. The news of what had happened to me spread, and it strengthened the faith of everybody who believed. I have been cancer-free since then, and when I hit five years they considered me cured. If it had not come back by then, it was not going to come back.

A year after my cancer disappeared, I had the opportunity to go to a church in Nashville to give my testimony on the grace of God. When I came to the end, I happened to mention Dr. Myers, the orthopedic surgeon. Someone came up afterward and said, "Molly, Dr. Myers goes to our church." I said, "You're kidding!" She said, "No," and told me, "Molly, after that he became a Christian." God knew what He wanted to accomplish through this, and I leave those results to Him.

God is in control in my life. When I trust God, it is a daily walk; I grow with the Lord Jesus day by day because it is a relationship. It is not what I do for God; it is a relationship. The prayer I had more than anything through my experience was, "Lord, whatever You do, bring glory to Yourself where people will see You, not me. Let them see You and know that there is a God." I remember one particular time at night, I was talking to Frank in bed, and I said, "Honey, I don't believe I have enough faith to make it through this," and he said "Molly, there is a hymn that has been around for a long time that says 'Great is thy faithfulness.' It doesn't say great is your faith; it's great is *thy* faithfulness." He kept bringing me back to His faithfulness; not me, I am human; I am going to have emotions. It is God who works; it is not me. When we ask the Lord Jesus into our hearts, the seal of that is the Spirit of God in us. The Spirit of God comes to dwell in us. My life is so different because of the Lord; there is a higher purpose in my life, and there is a peace and joy that I had never experienced before.

Because I went through this, I am much more aware of how life is but a breath and a vapor. There is some freedom in that for me; I do not have to worry about tomorrow. Why worry about tomorrow? He is the one who has already planned out our lives. You plan as if you have tomorrow, but you live today in light of eternity. That has given me a lot of joy and contentment in my relationships. It keeps bringing me back to what is really important in my life. I want to be able to say when I am old that I walked life with the fullness of each day.

Molly is a white Southern Baptist in her 40's who was interviewed by Andrew Cousins in the Spring of 2002.

Jesus Gave Me Life
—Linda Johns

When I was six years old, I was struck by a car while coming home from school. Shortly after that I started seizing; they said that over time it would eliminate itself, but I would be on medication until then. I was put on a tranquilizer, as well as an anticonvulsive. By sixth grade I was seizing a lot more; the medication went up, and I had spinal taps. As I got older the seizures progressed. In ninth grade I was having petit mals all day long, and I could not maintain concentration. I graduated high school, and I really had to bite the bullet to do it because of these challenges. But I graduated from high school, and then I married.

At age twenty, when I was pregnant with my third child, one Saturday night I had come home from a choir rehearsal. I started to say, "I don't feel right," but just as I was about to say that—pow, there I was!—I was seizing, and the seizing wouldn't end. I had to go to the hospital, and when I got there my vital signs shut down. While the doctors and nurses are experiencing my dying, I am experiencing my body lifting up. I am going at the same time left and right; I am going fast, and I am going slow. I am looking at myself come off of myself, and it was so cold. I am seeing colors. There is no color on earth to compare to the brightness. There is no aura to compare to the fragrance. I am traveling over crystal waters and the blues are so—ah, it's beautiful!—and I'm going slow and fast at the same time.

Then I am gravitating to a huge light, and I realize, "Oh, my God, I'm in the presence of the Lord!" I thought, "Let's make sure I'm looking all right because of His majesty." It is like you are in the Fred Flintstone car, and you are about to go over the curve. You are about to go over the mountain, so you stop yourself; you stop yourself, and you are braking, and you hear it. Then I am going backward fast and slow. I am approaching the dullness of color, the faintness of smell. I am crying, "Wait, wait, wait, I want to go! I want to be with You! Wait, wait, wait!" Then I am back in the hospital room, and I am boarded down because I am seizing so bad they have me restrained. I am crying because they couldn't get my veins. They had to go into my neck, and that's so painful, and I am saying, "But you don't understand what I saw!" What was amazing is that they said that my vital signs had shut down, and I was dead for 4 ½ minutes. Legally I was supposed to be brain-dead. One of the nurses had dropped a pen during that time, and I told her where her pen was because I saw it. She didn't know where it was; she was looking for her pen, and she couldn't find it. I knew where it was, and she said it was impossible for me to know because I was dead. But when I was lifting up, I saw her looking for it; I told her, "It's over there." I recovered, and life went on.

Soon after, my marriage ended. When we broke up, that was more stress. I had three children, one with special needs. I was on many drug cocktails, trying to get the one suited for me. Eventually, I had to go into the hospital because I was up to twenty seizures a day. The medication was not working, but they wanted to hold off on surgery. They would have had to go in and take portions of the frontal lobes that were shorting out in my brain to keep me from having seizures, and they weren't ready to do that.

However, the doctors decided not to do the surgery. Shortly after I was released from the hospital, I was singing at this "light club" (they call it a "light club" because of Jesus Christ the Light), and a woman came up to me. She said, "You have a beautiful voice; we would like for you to come to our church and sing." So I went and I sang, and it was cool. I went to this church, and I loved it. The pastor said, "I love your spirit; I want you to come to my School of the Holy Ghost." I said, "Okay, I'll come." This was in October of 1998. I was in his class, and he said, "I feel a demonstration of the Holy Ghost. You come here," so I got up, and I was submissive to the Holy Ghost. He began to prophesize to me that God was going to heal me from my seizures, and I was thinking, "How does he know that I have seizures?" That was amazing to me. Instantly, I felt a surge, a warmth—hot, I should say—from the tips of my hair follicles all the way down. When the pastor laid hands on me, he did it gently, but the surge that came through was magnified a billion times. It was like a burn all the way down, and you can't stand against it; your legs will give way. You are not pushed by any means; he has a firm hand on you, but it's not the hand. It is what is transferring from the hand. But it's amazing! It's amazing!

It's like electricity, warm, numb, closer to hot energy. I don't know how to say it because sometimes it's quick. Once I got one of the sisters, one of the ministers at the church, to pray with me; that was slow, warm . . . it was almost like when you put your hand in hot water, but you think it is cold, without the flesh burn. It's an inside slow warmth that penetrates the body. I breast-fed my children; it is that kind of warmth, something real intimate. When that rush comes on, you can't stand against that power. God ordained it; God initiates the healing.

There is no way that the pastor could have known about the seizures; he didn't know me from Adam's housecat. Nobody in the church knew. He just asked me to come to the school while I happened to be at his church.

In the past, I had not prayed to be healed of the seizures. I always thought that the epilepsy was a part of my life and that whenever a seizure was over, I could still function. It was like being dyslexic, like being me. It was a description of me, so I didn't know it was something I should ask for. I thought it was a part of my personality. I thought it was a part of me.

A few months later, it was time for my check-up. You have to lie on the table, and you have to be plugged up, and they eventually start a flashing light. You seize every time because the light is going real fast like a disco thing. It doesn't matter because you'll never get to the third repetition; I am usually seizing by then. But nothing happened! Nothing happened! They asked me, "Are you keeping up with your drugs?" The first time I lied; I said yes. Then I admitted, "I went to this service, and I got healed from seizures, so I don't have seizures any more. Even the petit mal, I don't even have those any more." I said that, and they studied me for about three years. They still have it on my chart, "seizure disorder." I haven't had medication since. That was phenomenal. I was very surprised because, for me, it was like clockwork, with as many seizures as I had had as far back as I can recall. One of my doctors said, "I cannot believe it!" He is a Christian too, and he said, "God can do miracles." He told me once that he really expected me to be dead by now. He said, "You are a very strong woman." And I ain't going to stop now!

The day that it happened, as I drove home, a presence and a fragrance were with me, and they didn't dissipate for a really long time. When you are in a service, and you worship and you praise and you're excited and you're dancing and you're singing, you can feel a wave of Him, but not concentrated as at that moment. This was different because Jesus gave me life. I had life all the time, but now I had life without seizures. How cool is that! I'll never ever have another seizure. I can't because I got life that Saturday in October.

Linda recalls one other incident that brought a different kind of healing to her life . . .

God put a woman in my life who works for the Department of Social Services as a case manager; she helped me find my adoption records. She told me to write to Children's Foster Care; they give you non-identifying information about your birth family. I did, and they sent me everything about myself, my mom, my sisters, and my dad. I knew everything; I knew my mother sang, and I knew she had three other children. She was tall and lean and had an aggressive walk. Through other searches, I also found out that I was from Charleston and what my parents' last name was.

Two weeks into the hospital stay that I mentioned earlier, a lady came in to visit the woman who was sharing a room with me. My roommate said, "Why don't you tell her all the family stuff that you've told me? She knows everybody in Charleston." I started sharing my story, and the visitor said, "Honey, take off those shoes and walk right over there; walk right there and turn around, child." So I walked and I turned around. She kept talking and kept looking, and about twenty minutes into the conversation she said, "Oh, my Lord, child! I know your momma; I know your momma and your daddy, child. I have known your momma for over twenty years."

She had pieced things together from my appearance and from the last name, Sanders. So I asked for my mother's phone number, and she said, "Baby, I can't do that." I said, "Why not?" She said, "Because they don't know what kind of circumstance you've been living in, and I can't put myself in the middle like that. I tell you what: you write a letter, and I'll go to the house and bring the letter. If they read the letter, then they can contact you, so I won't be in the middle." Smart woman. I did it, and I sent pictures of my children and me. Later that week at the hospital, they said, "You got a call from your momma," and I said, "Yeah, okay," thinking it was my adoptive mother, and they said, "No! Your *momma* called." I said, "My momma! Oh, my God!" so I dialed the number, and I said, "Mrs. Sanders . . . I mean, Momma." Her voice is sultry, and there is really no distinction in our voices.

She said to me, "Hi, baby." I said, "Hi, Mommy!" I was crying, and she said, "Tell me where you are. I am coming now; I live ten minutes from the hospital." I knew I would know her when I saw her because she is my momma. I went to the very end of the corridor because I wanted her to search for me. She didn't know my adopted name; I forget to tell her because I was so excited. She said to the front desk, "I have come to visit my daughter." They said, "What's your daughter's name?" "I don't know." When she told me this story I just burst out laughing. "I don't know because she's my birth child. She was adopted, but she is here because she has seizures, and they're going to do surgery." So they looked up the records, and they found me. I was at the end of the corridor when she walked in. She swings poetically. When I saw her, all I could say was, "Oh, God, that's my momma; that's my momma." I got up and then I ran. The doctors were crying and the nurses were crying; everybody was crying, not to mention my mother because when she embraced me, it was like I was born for the first time.

Linda was interviewed by Vivian Moore in June of 2002; she is an African American in her 40's and a member of a Full Gospel congregation.

You Have Been Delivered
–Sally Gordon

During the summer before seventh grade, my mom committed suicide, and my dad, who left ministry as a full-time occupation, remarried three months later. I remember thinking, "I thought we had done it right; we were the Christians, we were following the rules, and we were going to church and serving God. What happened here?" Then during my eighth grade year, I started eating and throwing up, pretty secretly. It was not a daily occurrence at this point. It would be after a party where I had eaten a lot, or Christmas or Thanksgiving, and then wanting to lose weight and be thin, thinking I was fat.

My dad had gone from ministry to real estate. He made an investment that fell through, and we lost money. We had to move to his hometown, which was really small, and I thought, "I don't have quite the same pressures, so I am going to stop eating and throwing up." But, lo and behold, I was not stopping, and it was getting a little more regular, maybe monthly. Then I got into college and thought, "Finally I am away from my family, and I will be fine. I am out of this environment," but when exams came around or a guy asked me out, I was nervous and eating and throwing up. I was living in a single dorm where we each had an individual room with a hall bath, and because I didn't want anyone to know, I would throw up in a trash bag in my room and then carry it out to the dumpster, the whole pattern of secrecy.

I was three, almost four, when my parents taught me the verse, "Behold, I stand at the door and knock and whosoever opens the door, I will come in and dine with him." So being a literal child, I pictured Jesus actually knocking on my heart, and I asked Him to come in. My mom had also told me another verse, "The angels in heaven rejoice over one sinner who repents." I didn't know what that meant, so I crawled behind the couch. My eyes had been shut really tight, and I looked up at the ceiling, and I expected to see angels going, "Ta dah!" with noise makers and confetti. I didn't see any of that, but I still knew it was very real. My brother and I learned Bible verses, and there was a reward system: you got chocolate for learning it, and so I learned the whole Bible.

I am thankful to God for giving me a sense that He was real, cared for me, and knew my every thought, listened to my prayers, and walked with me to school. I was thankful that God kept me close, despite what was happening in my family. During my first year of college, I was sharing my testimony about how God had helped me through my mom's suicide, and I would be up in a semi-public place; for instance, I was the president of the youth group. People would ask me to share, and then I would go home and have my head in the toilet. I had this double life, felt I had been a liar, and held a real sense of shame. I would be home crying about it, but I was too ashamed to admit it or say it publicly.

I went to college my first year, and that summer I went to see my eldest brother, who had gone to live in California. He invited me to come and live with him and his wife for the summer, and I worked there as a waitress. While I was living with them, they had their one-year wedding anniversary. They had saved the top layer of the wedding cake, and while I was there, I ate the whole thing. It became obvious that I was not eating right. I finally told him; I tried to tell him nonchalantly. I was talking about everything under the sun, and I said, "Oh, by the way, sometimes I make myself throw up. So, how is work going?" He stopped me and tried to talk about it a little bit. When I flew home from California to South Carolina, he told my dad, "Sally has been out here, and she is eating and throwing up; you may want to get her to talk to a counselor, and help her." My father came to me, and he said, "I don't know anything about this, Sally, but I don't want you to die."

When I flew back from California to South Carolina, I was supposed to go to college in four days. My father sat me down and told me he had declared bankruptcy. We didn't have the money for me to go back. That was a shocker. I liked my college and was very proud of being there. When I couldn't go back, it was a time where everything that I had put significance in was stripped off me. I would think, I am okay because I am making the grade and having people like me. I am having this little thing where I am eating and throwing up. Then I was home, working, trying to save money to get in the state university for a semester. I had told my brother, and my brother told my dad, so the cat was out of the bag.

On one level I was so relieved, but on the other level I was so ashamed—the ambivalence again. If you know the book *The Scarlet Letter*, it was like I had a scarlet "B" on my chest in a real sense. I couldn't kick it. I felt trapped and realized there was something in me that needed to change—and I couldn't, and I was terrified and ashamed. I was working seventy hours a week. It became winter and I would wake up in the dark, drive to work, drive home. We were living in a really small rural town. All of my friends had gone off to school, so I was very much alone and in a routine, and I was depressed. I remember saying to a friend, "I feel like such a failure." We were spending a night together at our house. She sat up in bed in a pitch dark room, and she said, "You are not a failure." She went on and on; any loving friend would do that, but I think it jarred me to think, "How is it that I define success?" If I say that as a Christian, my significance is in Christ, and He loves me unconditionally, then I can never fail by Him. Why is it that I am not at college, and I am not weighing 120 pounds? I started putting a mirror to what I based love and significance and success on.

I felt pretty broken about my eating disorder, in terms of the lies I had told myself as a coping mechanism. Sometimes because I had eaten so much and thrown up, there would be days when I wouldn't eat anything. Talk about eating disorders, anorexia and bulimia and the spectrum. I would do the starving thing, so there was nothing to throw up. I had made a vow that I wasn't going to throw up, by my own volition. I could hold off for a day or two, or I wouldn't eat anything or eat lettuce or something that was not caloric.

I worked, saved money, and got into the state university that next spring, the spring of 1991. I walked to class the first day, and there was a flyer on the wall for an anonymous overeaters/eating disorders support group at the university's psychological services. I was astounded: one was sitting right there by the elevators, staring me in the face. I didn't have any money, and it was free. I said, "Okay, Lord, I believe You will give me the discernment and help me, so I will go to this, and we will just see." I tried to sneak over in the dark and not be seen going into the house where the support group met. It ended up being a group of eight to twelve young women, whose stories were much more tragic than mine, and yet they were doing the same thing that I was doing. I felt like less of a freak, knowing that I wasn't the only who was struggling with this, and I was seeing how other people were dealing with it. It was okay to admit it, and also to hear how you were struggling.

I thought about my weight, food, or how I was failing in this area—or the shame—all the time. Any time I thought a guy was interested in me, it was a sense of, if you really knew me and what I did, you wouldn't want to be with me. Because my mom had been depressed and had committed suicide, I was scared to admit that I was depressed; I was afraid that maybe I would be suicidal. It was never a non-functioning, not-get-out-of-bed thing, but it was a real time of struggle. No one ever clinically diagnosed me, but I did eventually start going to counseling.

I took a "History of the Bible" course in the Religious Studies Department. It was my first exposure to higher criticism, deconstructionism or "demythologizing" the Bible. The professors had very systemic, intellectual arguments for why the Bible was a book made by humans, and certainly not by God, and could not be trusted—that you would be a fool if you believed it. I had never heard arguments that were that "sound," backed up by academia. This professor talked about how miracles were not real and how Christ could not have healed people. Jonah was not swallowed by a fish. The crossing of the Red Sea was actually a crossing at an extremely low tide. There are very natural explanations for supernatural phenomena. It was really, really shaking me. All that I had believed in or trusted had been stripped from me, whether it was my parents' marriage, or my mom leaving, or even my own eating disorder. All I had left was God. I felt like I was clinging to Him desperately. I felt very fragile being at school; I was afraid I would have to leave again, that I wouldn't have the money or make the grades. I was weeping and praying to God daily to help me, and then this professor was trying to show me that the Bible wasn't the revealed Word of God, and maybe there wasn't a God.

I would read my Bible and pray for discernment. I remember thinking, "If Jesus is true in terms of being a person and being God, and what He did was true, that truth will be bedrock. If I dig hard enough and long enough through all the layers, I will hit it. If it is a lie, I will dig straight through the earth and be free falling." A lot of what I believed in the Bible I believed from my father, and I had grown to find him a pretty untrustworthy person. I started being afraid that I had just believed my father about God. I had not had the responsibility to find out on my own, so this of course was shaking me up. But I was still reading my Bible, and I remember coming across a verse in I Chronicles 28 where David, who is the king, is handing over the kingdom to his son, Solomon, who is going to build the temple. He says to him that God knows your thoughts when you are rising up and lying down, and if you seek him, He will let you find Him. So I decided, "I am going to seek You, and if You are really there, You will let me find You, but if You are not, my whole world has been a lie."

Then one day, I went into class, and the professor started speaking. I opened my notebook, and he began lecturing, and the front of the room became this exceedingly bright light. It enveloped me, and the spot where the man had been lecturing became almost a focal point. It was the purest, brightest light I have seen. It enveloped me and the whole room. I could have been lifted in the middle of space. I have never experienced anything like it on Earth. It blinded out everything in the room. It came on suddenly. It seemed to move like a mist, almost as if a cloud had come in, and maybe it lasted ten seconds. I remember a sense of weight or being pressed into where I was sitting, but I didn't have a sense of sitting. Maybe I am reading into that because the Scriptures talk of weight of glory. I don't remember warm or cold, just really being impressed, like an impression upon me. It wasn't a sense of haunting or disturbing fear, but it wasn't like a soft fan blowing on your face, or comforting. It was like somebody getting your attention, grabbing you by the back of the neck. That sounds hostile, but it wasn't hostile; it was just such a grabbing of my whole attention—shock—so fast, almost somebody taking your head and turning it to see something, but that changes your whole understanding and perspective. It was so much bigger than me, and I felt so small and taken up into it. There wasn't a bodily corporeal form, but it was like the speaker was being replaced.

Someone else had come to speak to me. It was definitely something outside of me. It was speaking to me and through me. It was through my whole body. It wasn't like a whisper. I heard, "You have been delivered." It was definitely a voice, a voice that was rich and full, but it was not loud. It was very clear English, and I am very humble and thankful for that. We talk about God bending down, being the King of the Universe, to let us know that He is real and to accept Him. He spoke my language. He didn't make me learn Hebrew; He didn't have a divine language. He spoke to me in what I needed and did what I needed, but it was just plain.

I wanted to sob. I felt loved and humbled at exactly the same time, more intensely than I have ever felt in my whole life. And freed, the sense of having carried something for so long and then having someone just take it off, almost like something was lifted off me, and I am a new person. The lifting off was a new, a free, a holy and terrifying thing, but I did not feel that it was going to crush me. Then the light dissipated, and he was still there lecturing, droning on.

At that moment I had three thoughts, exactly at the same time. One was, "Oh, my God, it's the beginning of the end of my sanity. I am starting to have delusions and hallucinations, like my mom. Maybe I am schizophrenic." The second was, maybe the angel of light was deceiving me, tempting me because I wanted to be delivered from my eating disorders so badly, almost like a carrot dangling in front of my face and not being true. The third thought was, this was of God, and it was real. I got tears in my eyes and I was shaking, and I looked around to see if anyone saw what I saw, and people were asleep or taking notes.

As I was walking back to my dormitory, I remember thinking, "Was that real?" and the sun came back out from behind the clouds and the wind blew. It was almost a reminder of God's Spirit. The sense that I had when I was told, "You have been delivered," I immediately associated it with my eating disorder. I believe it was God—it may have been one of His angels sent to minister me—who said, "You have been delivered." For some reason, He knew I needed that, and He graciously lifted the eating disorder off me immediately. He had to come rescue me. "You have been delivered" was in the past tense. At the time it was the immediate, "I am taking this off you," which was true, but it was also speaking of my identity. "You have been delivered; you don't have to fear." It was that process of being delivered.

I saw the irony and humor of God performing a miracle, where I was physically changed, in the class where the professor was saying miracles don't exist. It was so hilarious, but it is like God, and He is so gracious that way and the way He takes care of us. I am so thankful. From that point, ten years ago, I did not throw up ever again, even from a stomach virus. I find that pretty miraculous.

Even though there was an immediate miraculous deliverance, there was still a working out in my mind about how I approached food and my family. I started going to a counselor who was a Christian. I still felt self-conscious about eating in front of people; I was still worried about being too fat, but I knew God had freed me, and I knew that I would never go back to being the same. There was a definite new freedom and an ability to start looking into the other things in my life, like family. That experience with the professor, as well as the deliverance, made me want to know more about God and Scripture, so I wanted to go to seminary; then I changed from the seminary program to the counseling program.

There is nothing bigger than God that can hold you. God has to break through fear, and He can. I think of my mom; God loved her as much as me, but He allowed her to take her own life. Whereas with me, He did not allow me to self-destruct, and I don't know why He does different things with different people. God is alive, and He is living, and He is far beyond what we think or imagine. One of my missions in life is to help people understand that God is good. This experience gave me a sense that God was for me and not against me. Nothing is as scary anymore because I know that God is for me and that He can supernaturally intervene if I need it. It gives me a sense of courage. I know that there is purpose in suffering. When you go through suffering, whether it is by your own hand or someone else's or a combination, the fact that you can be made a better person is a sign to me that there is a God. God redeems and can bring life out of death, and that is a miracle.

Sally was interviewed by Andrew Cousins in June 2002; she grew up in an evangelical, non-denominational church and is a white woman in her early 30's.

Trust in Him
–Richard Walters

This happened October 6th, 1990. My field was master craftsman; I did plumbing, electrical, and carpentry. I was on top of one of the buildings, and I went up the scaffold. On this day, the scaffold felt so weak going up, and when I got up there some guys were already up there working, and I told them, "Y'all, this scaffold doesn't feel right." Something in my heart told me it didn't felt right. I didn't step down on it; I stayed up there and worked with them for a while. Then I got paged, and it was about 10:00. I thought about that scaffold being so weak. I said, "I'm not going to use that scaffold; I'm going to use another one."

On my way down from the other one, it sort of opened up. This scaffold was weaker than the first one. I don't know if you have ever seen a scaffold; they have their little safety bars around them. You have to go down on the safety bar on the proper side. So when I went down on the safety bar side, it sort of opened up; it swung open. While it was swinging open I was on the end of it, holding on with my left hand, over twenty-five feet in the air. At the time it swung open, they had some guys on the top, but they couldn't get to me. The only thing that was holding me was that one end and me holding on.

So I began to pray and talk to the Lord. I said, "God, I don't know what I am going to do now. There is no other way for me to go but down. God, I am going to trust you and believe You will work this thing out. I believe my soul is right with You, so if anything should happen to me . . ." I'm making sure my soul was right still. I'm still holding on with the right hand, and I couldn't grab with the other hand, so the skin began to dig down, and you could see the blood running down my arm. At that time I thought about Jesus on the cross and how they nailed His hand to the cross, and how it began to bleed. So I said, "Father, I am going to trust You." I began to quote Proverbs, chapter 3, verses 5-6; it says, "Trust in the Lord with all your heart and lean not on your own understanding; in all your ways acknowledge Him, and He shall know the right path." So I was quoting Scripture and praying, and I said, "Father, I am going to trust You if I fall. Whatever happens, I am in Your hands because I know I can't hold on any longer." I let go because there was no other thing to do but go down now. It is too much weight now, and my hand is cut down almost to the bone.

I let go, and as I began to fall, I was falling flat. I closed my eyes. I wasn't screaming or hollering or anything because I had already turned it over to the Lord. I felt comfortable with whatever happened; if I should die, I knew my soul would be right with the Lord. It seemed like it was five or ten minutes in the air. I began to pray to the Spirit on my way down, and as I did, all of a sudden, I felt a wind or something come up under me, a mighty wicked wind. October was hot that year. I felt a breeze come over me, so I opened my eyes. I was looking to the right when I opened my eyes, and I saw an angel up under the right side of me. He was up under my arm, and then I looked to the left, and I saw an identical twin angel. Once I saw the angels I began to pray to the Lord, "I'm still falling now; realize I'm still falling here." I got God to show me all these things while I was falling.

As I fell, I decided that I would thank the Lord now because I knew my help had come to me. I realized that the angels would protect me, so I began to pray and say, "Thank You, Jesus; thank You, Lord," all the way down. By the time I hit the ground it didn't feel like a hard hit; it felt as if I had just run and jumped on the bed or something, like a little cushion. So I'm down on the ground now, thanking the Lord. Everybody is rushing out, and I talked to a lot of folks after the fact. They asked me, "While you were down there, you were thanking the Lord . . . ?" I said, "If you knew what I saw and knew what I have been through, you wouldn't ask me that question." They didn't move me. The ambulance came, and I was still there, and I didn't feel any pain; I was just praising the Lord.

We got to the ambulance, and they took me in to have surgery. Once they did that, they had to put me to sleep, so I didn't know anything from that point until I woke up in the hospital. Then I saw pins in my arm and a bar going across my hand; I had pins everywhere. When the doctor came, I didn't see my face and didn't know what it looked like. (I finally looked at myself when I got home. My head was all swollen; my eyes were bloodshot red and everything. It was a terrible fall, but I never felt a thing—but it was there to see afterwards.) The only thing I knew then was that surgery was done on my hand; it was all swollen up, and everything was completely black like it was dead. I asked the doctor, "Doctor, what is going on with my hand?" He gave me all these medical terms, and I said, "Tell me in English what you are talking about." He said, "It is like taking a glass and throwing it up against a brick wall . . . it just shatters completely." He said, "Your wrist was shattered; bones came out on this end here on this side of it. You won't be able to use that hand again. You won't be able to use that wrist again. It is damaged completely. But we went in and replaced some bones with metal plates." They tried to do what they can do, but he said, "The way it is, you won't have 100% in that arm or that hand again."

I was beginning to have doubts because I had asked God to take care of me, and I'm saying, "Lord, what am I going to do now?" I'm praying, "Lord, what am I going to do? I'm a master craftsman; I use my hands. How am I going to take care of my family? What am I going to do now?" I have done this for twenty years now, so my career is gone. How am I going to support my family? All these things were flooding me. I didn't get an answer; I guess because He says, "I already answered you when I saved you from the fall."

One night while I was lying in bed—it was 1:30 in the morning, and my wife was lying beside me asleep—I began to talk to the Lord. I said "Lord, what am I going to do? I asked You a question, and I'm looking to hear from You. What can I do now?" I said, "I'm out of work for now. The doctor said I can't use this hand again. What am I going to do, Lord?" He starts talking to me. The voice was so clear—and I was wondering how come my wife didn't wake up and hear this. The voice said, "Didn't I make the lame to walk?" And I said, "Yes, God." He said, "Didn't I make the blind to see?" I said, "Yes, Lord," and He said, "Didn't I create man in my own image?" I said, "Yes, Lord." He said, "Didn't I even raise Lazarus from the dead?" I said, "Yes, Lord." He said, "What you are asking me to do is nothing. That is something simple. What I want you to do is not worry about your hand and just concentrate on being a witness for Me."

So I realized then what He was telling me from the beginning of my path: begin to trust in Him. In His own way, He came to me and told me those things. So I said, "Okay, Lord, I'm not going to worry about my hand; whatever happens I know You are going to take care of me and provide for me. Now I remember because I asked You from the beginning. Now I understand that You never left me; You were always there."

I began not to worry about anything and went to my therapy. I began to work on my hand, and it didn't seem like any progress was being done, but I wasn't worried about it. Whatever they told me to do at home, I did; I exercised, whatever I needed to do. I went to the therapy three days a week. I began to give my testimony to folks, like I'm telling you, and all of a sudden I saw my hand move, my fingers. I still couldn't make a fist, but when I saw that, I began to praise God for that. Then later on—months have gone by—I began to make a fist. I'm still not worried about it; I am doing normal things, trying to feed myself, and I'm beginning to come back. Everything eventually came back. I can make a fist now. I can move my hand. I can't turn this one completely over, but I'm still not worrying about it. At one time, I couldn't go but this far, and now look where I am at! It is still getting there. I'm still not worrying about it because I know God will give me everything back that I need. I praise God for what He has done.

Richard was interviewed by Vivian Moore in July of 2002;
he is an African American Baptist in his 40's.

Put Every Beam of Your Faith in Him
–Roxanne Wilmer

I had been going through an awful difficult time in my life. I had a big tumor that was reaching from the middle of my shoulder blades all the way down my back, and I was in what they call chronic pain, day and night, no relief. I couldn't sleep at all. I had to sit up in bed on three pillows to get any rest at all. I couldn't get any relief from the pain. The doctors had given me some medicine to take, and it seems like the medicine wasn't doing any good at all. So I put it in God's hand; I always put everything in God's hand because He is with me. He helped me get through what I went through. I went to one doctor, and he said there wasn't anything he could do for me. He wanted to send me to a surgeon, and the surgeon told me, "It's what they call a major operation; that's the only way you're going to be here very long." And he said, "It's very dangerous. You may not get off the operating table, but I'll give you some time to think about it."

I kept talking to God about it. I would go on my back porch, and I would sit down, and I would talk to the Lord. He would let me know He was there, that everything was going to be all right. I said the Lord's Prayer over and over. I pictured Jesus at that time when He was going to be crucified, kneeling at that rock; He didn't want to die. Nothing wants to die. Not even my Jesus Christ wanted to die; He wanted that cup to pass from Him. I felt that feeling; believe me, I felt it. But I accepted it. I told Jesus, "If it's Your will for me to go, I'm ready."

My parents had started teaching me about Jesus when I was a real young little girl. My mother had a good education, and when I would be home with her, she would say, "It's time for us to read the Bible." I looked forward everyday for her to read the Bible, and I grew up with that all my life. My mother believed in Jesus with all her heart and soul. She was paralyzed when she was eleven years old, and she said that God blessed her by being with her at all times. She prayed all the time. In those days, we had a wood stove; we didn't have electricity or running water. My dad, he was a hard worker, and he was always talking about God. Daddy had a big, beautiful family Bible. He made a rule: it made no difference how tired he was, but every evening before we went to bed, he would take that Bible down, and he would read two or three chapters of it. He would go all the way through the Bible.

I was going to go back to the surgeon the next day; that night I had talked with the Lord outside, walking around talking with Him, praying. He was right with me. That night in my room, I was propped up on the bed, hurting, and I was saying my Lord's Prayer. What did I see when my eyes shut? One of the brightest white lights you have ever seen in your life! Oh, I wasn't scared. It was a good feeling; it was a happy feeling. I remember opening my eyes, and at the corner of my room, I saw a bright light that came from way up there. It came right down, the brightest white light you have ever seen. I kept looking at it, thinking, "Praise God!" and when I looked, I saw steps. The steps were going up. On both sides of the steps were angels: angels on this side, angels on that side. Some of them were men. Some of them were women. Some had wings. Some didn't. Some had musical instruments, like harps, like violins.

I was looking at the beautiful sight going up those steps with those angels there, and about that time, who came walking down those steps but my momma! That was the first time I had ever seen my momma walking. She came walking down those steps, wearing a long white gown. She came to my bed, and let me tell you, she's a beautiful lady. She was young. She had long, black, curly hair. I looked up at her face, and she was smiling down at me. I was thinking, "What a beautiful person! Thank You, God, that You let me see my momma walk." It was wonderful.

She turned her hand towards the steps. She never spoke; everything was just completely quiet. She just was smiling down at me. I looked back up at the steps, and I kept going up with my eyes, and at the top of those steps way up there, stood Jesus Christ. Jesus had a white gown on too, but He had a rose-colored robe over it; it wasn't completely around Him. I did not see His face so plain, but I knew it was Jesus. Behind Him were the great gates of heaven, the solid gold gates. And they were wide open, telling me you can come in. That's the feeling that I got from it. I was praising God and looking at that, and my momma turned away from me and went back to those steps. She was going back up the steps, and everything went away that quick.

I was healed that night. I was healed from that vision. The pain that I had was gone. I got out of bed. I got down on my knees. I praised God for what I saw. I praised Him the rest of the night. That pain was gone. The next day, this lady came to get me to take me to the doctor. I had had to walk with a cane and with people holding on to me, but I came down those steps like it wasn't nothing to it. And she said, "Where is your cane?" I said," I don't need it." She said, "I'm scared you're going to fall, and I said, "No, Ma'am, I'm fine. I'm fine. The pain has gone. I'm not hurting." She acted like she didn't understand what I was talking about because she knew how bad off I was.

We went to the surgeon. He came in and examined me a little bit, and he said, "Everything's fine. Let's look at the two x-rays." He put the first x-ray up, and it showed the tumor. He said, "How are you feeling?" and I said, "I feel great. Just fine." He said, "Well, let's look at the other x-ray." He put the second film up there, and when I looked at that, everything was gone completely. The tumor was completely out of my back. It had made an awful curve in my back. He said, "Your back is not like it was. The growth that was in there is gone. You don't have to have an operation. There's nothing there to take out at all." He said, "Now I can tell you. I didn't have the heart to tell you before. If you had gone through that operation, I don't know if you would have gotten off the operating table. If you had gotten off the operating table, you would have been paralyzed for the rest of your life." He put his arms around me and said, "Do you realize what kind of miracle God has done for you?" I said, 'Oh, yes, sir. I knew it ever since last night."

I have really enjoyed life since then. I can move. God has really blessed me, and I just want to share that everywhere. God left me here for a reason, and I think the reason is to let people know what a wonderful, loving, sweet God He is. He is there for you to see you through your troubles. You got to put every beam of your faith in Him. You got to talk to Him. You got to walk with Him. You got to read your Bible and understand what He's trying to tell you. He's there for you, and He'll take you by the hand and lead you every step of the way. He works things out for you. So that was my miracle. I felt the presence of the Lord with me, letting me see the miracle that He was. If anyone has had a happy thing happen to them and felt a wonderful happy feeling, it's glorified a million times more than that. It's one of the wonderfulest feelings on God's green earth to experience. One day, whenever the good Lord is ready, I'm going to see the steps come back down. The angels will come back down, and my momma is going to come down those stairs, and she's going to grab me by the hand, and we are going to walk up those steps. I'm going to grab Jesus by the hand, and all three of us are going to walk in the gate to heaven. Yes, sir, I'm ready to go. What He wants me to do right now is let people know what He can do for them.

When I was a girl, I had another tumor that was down in the lower part of my right side. The doctor said I was going to have to go to the hospital for an operation to remove it. It was what they call a bleeding tumor; I was bleeding to death. I had got down to about 103 pounds, skin and bones. Everybody is scared of surgery. I don't care who they are. I knew it was going to be another bad surgery.

I have always believed in God, and I always go to Him with anything. The night before the surgery, I went to him and said, "Lord, show me if I die, will the gates of heaven be open unto me?" After I got through praying, what appeared to me was a wall. As far as I could see it went; it was far, and it was down in the hard ground. I said, "I can't dig under there, and I sure can't climb over the top of it," and I knew heaven was in there. As far as I could look, it went on and on—on and on both ways—but there was a door. The door was shut. I was praying, "Lord, I know that was heaven. Why wouldn't the door open for me? I love You so much, and I've done everything that I know that You wanted me to do. Give me some kind of sign."

Before I went to the hospital, I told my momma, "Momma, I'm sure that I'm going to get some sign from the Lord Jesus," and I told her all about the wall and the gate. She said, "Yes, you will." That night in the hospital before the surgery I went to sleep and, sure enough, in just a little bit there was that wall again: right in front of me, and I was right at the door. I said, "Lord, is this door going to open for me?" It swung open, wide open. I didn't go in it; I wasn't supposed to go in it. But I got to see a little inside, and it is beautiful. It is one of the beautifuliest places . . . Now we've got beautiful places here on earth, but it's no place like that. There was a long table with a lot of chairs and plates, and everything was on this table. I could hear people, but I couldn't make them out. That showed me and let me know that the gates of heaven were open to me at that time, and if something happened to me, I was going to go right on in. I wasn't worried about the operation. I was fine. I had the surgery. I had a big tumor removed; it weighed a little over a pound. But thanks be to God it was benign; it wasn't cancerous. It could have been. The doctor was afraid it was cancer.

God has sent a lot of miracles to me. I believe in Him in every way there is to believe. Lord Jesus Christ is with me at all times. He is my shield, keeping all evil and especially the devil away from me. Believe with all your heart and soul, and you see things happening. Ask God every day to take you by the hand and show you the right way to go. Believe with all your heart and soul, and He will come right in; He will take you all the way. It's one of the wonderfulest relationships anybody could have.

Roxanne is an African American in her 60's. She was interviewed by Andrew Cousins in the summer of 2002 and attends a Free Will Baptist Church.

Chapter 2

RECEIVING PRAYER

When [Jesus] returned to Capernaum after some days, it was reported that he was at home. So many gathered around that there was no longer room for them, not even in front of the door; and he was speaking the word to them. Then some people came, bringing to him a paralyzed man, carried by four of them. And when they could not bring him to Jesus because of the crowd, they removed the roof above him; and after having dug through it, they let down the mat on which the paralytic lay. When Jesus saw their faith, he said to the paralytic, "Son, your sins are forgiven." Now some of the scribes were sitting there, questioning in their hearts, "Why does this fellow speak in this way? It is blasphemy! Who can forgive sins but God alone?" At once Jesus perceived in his spirit that they were discussing these questions among themselves; and he said to them, "Why do you raise such questions in your hearts? Which is easier, to say to the paralytic, 'Your sins are forgiven,' or to say, 'Stand up and take your mat and walk'? But so that you may know that the Son of Man has authority on earth to forgive sins"—he said to the paralytic—"I say to you, stand up, take your mat and go to your home." And he stood up, and immediately took the mat and went out before all of them; so that they were all amazed and glorified God, saying, "We have never seen anything like this!"

Mark 2:1-12

Wholly Rely on God
—Shivani Chowry

I am from India. I got married in 1996, and we left for Canada because of my graduate studies. All of a sudden, I started getting sick quite often. The sickness began with severe sinusitis and very frequent colds. We set an appointment with a doctor; I went to her and she said, "I need to do a blood test." She took the test and said, "I'll call you back and let you know the results." After a week—I was home, and my husband was still at work—I got a call from the doctor saying that your results are all abnormal. She was blunt from the very start. So I said, "What's wrong?" She said, "All your blood reports and readings show that you have a brain tumor." It was a terrible shock to me because I felt perfectly normal.

After she hung up, the only thing I could do was sit and cry. I waited for Prasad to come back from work, and as soon as I heard him coming, I started getting myself busy. I wanted to avoid the topic and did not know how to tell him. I tried to keep avoiding but he said, "Something is wrong; I know." I said, "The doctor called and said that my blood reports were all abnormal; I have a brain tumor." The only thing Prasad did was hold me tight. He didn't say a single word. He was equally shocked and shaken, but I believe that the kind of strength God gave him was not to break down. He said, "No, we are not going to accept this. We are going to pray about it." There is a Scripture that says that in the name of Jesus, you bind things on earth. If you bind things on earth, God releases positive things. God releases healing. You take shelter in the Word of God because it sets you free.

So we prayed, and we bound the spirits of sickness, and there was an assurance. You get that feeling from inside, and that is God's Spirit working within you. It assures you, "You have faith in Me; leave it to Me, I will work it out." The next thing I did was call my mom, and I said, "I have a brain tumor, and I'm going to die." She immediately prayed with Prasad and me. She said, "Let Prasad take up the other phone, and let's all agree." When you pray alone, it is one thing; when you pray with another person, you have added strength. The Word of God says one can put a thousand to flight, but two can put ten thousand to flight. There is power in agreement, and there is power in strength. Our pastor also called us, and he prayed for both of us on the phone: "I bind all negative news. I bind all wrong reports. I bind all things that seem to be coming against the Word of God. And I release healing; I release faith, hope, and that spirit of satisfaction."

Soon we met with another doctor, and he said, "Even without seeing your reports, I can say that it is a little brain tumor that has been growing in your pituitary gland at the base of your brain. You have to go in for a CT scan. However small the tumor might be or however big it might be, we have to make sure that it's not growing and it's not cancerous." All the way back home on our bus ride, we kept holding hands and encouraging each other. We know we can overcome it; we can overcome it with the Word of God. When you start dwelling on the Word of God, God sees the little faith you have; though it is as small as a mustard seed, you can move mountains. The Word says it. You have to believe and act on it and trust.

Prasad and I decided to go to New York because our family was there. It was arranged that the CT scan would be done at Long Island Jewish Medical Center. I went in for the CT scan. It hardly took ten minutes, but they said it would take another two weeks for the reports to come. Finally the lady called and said, "You can come and pick up your reports." So Prasad and I took a taxi. My mom was at home; she was praying, as was everyone else who knew. They were constantly on their knees, having their supplications toward God, lifting us up. We brought the results back home, and the results read that it was a 10-mm tumor in the pituitary gland, but it was non-cancerous.

That was the first victory. We kept thanking God and rejoicing. We came back home and shared with our family that God has been so good; in His mercy and in His grace, He has healed me. We decided that we would stay in America. I wrote back to my professor, and he was disappointed that I would not be going back to Canada, but he said, "We are happy that you are fine." We settled down in the States, and the biggest strength we had was our church. You get the feeling that you have people who care for you, who love you, and above all, who are constantly surrounding you with prayers. We used to come up and ask for prayer shamelessly. If you are shameless for God, then He is shameless for you. He says, "You have a need? Come to Me, ask Me, and I will do it for you." Our families kept us in prayer constantly.

Later, there was a doctor in Atlanta, Georgia who checked me. He said, "You have to go on hormonal medication for the tumor to be dissolved." The other thing he saw during the tests was that I had highly abnormal ovaries, surrounded with thirty to forty follicles that looked like cysts. That condition is called polycystic ovaries, and because of this hormonal imbalance, I was told I would never be able to have a child. He said, "You might have to be on this for the next two or three years." My reading was 313; the normal text book reading is 2 to 26. It was absolutely berserk. It was skyrocketing. He said, "I don't understand how you are even standing because with such readings, it starts affecting the brain." I prayed over the medicine: "Lord, I know that the medicine is going to work, but You are going to work through the medicine. I am not wholly relying on the medication. I only rely on You. I wholly rely on You, that You are going to heal me." It was a month that I took it, just a month. When the doctor took the reading, he said, "Did you take an overdose of these drugs?" I said, "No, it's what the prescription said." He said, "Something's funny over here. Because your reading was 313, and now it is 16. 13 is the perfect reading." There are so many things you cannot understand. You do not have the proof of it medically. But God had already acted.

The doctor said, "Fine, go your merry way, but think about that what I told you: those cysts have to be taken care of." Until that time we had not decided on starting a family because we had been married for a year and a half and were all set on our careers. But when someone tells you, "This situation seems impossible," then you start dwelling on it. That had become a fear for me: I will never be able to have kids. That kept discouraging me so much that I went into a depression, and I shared this with Prasad. He said, "You are healthy; God has proved it. But we will pray. We will believe that when the time comes, God will bless us with a child." In our church, there are people who are blessed with the gift of prophesying. One day we went up for prayer because, by that time, I could not see anything else; I wanted a child. God has to do it because the Word of God says, "Ask anything in My name, and it will be given to you." I had forsaken everything else. I was wholly relying on God, and He had to do it. If He could do other miraculous things, why not this too? So we went up in front for prayer.

There was a couple in our church, Chris and Karen. We had never met them before. They did not know what my symptoms were. We went up and asked for prayer that everything would go fine with us. He looked at both of us, and he said, "Lord, I pray for divine healing and that everything goes okay with them." His wife looked at me; she put her hand on my head and closed her eyes, and she said, "Lord, I see cysts in the ovaries, and I refuse it, I reject it; I renounce it in Jesus' name." When she said that, I literally shook all over. I opened my eyes, and my husband and I looked at each other: how did she know? She is a stranger to us, and how did she ever know? It was definitely God confirming it through her. After a short time, we came back to church and said, "We need to share something." We went up and shared that we were expecting. You have to let go and let God, but have the faith. You forsake all the signs and symptoms of the world. You make yourself blind to it and wholly trust and rely on God, and then He works. It doesn't stop there. The other part of faith is finding another to tell about Him. That is how faith increases, by hearing the Word of God. That was one big victory we had: that I was pregnant and that our little son was on the way.

In the fifth month, I had a sonogram and a blood test. The nurse called me and said, "The doctor wants to see you and Prasad in the office," so I thought it was something to do with me taking more multivitamins or something. The doctor had this file out, and he said, "Your readings are all abnormal. According to this, your baby has Down's Syndrome. You think about it; either you want to go through with it, or you want to terminate your pregnancy." The things that were going through my mind were, "Lord, if You have blessed me with a child, then the child has to be perfect. Otherwise I don't want this child." That's the human tendency. All the way back home in the car, we were praying, and I was crying and angry. I was so bitter with God. At that point, I told Prasad, "I am not going to give birth to an abnormal child. It's not because I don't love the child, but I don't want anything abnormal happening to me; that's it." And he said, "Whatever you do, we are not getting rid of the child. You calm down; believe and trust God." From five months to nine months is a long time of believing and trusting.

That night we were visited by an elder of the church, and Chris and Karen came also. They told us, "You're going for a battle. When you go for a battle, you don't go with the feeling that the enemy is stronger, and you are going to lose. You go for a battle with the impression in your mind that you are going to crush the enemy. No matter what, you are going to win again through the Word of God." From that day onwards, we prayed and believed that we would have a perfect child. It was like boot camp. But you have to do that to show the evil one. Again there were people praying for us and upholding us in prayer. We prayed. We gave thanks that our child is perfect.

In the seventh month, I was diagnosed with gestational diabetes. Nothing seemed to work, not diet, not exercise, nothing, so they said, "You have to take insulin injections." Every time Prasad would give me an injection, we would pray, "Lord, don't let it affect the baby in any way." Finally, I went into labor in the eight month. Our son was born exactly one month before the due date. We went to the hospital at 12 o'clock, and at 2 o'clock he arrived. It was a normal delivery. He was a big baby, and the doctor said, "He is healthy, but let the pediatrician come and check." When the pediatrician came, he walked in and said, "Prasad, I want you to come with me." My husband was shaking then. We believed that our son was okay, that he was fine, but we were thinking, "God, You have to prove it again." So the doctor went in and did whatever tests they had to do. He came back, and I was all exhausted and tired. He said, "Ma'am, you have a very healthy baby boy, and you must thank God for it." We knew; we had the assurance that God had done it, but the doctor said, "You both must thank God."

The physician in Atlanta had told me, "When you want to have a kid, come back to me, and I will put you on a fertility pill." When I called and told him about my son, he asked if I had taken any pills. I had not. He said, "It's amazing. It's really amazing. It's the hand of God." This was an impossible case. But it's simple faith. Prayer and faith, that's what we believe. On February 24th our son will be three years old, and he has no health problems, no abnormalities, nothing. They checked me for gestational diabetes again after I delivered. It is gone. Even with my hormone imbalance, all my body functions are perfectly fine as they should be. This is definitely a miracle. The cysts on the ovaries have also disappeared. That was prayer.

When we are out of words for prayer, that is when we speak in tongues, and the Holy Spirit takes over. When I start speaking in tongues, I see myself at the throne of God. Everyone has different experiences, but I feel like a child who is helpless, who does not have anywhere else to go, and I come to my Father. He is all supreme, and I know He has the way, and I know I am in the best of care. I feel I have come so close to God that I am talking in tongues, and I am communicating easily with Him. I know I have made my supplication clear before God, and He is going to take over from there. It is communication with God, and it is very comforting. You feel that warmth coming all over you. I very strongly believe that from the day of my diagnosis till today, I have come closer to God. The Word of God came alive to me. In His mercy and His faithfulness, God saw and knew the innermost desires of our hearts, and He brought healing.

Shivani was interviewed by Andrew Cousins and Puja Verma in February 2002. She is a non-denominational Indian woman in her 30's

Open Your Heart–
Amelia Cooper & Susan Landers

Amelia begins her story . . .

In November of 1996, I had an accident. I was working for a chicken processing plant in the quick freeze. It is between 25 and 30 degrees back there, and the frozen chicken is in a big bin upstairs. It comes down this chute, and bags go up and come down, and we catch them in bags and weigh them. Sometimes the metal piece that releases the bags gets stuck. The mechanic had come in, and he thought he had fixed it. When I went to reach up for the bag, my wrist was struck. Because of the cold, I had on thermal liners and a plastic glove. When the metal bar hit my hand, all I did was shake it off and keep going. Then, about two weeks later, my hand started to hurt, and everything started to go bad.

I kept going back to work, doing the same job. They sent me to a few doctors, but they said that nothing was wrong. My hand turned blue and swollen, and I could not use it. They gave me an x-ray, but they still told me nothing was wrong. The doctors here knew very little about this particular condition. The pain ran from the fingers and palm of my hand, up into the shoulder, up into the neck, and down my back. After several months I finally got in touch with Dr. Cooper; he diagnosed it right away as RSD, reflex sympathetic dystrophy, and told my employers that they had to take me out of the cold. The bone had broken; it had severed the radial and medial nerves, and the pain was unbearable. I had no use of my hand. The company did not want to believe him. He set me up with therapy. That is when I met Susan; she was working as the therapist in his office.

Reflex sympathetic dystrophy is when the autonomic part of the brain shuts down the nervous system because the pain is so bad. There is nothing you can do. RSD can completely shut down one side of your body. My hand looked like dead bones, with no color; it was small and ugly. The doctor said that a lack of circulation in the hand causes it to be like that.

It is something that can't be cured. You have to learn to live with it. For me, it went from bad to worse. They started sending me to get stellate ganglion blocks. For that procedure, they would give me an injection here in the nerve to deaden the feeling. The pain was so bad, and that was the only way they could calm everything down. I had no motion. Susan had to make a splint to cover this area because of the pain. I had to sleep at an angle. There was very little that I could do for myself; I had to depend on others. I was a very angry person for a long time.

The stellate blocks would quiet the pain. Sometimes they would last three weeks, sometimes four. Very seldom, they lasted five weeks. Then all of a sudden the hand would start to sweat; it would drip, and I knew the pain was going to resume. Sometimes the pain would be a hot, searing pain. It was never dull. I had to wear thermal gloves because I couldn't let any cold touch this hand. There is no control of the pain; it all comes from the nerves. Sometimes I would start to pray, but I wouldn't finish. I did not feel that I had the right to ask God to do anything for me because I had not done what I was supposed to. I had not let go of the anger and the bitterness, so I didn't feel like I had the right to ask Him to do anything for me.

In June 1998, my husband and I had a car accident. A man ran into us from the back, and the back seat of the wagon was pushed into the front seat. Glass was shattered. When I realized what had happened, I was standing outside the car. Things happen, and you stop, and you think: He is always with me. Soon after that, I got fired. I couldn't get unemployment. And they closed the case three years into it because Workman's Comp said they had already spent X amount of dollars, and there was nothing they could do. But it didn't matter. I knew everything was going to work out.

After the incident with the car, I let go of all the anger and bitterness. The pain was still there some; it would come and go. When things would get real bad, I would pray and try to keep myself calm, to keep the pain away. I started to sit down and evaluate things. I asked the Lord to help me get rid of the anger. When I started to let go, there was a calm that I finally got. I started praying more and reading more, getting into my Bible. My God, He does not lie, and His Word is my nourishment.

I finally realized that only through Him could any of the pain be taken away and any healing be done, and that I had to let go all the anxiety and frustration that I had. Everything was going to be taken care of. When I finally did that, it felt like somebody took a weight off me. There would be days when, all of a sudden, I would catch a sharp pain. I would laugh and say, "Not today." This past January, my husband went to church one Sunday. When he came back home, he said that he had gone up for prayer that morning. He said to me, "The Lord told me He was going to heal you." I told him, "I know that." With every fiber that was in me, I knew that.

On Sunday, May 6, th my husband got up and went to church. Every Sunday at 2 o'clock, I would listen to Pastor Parsley of "Breakthrough Ministries" That day he was at a crusade in Anderson, Florida. He was preaching, and it was a healing service. I love to hear him; he is the type of speaker who I can listen to every day, all day. When he is talking, you can feel there is some sort of presence with him. He was talking about being at the Jordan River and having to stay there three days before passing over. He was saying that we should be third-day Christians, ready to cross over, ready to go into whatever the Lord has for us. He talked for a while, and then he said, "Right now I'm going to pray for you. Wherever you are hurting, or your injury is, put your hand over that area, and begin to pray with me." This was about 2:20.

I started to pray with him. First I had a sensation that was like the feeling you have if you run and run and then you get tired, and you go to take a deep breath, and it seems like something cuts it off and stops it after you inhale. Then I started to feel warm all through. The warmth just enveloped my whole body. And it didn't let go; it hasn't let go. I kept praying and thanking God. The warm feeling started in the tips of this hand and then went throughout my whole body. Everything happened at once. I felt myself rocking, and I stood up and looked around, and all I could do was thank Him.

I thanked God aloud, and then there was a voice in my head from God. He said, "Move your hand," and I moved it. I moved my fingers because I had had no motion in my hand; the only one that would move a little was the baby finger. I hadn't been able to move it in four years because it was splinted. At a quarter to three, my husband came home, and I was standing there crying and flexing my hand. When he came into the house, I ran and grabbed him, and I held him close. He didn't know what was going on, and I caught his hand and squeezed it. I held my husband's hand for the first time in four and a half years. He didn't say anything. I told him what had happened, and he sat there and looked at me. We both started crying and started praying. We prayed and we laughed and we talked.

After that I went and dialed the number to "Breakthrough" with this hand. I called to let them know what had happened. Then I enjoyed all the little things. I scratched my back. I put on my own shoes and tied them. I was able to put my earrings in my ear for the first time in four years and fasten them. I went in the kitchen to pick up my coffee cup; I wanted to see if I could lift it. I don't believe I slept that night. It was like I wanted to take a deep breath, and I could not. I have never had a sensation like that. You have something, and you are afraid you are going to lose it. The next morning I got up, and I looked around and said nothing. I went to my mom. I didn't tell her on the phone; I just went in.

My muscles were not weak at all. I remember cutting the rose bushes back, and a thorn pricked my finger. I felt the pain. I felt something touch my finger. Anybody who passed that road must have thought I was crazy. I was standing in the yard, laughing and crying and praising my God because I felt it. For four years I felt nothing in this hand. Unless you've been there, you don't know. My God is an awesome God; yes, He is! I went to church the next Sunday; that's the first time my brother had seen me, and when I walked in, he started to smile. I grabbed his hand, and he looked down and said, "Which hand was it?" And I started laughing.

I did not want to tell Susan on the phone. I just called and told her I needed to bring my splint in to be repaired. I wanted her to see. In a period of seven days my hand went from a chalky white to where the color was almost back. It is only because of God's grace and mercy. No doctor was able to do this for me.

Her physical therapist, Susan, shares her view . . .

RSD is caused by a trauma; your body becomes hypersensitive to being in pain all the time. The autonomic nervous system keeps responding to the fight/flight system, so whatever pain you feel becomes exaggerated and heightened. It is a continuous response, and you have increased swelling. You have sweats. It changes the vascular input to the hand. There are three stages; if you can catch RSD at a stage-one level, even a stage-two, you can reverse the symptoms. I have seen people recover from RSD, but not when they get to stage three. Amelia's condition was a stage three; stage three involves a fixed atrophic hand with severe osteoporosis. By the time I saw her, the original injury was about four months old.

When she started therapy, she was coming three times a week for a few months. The RSD kept progressing, and she kept getting worse. At the time of her healing, it had been months since I had seen her. She had been improving, but that came to a stop, and then she regressed. She ended up getting worse and worse and worse. There was nothing that could be done. All I was looking to do was pain management, and it was always short-lived.

One day, she called to make an appointment. I had repaired her splint many times, and in my brain was, "We'll make a new one." That's what I was thinking. She walked in, and she grabbed my hand and squeezed very hard, which was not like her at all. I looked down, and I looked at her hand. I kept looking at it and said, "What happened to you?" I never met her with any grip strength because of the injury. She said, "I was healed." I cried because I knew: this could only be of God. This is not humanly possible, to fix her hand. We sat down, and we talked and cried. I had never seen her left hand look like her right hand. All the swelling, all the discoloration, they were all gone.

I had given her a functional capacity evaluation while she was still injured, on April 27, 1999. Then I gave her the same test just a little over a month after her healing, on June 11, 2001. This test measures grip strength compared to what would be normal for her age and sex. In 1999, on the left hand she was 80% below standard for age and sex. Then in 2001, she was 22% above on that same hand. I also did a test of pinch strength. It's a lateral pinch, "lateral" meaning pinching from your thumb straight down onto the first finger. So in 1999, the left hand was 80% below standard for age and sex. But in 2001, she was 38% above on her healed hand. Finally, I did a manual muscle test. In 1999, she had about 60% function overall: in the wrist, she only had 40% function, in the elbow, 60% function, and the shoulder, 80% function. She was at zero function in her hand. But as of 2001, in terms of her actual strength, she has come to a complete recovery, from 40% function to 100% function.

Amelia is the only patient I have ever had who has received supernatural healing. There was no medication. There was no therapy. There was no surgery. The damage she had was past medical intervention for recovery. You cannot transplant capillaries. The capillaries were irreparably damaged. There was nothing they could do to replace it, so they left it alone. Only God could have fixed her hand.

Amelia concludes her reflections . . . My healing was exactly four and a half years to the day after the injury, from November 6th to May 6th. That period of my life was like climbing stairs, and when I finally got to the top, that is when the Lord healed me. Our pastor was preaching the other Sunday about the potter's house. When he starts to mold that lump of clay, he has to get it smooth. He has to take out the lumps. That is what the Lord had to do with me when I asked for a healing. There were other things in my life that had to be straightened out first. It was a gradual thing, but I would not change anything that I went through because of the peace and the joy that I have now.

With what is left of my life, I want to do something that is going to change somebody else's life in one way or another. I know that the Lord has something for me to do. Whatever it is, I am ready and willing. I keep remembering the verse, how God does not give you the spirit of fear, but a spirit of peace, joy, and a sound mind. Everything is different now. There is a calm and a peace within me that I once knew nothing about. No matter what, I don't look at things negatively anymore. I don't worry about things. There is an energy and a joy that I have never had. It is a feeling I don't ever want to lose. Every day when I wake up, I look around, and I thank God, and there is always a song playing in my head in the morning. The feeling is still there, and I praise Him and continue to bless Him everyday. I don't ever want to lose the peace and the joy that I feel now. This can help to strengthen someone else's faith and to let them know, don't give up on yourself. You never give up on the Lord, but don't give up on yourself either. That's what I did. I did not think that I had the right to ask Him to do anything for me.

Instead, you continue to ask and be persistent about asking God. I pray aloud wherever I am, wherever I feel like it. I know my God is a good God. I didn't give up on the Lord. The Lord was saying, "Yes, you can keep going," so I would not rest. I kept moving forward. I kept trying. I kept reading. I kept believing. And there was a warmth and an inner peace that I had never experienced before. The prayer and peace that I had found on the inside, that is what kept me going. My life was in His hands. The healing was there and was already mine. All I had to do was accept it. The Lord did not give up on me. All I had to do was stop, open my heart, have faith, and accept.

Amelia and Susan were interviewed by Andrew Cousins and Puja Verma. Amelia is an African American Baptist in her 50's.

The Power of the Lord is So Strong
—Caitlin Jackson

My friend and I go to the local community center, and some of the residents come and listen to us lead a Bible study and pray for them, and we give out groceries. My pastor encourages my friend and me, saying, "You ladies need to know that before you started coming here, the women who come to your Bible study didn't even speak to each other. They didn't even know each other. What you have done is create a community." I am also realizing that I can't get in a hurry. I can't rush God to do anything with these ladies, but they trust and love us, and sometimes they thank us to our faces for coming. They will say, "You could be with your family, and yet you choose to come and be with us." We really like them. They needed to see that we were going to continue to come.

I have a story to tell of what the ladies did for me. When my daughter, Helen, was nine or ten, we were at the pediatrician's office, and the pediatrician happened to notice something amiss. She had Helen do some simple bending exercises, and she said, "I think I see something not right here. Why don't you go to the hospital and get x-rays?" We went to the hospital's x-ray lab; they took x-rays and her spine was curved, which is scoliosis.

The pediatrician told me to get a second opinion. She said, "The hospital did the x-rays, but the orthopedic center will set a baseline and begin a treatment." Right after I got that report, it was time for my friend and me to go to the community center. When it is time for prayer, sometimes these women, one or two, will ask for something. They are still shy, and they rarely pray aloud. Sometimes they will. I shared with them and said, "I have a prayer request tonight. My daughter has been diagnosed with scoliosis and curvature of the spine. It is not so critical right now, but as she grows into her teen years and her skeleton begins growing, there is the possibility of some problems." I said, "I know God can heal her, and I ask y'all to pray." One of them just took out and started praying. She said, "Lord, You know." My daughter was there, and they all came over to Helen and prayed with her; they asked the Lord to heal her and make her spine straight.

A few weeks later we went to the orthopedic center. The doctor said, "May I take x-rays again?" I said, "That's fine." He took the x-rays, and then he said, "Helen, I want you to bend." She did the bending exercises, and he said, "I am not seeing what your x-ray is showing. Get those pictures, Helen, and come with me." We could see the wall on the hall where they place the x-rays. I saw the first x-rays, and you could see the curvature of the spine. Then I saw the x-rays they had just taken, and there was no curvature of the spine. You can't curve your spine the way scoliosis does it. You can't stand lopsided; you can't manipulate it because your spine is straight. He was consulting with another doctor, and he came back and said, "I don't see any curvature of the spine. She has no scoliosis. It is just not there." That was definitely the hand of the Lord because there was nothing else that was done to her, not chiropractic, not anything.

The next year, other health problems came up for my daughter. She was having frequent urination and rectal bleeding. The doctor said, "I have some reason to be concerned. I want you to go to a pediatric gastroenterologist." We went to see him, and he said, "We need to do a colonoscopy. I have some ideas about what this might be." The doctor came out after the surgery, showed me the pictures, and said, "There are ulcers in her colon. We took some tissue samples, and I will give you a report." She was diagnosed with Crohn's disease. If you are looking at diseases of the intestinal tract, this is the second worst: colon cancer and then Crohn's. It is incurable. It causes ulcers, holes, bleeding, and scar tissue, and this can cause it to constrict; people get parts of their colon removed. It is a very, very debilitating disease.

I started researching Crohn's disease. It had to be treated, or she would be one sick kid. She was getting worse—stomach cramps, a lot of pain, passing blood—and you cannot let that go on. She was very pale. On the internet, I found a diet from some German physicians called the Specific Carbohydrate Diet. You take everything out a person's diet except for monosaccharides. That means no starches, no breads, no rice, no whole grains. If you stay on it for two years, your colon will heal. I was giving her pure food, and it was very healthy. Our family doctor would check her periodically.

Then I came across a book; the table of contents lists specific diseases that the sponsoring ministry has had success with, and I saw Crohn's disease. I said, "Hey, Lord, are you going to tell me something?" I flipped to Crohn's disease, and it says that Crohn's disease is an autoimmune problem. The author of this book is a man named Henry Wright. He is a pastor who has a background in pharmacology and medical knowledge. His theory is that as we attack ourselves spiritually, our body also begins physically attacking itself. In regard to Crohn's disease, he believes that it is caused by self-rejection and guilt, by feelings of abandonment and hopelessness, and often by lack of self-esteem from one's father.

Helen felt hopeless because her parents were split, and her dad sometimes hurt her when she stayed with him. There was nothing she could do about it at her young age.

What this book taught me was that we are all dealt hands in life that aren't fair. But it is not what is dealt to us; it is what our reaction is. What Helen was going to have to learn was not a stuff-it mechanism, but that when life is unfair and when it hurts, she needs to go to God right away. She needs to ask God to forgive whoever did it to her and to come in and heal the hurt in her heart. Otherwise, it is the hurt from that incident that eats her up. As I read the book, I thought, "I would love to go down here and let these people minister to Helen."

So we drove to Pleasant Valley. They were very gracious to us. First we sat in a room and listened to tapes that described the ministry's teaching. Then we had personal ministry time with two people on the staff. We got this wonderful woman named Andrea; another friend of hers was there. They ministered to Helen, and they had me sit in, as the mom. The other woman would be interceding, and then Andrea would minister to Helen and me. I was impressed by how real they were; they just ran a conversational tone with their eyes open the whole time, asking us questions. They asked about Helen's birth experience. They asked about things that had happened in her childhood, and Andrea's eyes were lighting up: "I see things right here." Then she asked me other questions because you had to complete a history. She said, "I see things where the enemy has come in and had a heyday with this little one."

She told my daughter, "Helen, this is going to stop. I am going to begin to pray for you, okay?" and they prayed with their eyes open. It is just so natural. She began to pray, "Helen, I see things that have happened in your life that were no fault of your own. I come against that spirit of rejection. You are not rejected; you are accepted and beloved." She started telling her who she was in the Lord. Helen began to weep, and Andrea would stop and let Helen cry, and she would say, "Helen, is there anything else you can think of that caused you a lot of pain?" Helen began to weep again and mentioned a difficult incident that had happened. Andrea was so precious, and she was able to minister to Helen in that area.

On the way home, we went through a little college town. Our friend said, "Are y'all hungry?" I said, "She has eaten all her food." He said, "What do you want to eat?" I said, "I don't know how to tell if she is well, except to let her eat what she wants and see what happens." So I said, "Helen, what do you want?" The choices were a pizza joint and a Mexican restaurant. Helen said, "Mama, I want Mexican food." She hadn't had tacos and burritos and all that. We went into the Mexican restaurant, and she proceeded to devour the basket of chips. She had a bean burrito and a taco and a Sprite with sugar. On the way home, we stopped to go to the restroom, but she never did. We got home and then got up the next morning. She passed a totally solid stool. We already had a standing appointment with the family doctor and went to him. We told him about our visit to Pleasant Valley, and I gave him a copy of the book. After that, Helen continued to walk in health, complete health, eating anything that she wanted to.

I have a story of my own healing experience to share. I used to have psoriasis, which is an autoimmune disease that is incurable. Doctors can give you medication to make the scaliness go away, but if you quit rubbing it on, it will come back in times of stress; it is cyclical. It is real itchy, and it will bleed. I would be embarrassed to take change from a cashier and would always hold out my other hand. I had prayer for it; I kept asking the Lord to heal my skin.

A man named Mahesh came to Columbia. Mahesh would pray for people, and people would just fall out on the floor: boom, boom, boom! He had a multi-day seminar, and I managed to go to one of the evening services. Mahesh came up to the podium and said, "There has been prayer here. I can always tell when I go into a city, and the warriors have already opened the heavens for me. God is here; His presence is already here. This place has been prayed over." He said, "I feel a real strong impression of the Lord that He wants to heal eczema and psoriasis tonight." I started walking from my seat down to the front. We were all queuing up in front of him because he was going to pray. He hadn't prayed; he was still talking, and the power of the Lord came on me, and I just went out. Boom, I hit the floor, and Mahesh said, "Boy, the anointing is really strong here today."

When you are out like that, you can hear, and you are aware, or at least this is my experience. I was aware, but I wasn't aware. I didn't know how much time had passed. I don't think he ever prayed for me. Eventually, I got up and looked; there was a seat on the front row, and I sat and was trying to come out of it because the power of the Lord was so strong. I have never experienced anything like that before or since. It was really wonderful. It was like a lead blanket was on me.

I didn't want to get up. I could have lain there forever. When I sat in the front seat, the band was packing up off the stage, so I had been down a long time.

I had a sensation of being drunk. I was sitting there thinking, "I don't know if I can drive like this." The auditorium cleared out, and there were little pockets of people talking. People would come and talk to me, and they would say, "Do you need a ride home?" I said, "Nah, I think I will be all right in a little while." At some point, I managed to get up and get myself home. There was nothing immediate that happened, but a week or two later, I noticed that it wasn't there anymore. It has never come back, never.

Caitlin was interviewed by Andrew Cousins in February of 2002.
She is a non-denominational white woman in her 40's

Faith Affects the Way You Do Things
— Wayne Cannon

The warts first appeared when I was around eight years old. It started out with just one, and then they started popping up all over my hands, on the backs and palms, but just on my hands. When I saw a dermatologist, he froze the first one with liquid nitrogen, and it swelled up like a blister. When the blister broke, I had a ring of small warts around the scar. Then they spread over my hand, and they started popping up on my left hand as well. I saw a dermatologist three times, the one that did the freezing. I went back to him and showed him what had happened. He froze it again, and it went away that time. But there were others that he couldn't get rid of. The blisters would swell up, and they would come back.

It didn't bother me much as a kid, but after adolescence it started bothering me more. I was very reluctant to shake hands with people, and it prevented a level of intimacy as well. When I got to college at eighteen, I saw a plastic surgeon and had them removed from the tops of my hands; on my left hand, three; on my right hand, four. On my left hand, I have a scar on my middle finger. That was the one that was enormous; it covered the joint, and the plastic surgeon told me that the roots were wrapped around the bone. There was no way to remove that without causing some serious damage to my finger. I would probably lose the feeling and do some serious nerve damage, especially with the ones that were on the pads because those ran deeper than usual. These were painful, but they weren't excruciating. If I bumped them hard, sometimes they would bleed. It was mostly unsightly; it wasn't a debilitating condition. It's a virus, and I have been told that you can outgrow them. Eventually, your immune system is able to defeat the virus. I don't know how long it takes for that to happen because it happened differently for me.

I grew up in a small Baptist school, and it was very strict. It was a private school, up through eighth grade. All of my religious knowledge came from that school because we had Bible courses, like any other regular curriculum, and I grew up with prayer and regular worship services. My father's family was Assembly of God, which is very similar to Pentecostal, and my mother was Pentecostal. We also went to a Baptist church for about six years. Because my sister and I went to the Baptist school, they wanted to keep the same denomination, to keep from confusing us. I started going to church regularly with my parents in 1999, the year that this event happened, the year I moved back home from college. I had moved back to help my parents open up another business, and around that time, my dad had a motor vehicle accident. He fell out of a truck and was run over. His lower legs were crushed, and he had to have two chest tubes placed, so he came pretty close to the brink of dying. He spent a lot of time at the hospital.

In my family, we always have Sunday dinners after church. It is a large family get-together with twenty to thirty people who come over to my family's house. It's a kind of a potluck. At the end of one of those Sundays, right after my dad had been released from the hospital, we decided to pray for him. He was getting along okay, but his legs were bothering him. He still had problems from the orthopedic damage. The prayer session there was in a Pentecostal style. We gathered around my dad, and I don't usually participate in these sorts of things, but I wanted to show some support for him. My dad was sitting down, and I was at his back with my right hand on him, and my cousin was beside me. I don't know how many people were there, but I know it was my sister, my mom, and I, and there were other relatives. It was mostly a lot of people with hands on shoulders, standing shoulder to shoulder and praying.

My cousin led the prayer, but everyone was praying at once. The prayers that I heard started off with praise to God in some form, followed by a giving of thanks; then there is usually a request. They were requesting healing and requesting support for the family, God's support for my mother, my sister, and me in dealing with this, and for my dad. One person leads the prayer, and after he initiates, other people follow in out loud. My prayer would have been silent, something to the effect of, "Heavenly Father, thank You for preserving my father's life. Please help him deal with his pain and get back on his feet. Please help my father get through this."

Somewhere around the middle of that prayer, I remember feeling heat, and it wasn't on my hands; it was in my back. It was a lot of heat. I thought at first, maybe it's because I am a little uncomfortable here with everyone around me. I am in the middle of this new situation. I have seen it, but I have never been in it before. The heat was in the small of my back, and it felt like it radiated up through the back of my neck; it was a burning heat. It was very hot for about five seconds. I was sweating, but I thought I was having a nervous reaction. I didn't know what to make of it, but I passed it off. I felt odd because this was a new experience, and I don't recall seeing anything. I had my eyes closed and my head down. The prayer lasted two or three minutes. All of the prayer was toward my dad. Perhaps there was something like, "And help this family support him and get him through this time," but nothing specifically was directed toward anyone else.

The following day, while I was in the shower, I noticed that all the warts were gone from my hands! I believe I could have had close to thirty warts. I never counted them. If I had, I would have lost track. But when I was taking a shower, all but one of them appeared to have dried up and were gone. I have scars left from the ones that I had surgery on, but the ones that I had never had touched with a scalpel or frozen were gone without a trace. The exception is I had one on my right hand, a small wart, but that one has disappeared over the past week and a half, so now I have none at all. Maybe God said, "You have had these long enough. You don't need them anymore."

I mentioned the healing to my cousin and his mother within the week, as I realized what had happened. They said that it was a divine healing, and I didn't doubt it. I believe in the power of laying on of hands. I have told other people in my family, but I haven't gotten up in front of a church and spoken about what happened with my warts. It's not because I am ashamed of God or think this is really wacky. I'm bashful. I am more of an introvert, and I wouldn't feel comfortable. However, I would say that the level of faith that I have is pervasive about my being, and faith affects the way you do things.

Wayne is a white Baptist in his 20's who was interviewed by Andrew Cousins in September of 2001

I'm in Jesus' Hand
–Tonia Waller

In 1982, I was rushed to the hospital. They could not find what was causing the pain, but they removed my gallbladder. After the procedure, the pain continued, though it was different. From that point on, I was in and out of the hospital; they did several procedures on me to see what was going on in my system. They found out that my liver was damaged. The only thing they could do was give me antibiotics; I would go into the hospital for that because they gave it to me through IV. Any infection would affect my liver, so I could not catch a cold. For fourteen years I was in and out of the hospital for those reasons. At the time they first found out that my liver was damaged, transplant for liver was not possible.

In 1988 they found a cyst the size of a grapefruit behind my pancreas. They said immediately that they would take it out or drain it. They took an x-ray and showed it to me. The next day, I was in the hospital, and they took me down for surgery. I was already prepped to have the surgery, but they took another x-ray for their records.

That day, a man met us in the hall. We had never met him before. He told us that it was going to be all right. He knew some of our friends, and he knew a lot of things about us. He said, "Is it all right if I pray for y'all?" And I said, "Yes." So he prayed, and he said, "Amen." When we looked up and opened our eyes to say thank you, he had gone. The hallway was long, and nobody was in the hallway. We saw a friend later on that day who came to the hospital to have x-rays done, not knowing that we were there.

She said, "Oh, you're sick again?" I said, "Yeah, but it will be all right." We told her about the person we had seen, and she said she did not know who we were talking about. She had never heard the person's name. That was amazing. We had just closed our eyes, and when he said, "Amen," we thought we were going to have another conversation, but he had gone. We looked down the hall and said, "What is going on?" We were amazed. We believe that was an angel.

Later, they could not find the cyst. They said it had gone. The cyst had disappeared. Of course, my husband and I had been praying about the situation, and that was a miracle performed!

Another time, I was at the point of death. When I woke up, the sheet was already over me, but I heard a voice that said, "No, Tonia, it is not time for you to go." I felt myself leaving the body, but I didn't think it was death. I went to sleep peacefully, and I relaxed, but I felt that something different was about to happen. I saw darkness, and I saw my grandfather and my great-grandmother. They did not say anything. It was so peaceful, and I wanted to go with them. At the same time, I knew that they were dead. So I said, "Wait." Within seconds I had this conversation within myself. I said, "They're not living; how can I see them?" I heard the voice say, "No, Tonia, it is not time for you to go; I want you to repeat, 'The Lord is my shepherd.'" They had already called the chaplain, and he was praying over me at the time. They said they saw the sheet move, so they knew that I had come back. They did not hear what I was saying, but they heard me mumbling. They said I was gone a good ten minutes, but it didn't seem like that. A lot of things nobody knows but God.

A physician gave me three choices of hospitals to go to for the liver transplant when that became an option. I went with Alabama because they were more successful, and they could take me. That Saturday night I had my family come over, and we touched and agreed, believing that I would stay there, and that I would find a donor. We believed God for a healing. We were supposed to be going only to be interviewed to see if they would accept me to have a liver transplant. That Monday they examined my body to see if I was able to have the procedure, but they said that they would not give me a transplant because I was too far gone. I said, "What?!" They were very frank. They said they were not going to waste the liver. They wouldn't give me three months to live. They were very firm and to the point. You couldn't even say, "Please try to help me." When they told us that, I started crying, and my husband started crying. I said, "Oh, Ben, if you cry, I know . . ." So he said, "Wait, let's pray." So he and I prayed in the Spirit, and it seems like that doctor had one foot out and one foot in; he came right back and said, "We decided to put you in the hospital and wait for a donor." That was the moving of God.

I went to the hospital room and waited. I was so sick and in pain. When you are at the point of death, you are just miserable. When I would fall asleep, I could hear Ben reading a Scripture to me, and even if he were to leave the room, he would leave a tape on, and it would be Bible verses. I could hear the Word and fall asleep; way in the back, the Word of God was being read to my spirit.

Three weeks after I arrived, they had a donor. Normally it takes three to four years. I didn't know until after the fact, but each member of my family had taken a day and time to pray for me, and they had been praying around the clock. We also had church support from home, as well as churches in other cities and states with me on their prayer lists. They came in the room at exactly eleven o'clock on Sunday, October 5th, and said, "We have a donor, and you have to be prepped." I said, "What happened?" She said, "It was a white male; he was in his early twenties, and he was in a car accident." He and I were compatible with everything, so they started prepping me and took me down. You have to go immediately because of the liver transplant. As they were rolling me down the hall, a man said, "Are you okay?" and I said, "Yeah, I'm fine." I was praying as we were talking. In the operating room, there were twelve doctors. I said, "Wow, all of these people?" and she said, "All of them are doctors and have a part to play. There's nothing for you to be afraid of." I said, "I'm not afraid. I'm in Jesus' hand." I asked, "I have a tape; could you play it?" One doctor said, "No," and the other one said, "Yes," so they compromised. He said, "I will put mine on for a while, and then we will put yours on." When I went to sleep, mine was on. It was Gloria Copeland; she was singing a praise song on healing. One of the doctors said, "Oh, this is one of my favorite people." He knew the song, and that helped a whole lot.

It took twelve hours, but when I came through, I asked them if I could see my liver. They said not to show it to me because it was hard as a rock, and it had lumps sticking out of it. They did not know what kind of bacteria that was. They did not know how I had been living. They could not explain it. It is in the medical books because they had never seen a liver like that. The doctor said he was amazed how we handled things. After the transplant, he saw that it had to be God who did some of the things. After the surgery, my skin started to come back, and my color started to come back.

As my husband says, "God gave us favor. He opened up the windows of heaven and poured us out blessing." People have always come up to me and asked me to give my testimony. I told God, "God, I do not like to talk in public. I do not like the feeling." I said, "You are going to have to work this thing out, and it is going to be You who are doing the moving because I am not going to volunteer to do it." God is still moving in that because He knew my heart. I wanted to make sure that it was not of self-glory, that when I gave it, it would be the anointing, and that He would get the glory and not me.

I wanted to keep myself humbled because I know He did it. Just that little testimony can change somebody else's life or their faith in God.

Tonia was interviewed by Vivian Moore in May of 2002.
She is an African American Baptist in her 40's.

To God Be the Glory
—Denise Wolcott

Our son was born with his hips 45 degrees out of the socket. He did not need any surgery, but it would take years of wearing corrective shoes. The hips were there, and the legs were formed, but they were just not formed inside of the hip region. They had to be rotated. We could take the hips with our hands and rotate them in, and they would go into the socket, but it was something we were going to have to mold. He was put in corrective shoes when he was about eight months old, with a bar between those shoes that hooked to the bottom of the shoes, to help align the bone back into the hip joint. There was also a bar that went across the bottom of his crib, and the bar on his shoes hooked into the bottom of that bar. That's how he slept at night. They did not want him to be able to turn over in that frog position when babies lie on their stomachs because that would keep his hips out.

He stayed in the bar 23 hours out of 24. He learned how to maneuver and crawl with that bar in place. But it was bedtime that was really bad for him. He just despised having to get in bed at night with that bar, knowing he was not going to be able to move. My husband and I cried every night; it was a horrible ordeal. We were praying because we believe in prayer. I believe in faith healing and instant healing from God, and we had started praying from the beginning that the Lord would heal him. When he began to walk, he was very pigeon-toed still. The hips were still rotating out. He also had a large knot on both sides of his feet. It was about the size of a quarter and stuck out half an inch to a quarter of an inch at his ankle. It was a hard knot, and there was never an explanation to us why that was because he was never x-rayed for it. As he grew, it grew with him, but it did not grow any larger than his foot. When he was about three years old, if he would run, he would fall down because one tip of the toe would catch the bottom of the heel. He was constantly tripping.

One day, we were in revival at church, and we had an evangelist from Texas. Every night, he called people down to the front of the church, if you had a special request, or a need, or if you needed God to intervene in your life in any way. We went and got my son out of the nursery to ask for prayer for his ears because we were having a lot of problems at the time with tubes and things. We were not even thinking of his feet because that was something that we had become accustomed to. It wasn't that we had stopped asking God to heal him, but, right at that point, he was sick all the time with his ears, so we wanted this evangelist to pray for his ears.

When we got down to the front of the church and it was our time, my husband and I walked up with our child, and the pastor said, "What is your need?" We started talking about his ears, that we would like God to heal them, since he was having all these medical problems. He had been on antibiotics for months and months and months. The evangelist stopped us right in our talking and said, "That's not the healing that your son needs tonight." Immediately I knew what he was talking about, and I started crying, sobbing out loud. I said, "It's his feet; it's his feet!" and the evangelist said, "Take off his socks and his shoes." That's all he said; I began to take them off, and he said, "Do you believe that God can heal him and heal him right now?" My husband and I said, "Yes, we do, we do believe," and we started praying out loud, "Lord, please heal him."

By the time I had taken his socks and shoes off, the first thing I noticed was that both knots were gone. We put our child down on the floor, and his feet were straight as they could be. I didn't feel his hips; I didn't have to do anything because when I saw his feet . . . ! Whenever we put our child on the floor, his toes were pointed to each other, and now they were straight as they could be. There is no doubt in my mind that God healed our child that night, and I know it was because my husband and I had the faith to believe. The church was packed, and everybody who went to that church knew about my son's feet. We go to church every Sunday morning, every Sunday night, and every Wednesday night, and everybody knew he wore his tennis shoes backwards. He had been wearing his left shoe on his right foot and his right shoe on his left foot; that was part of his therapy. But ever since that night, his feet have been straight!

I took him back to the doctor. I said, "I need you to look at my child," and he said, "What's wrong?" I said, "I just need you to look at his feet." I had my son take off his socks and shoes, and he ran back and forth in the office. The doctor said, "What happened?" I said, "God healed him two days ago." The doctor put him up on the table; he felt from his hips all the way down, and his explanation was, "I don't know what happened, but I do know that his hips are in the sockets." I know God did it, no doubt in my mind. It was not a gradual thing; it happened right then!

We had been praying for three years for God to heal him. I don't know why God chose that time, perhaps because, in front of all those people, God could get the glory. People know my husband and me in that church, and they know we are not the type who would get up and scream and holler and shout and cry in front of the church like I did. If God had healed him at home, if he had awakened one morning and had been healed, would people believe me as much as they would have by seeing the healing take place right then? I know when he was placed on the floor, his feet were straight; the healing was there, and with it happening in a group of people like that, God is getting more glory for it.

Denise Wolcott was interviewed by Andrew Cousins in February of 2002.
She is a white woman in her 40's who attends a
Pentecostal Holiness congregation.

Nothing is Impossible for God
—Barbara Clayton

I had a normal pregnancy and a normal delivery. They immediately laid my son on my chest, and I noticed that he was making a low grunting sound. He wasn't crying. I realized quickly that it was because he couldn't cry. He could not get the breath to cry, so I looked at the nurses and said, "Something is wrong; he is not breathing right." He was turning a light blue. I thought, "This can't be good." I kept saying, "You need to take him; you need to take him and do something. He is not breathing right." They said, "Oh, he'll be fine; he'll be fine. He will catch his breath in a minute," but he never did.

Within five minutes, it went from "Oh, everything will be fine," to yanking him off my chest and putting an oxygen mask over his head. They were starting to get concerned because he couldn't catch his breath. Once the neonatal doctor got there, he said that he had respiratory distress syndrome, and it was very serious. He was trying to breathe on the outside the way that he had breathed inside me, and his lungs were not making the adjustment. They gave us a very grim outlook at first. The doctors said he would be in intensive care for months and that he would probably have major breathing problems, possibly asthma. They thought he had a hole in his lung and that one of the valves in his heart had not closed. They said the next twenty-four hours would be crucial, and he might not make it.

My husband and I prayed that evening, before we could even see him, after the doctor told us about the hole in his lung, the right chamber of his heart not closing, and all the breathing problems. I started to pray in the Spirit, and before the end of the prayer, there was a peace that filled the room and filled my heart. I was completely okay, and I knew he would be going home; I knew he was going to be fine. God had it all under control. I was told by the Lord that my son would be going home on Wednesday, six days later. When my husband opened his eyes, he said, "What did you hear?" I said, "You go first." He said, "Something about Wednesday," and I said, "Yeah, he's going home on Wednesday." We told the nurses, and they thought I had completely lost my mind. Some of them even laughed in my face, and someone said, "Oh, no, honey, he's not." And I said, "Oh, yes, he is."

At ten o'clock that night, we were allowed to see him for the first time because our pastor was there. They allow pastors in even when they don't allow parents, if they are going to pray. He very much felt like he wanted to go in and pray over our son. Our son was in an isolette; he had all these tubes, and a huge oxygen plate over his head, and it was horrible. He was pinned down by tubes, and our pastor went in and laid his hands on the isolette. He started praying, and he prayed the sweetest prayer. He was holding my hand, and I was holding my husband's hand; I had my hands raised because that's how I worship and pray. One of the nurses came over; she bowed her head in prayer with us, and she raised her hands, and I really felt the presence of the Lord. It is a very calming, sweet Spirit that comes over me; it is reassuring, and it completely calms my heart. I grow very calm and reassured that God has it under control.

The day after our baby was born, the doctor came in and said, "We have re-evaluated. He does not have a hole in his lung, and the chamber in his heart looks like it may be beginning to close." But in the days that followed, they would not let me touch him, and for a mother, that is horrible. I was not able to hold him; he was so sick that it was taking every ounce of energy to breathe. They could not feed him for five days; they could not bathe him for three. They could barely even change his diaper because everything was too much stimulation for his system to handle and sent him into a tailspin where he couldn't breathe. He was having oxygen supplied for him and IV food. But we kept clinging to the promise that we had received in prayer; every time we had a bad report, we would say, "He is going home on Wednesday." Every day was a little bit of improvement.

On Sunday we had a church service, and I asked for the pastors to pray. Our son was still in the hospital. The pastors and members of the congregation laid hands on me at 12:15 on Sunday afternoon, and they prayed in the Spirit; those who were not Spirit-filled prayed in English. When we got to the hospital at 2:30, the pediatric respiratory specialist was waiting for us. He said, "I wanted to make sure that I talked to you. I don't know what happened, but we took your son off of his oxygen today. Something happened at 12:15." I said, "I know what happened. At 12:15 I was prayed over for my son." The doctors said he completely turned around at that time; he was breathing better on his own than with the oxygen they were supplying, so they took it off. I said, "God is healing him, and he is going to go home on Wednesday." The specialist looked at me, and asked if I believed that. He said that he did not consider himself a Christian, but he believed that God had healed my son. There was no other explanation, once I told him that we were prayed over.

For the most part, for five days, every time the doctors would come in, they would say, "There is no change; there is no change," and I would say, "Oh, yes, there is. There are a lot of changes going on," and they would say, "No, there aren't." We would continue to go and pray over his incubator. On day five they let me hold him and nurse him. The day before he was supposed to go home, his heart had not closed, but he was completely off the oxygen, and most of the tubes had been removed. On Wednesday, I kept saying, "Okay, God, I am going to take my baby home today." I got there in the morning, and I said, "When are we signing him out?" and they said, "He is not being released today." My heart fell; I knew that I had heard from God that he was going home that day, and I assumed that when I got there at ten in the morning he would be ready to go. I thought that he would be completely healed, and everything would be fine, but they said his heart still had not closed up. There were a few other things that needed to happen.

But by the end of the day, the very last shift when they could release him—that afternoon at five o'clock—the nurse came and said, "Let's get him ready to go home," and he went home that day. His heart closed right before we got ready to leave. The nurses said, "We're going to miss you; we didn't think you were going home yet." It was exciting. They told us that his chest would be caved in for the rest of his life, but there is not one lasting effect that shows that he has ever been sick. He does not have asthma; he does not have any breathing problems, and his chest does not cave in. What happened with my son has strengthened my faith in God. I realize that absolutely nothing is beyond His realm of control; He can change any certain thing. It has really strengthened my faith to know that nothing is impossible for God; He can do anything.

Barbara was interviewed by Georgianna Jackson in April of 2002. She is a non-denominational white woman in her 30's

Chapter 3

PSALM 23

The LORD is my shepherd; I shall not want.
He maketh me to lie down in green pastures;
He leadeth me beside the still waters;
He restoreth my soul.
He leadeth me in the paths of righteousness for his name's sake.
Yea, though I walk through the valley of the shadow of death,
I will fear no evil; for thou art with me;
Thy rod and thy staff, they comfort me.
Thou preparest a table before me in the presence of mine
enemies: thou anointest my head with oil; my cup runneth over.
Surely goodness and mercy shall follow me all the days of my
life: and I will dwell in the house of the LORD forever.

The Lord is My Shepherd
– Anna Greene

I recently read something about Quakers and holding people in the light; that's what they say Quakers do, "hold you in the light." It is this image you have of a person in front of you, and you hold it there without trying to say, "Okay, God, it should go this way or this way or that way," and in the process you leave it open for God's action, without the human element in it. That's one of the things that I have worked on really hard over these years, to get myself simply to be open, and that's no easy task. Over the last six months or so, I have been trying to be more connected to my feelings because I have typically kept my feelings away and been pretty numb. I was talking to a family systems coach, and part of my life was not being able to say what I felt about things, not feeling it, and not knowing what it was. I don't know how we got to talk about my connections to my mother. I had had these conversations, but when we went into worship one night, I don't think it was on my conscious mind. What drew me to it was that a woman said, "Is everybody here in that song?" My immediate thought was, "No, my mother isn't here." I just stayed with that, and I don't really remember how the image came, except that there it was, this image of my mother holding me as a baby. It was the fact that she would have held me, and that she would have been doing her best to mother me, and that that's what we all need. I was very glad for the image, very grateful because it was gaining back a piece of myself that had been unknown to me. It was getting a part of myself, finding a part of myself.

It was a gift. It certainly didn't come out of my consciousness. It came out of something more than me, bigger than me. Maybe it was stored in my memory if I had experienced it: just my mother with her arms around me. One of the little pieces that I know about this holding was that I have always wanted to be held; it may have been a drivenness because of this lack of connection to my mother. But I haven't noticed that recently; making that connection with my mother holding me has more than filled the void. It made me more complete. Once I got that natural connection, I haven't felt the other. In that sense, it was resolved and healed. When I saw that image, I was crying. The tears were rolling down my face, but I just felt glad. It embraced the whole thing, the whole dimension, and my mother embracing me.

On a different topic, I asked for a meeting for healing with the Quakers. A meeting for healing is a long-standing Quaker tradition. The way it works is people come together, and you have to want to be held in the light. It is not done against your will, so you agree, and you can be physically present or not. I asked three other Quakers to come together with me, and we ended up with just three of us, two other Quakers and me. The worship took place in somebody's house. This was a first for all of us because none of us had done a meeting for healing. I had read about it, and I just said, "This is what's on my mind, and let's just have a go at this, and see what happens." I started out with a list. There's a list of affirmations and things that you need to let go of, so I was reading that list and asking them to hold me in the light, but they said, "Oh, Anna, you're talking too much." They said a couple of things to me, and I said something to the effect that I was hiding behind all the things that I was going over, so we settled in the quiet.

Then out of nowhere, I remembered this image of my parents. My mother and father fought when I was very young, about four or five. I would be in my room in the hall, and they would be in another room fighting. Out of the quiet, the thing that came to me that night was, "Anna, you don't have to hide anymore."

I had never really thought of it or perceived that situation in that way before, but I realized, "You don't have to hide. You're an adult, and you don't have to be afraid of what you've got to say." That was a real inspiration, a healing inspiration. It's an inner knowing. My response was: Anna, you don't have to hide anymore. It was a truth about myself that I didn't know. How did it make me feel? I was glad, relieved. I cried again. I felt relief—and released from this idea that, "You've got to keep quiet, so you'll be safe."

I have spent most of my life hiding and running. That's how I learned to cope as a little one.

Toward the end of the meeting, we talked about what happened to us as we were sitting there. One of them said she felt very moved by the experience, and the other one was saying things that were affirming of me. Since the meeting, I have thought of it a good bit. In some situations, it would come to me, "Anna, you don't have to hide. You can say your piece." It has stayed with me.

I don't consciously think about other people's healing. I am more and more conscious of inviting God to be present through me, and the healing comes with me just being the best I can be, the truest to my higher self. As I do that and relate to other people, then the potential for them to be healed is there. But it is not me focusing on their healing. If I am sitting with you and being the best I can be, we have a connection, just by the fact that we are here. What comes to my mind is that I am doing my best to relate my true self to you, the self that I know and experience. I am trying my best to put that out to you, to share that with you. I have always believed in being honest, in self-honesty. If I am being the best I can be, and I am connected to you, I am going to influence you, without trying to influence you. My presence and being will influence you. If I am being the best I can over here, and you are doing the same, then we have lots of room for God to be here, too. There is lots of free space, and we don't have to worry. I don't have to worry that I am hurting your feelings or that I am going to be hurt.

Healing brings with it peace, and you don't have repercussions. The only possible repercussion I see is that there is a part of me that is afraid to have another meeting for healing and do that in a worshipful way. I am afraid that I might not be able to be open and have the same good result that I had before. It is fearfulness that I might not have another inspiration. I am not ready for it because I haven't gotten there. I will know when I get there. You have to be open to divine inspiration, but you can't force it. I have been struggling with that. I believe that I can expect God to be there and give me answers. What happens if He doesn't? Then one waits for the answer. How long?—as long as it takes. Why no answer?—it could be several things. I might not be ready to hear the answer, or I might not be open enough, quiet enough, still enough, and calm enough to get my own stuff out of the way and have space for God's presence. Those are the two things that come to my mind because God is here.

When I was about 13 or 14, God called my name. I remember very clearly a candlelight service at a Lutheran camp, and my prayer at that time was this hymn, "Take My Life, and Let It Be Consecrated, Lord, To Thee." That was the beginning of my relationship to God and my awareness. I don't know that I felt that then, but I was very moved by the experience, and in a sense it was a dedication. What we had to do is get a rock along the path; it was a candlelight thing, and you put it on this altar, and you had to recite something. I chose that hymn. I give it a lot of significance upon reflection. It was the beginning of my spiritual life.

My more recent spiritual questing began sometime before August 1998 because, at that date, I quit my job as a home health social worker. I quit because I couldn't do it anymore. It just didn't fit; it didn't have any life, and it didn't have any meaning, so I quit. I had money saved. I was working a little bit part-time, and I saw the whole thing as my effort to be led by God and to see where I was to go and what I was to do. That was a drastic move for me to quit my job, and then I got laid off from my part-time job. I was drawing unemployment, and all this time I was still trying to be led and asking, "What am I to be doing with my life?" The Christmas of 1999 I was stuck. Nothing was happening. The way was not opening to anything, so I made a head decision; I said, "You have to do something different." Within six weeks, I made arrangements and moved to another city.

In the process of all that, part of what I learned was that I was trying too hard. I was trying too hard to see what the way was. I have gotten more relaxed about it, and it seems the more relaxed I have grown, the better, and the more pieces have fallen together. When I went on the retreat, I got really clear about my vision for myself. My vision is a life that is gathered, and that's a Quaker word; it's gathered, so that all aspects come together into a living whole. Every part comes together into this whole that is bigger than any one part. This has been amazing to help me stay focused and to get clear about what does matter. I am trying hard not to do things out of duty but out of love because I believe that's where God is. It would go back to that potential to be the best you can be, however that unfolds. If you have to struggle against it, or with it, it is probably not toward your best self. Another way of listening to God is noticing what draws me to it.

I have been journaling since 1975, writing in a journal almost daily. In the last month, I have been clearer about how I wanted to use my journal time. When I was on retreat a couple of weeks ago, I developed my morning discipline: I write in my journal, and I say, "Good morning, Great One. I am dependent on You." Then I write, "I invite God's presence and welcome it," and I talk about things that I am grateful for. If there are things on my mind, I try to think about them on paper, and then I ask for clarity to discern the way forward and the ability and the strength to carry it out. That is in the context of believing that God does know the next step and the way forward. Usually I am sitting and being quiet; that works pretty well for me. Quakerism is about inner guidance, and then you act it out in the world. So one of the things that works well for me is to do my thinking, to try to be in touch with feelings, and then to go into the contemplative quiet. That is what I do in my morning quiet time. The journaling has been one of those practices that I am drawn to.

My life is getting more and more like that: gathered. It takes a lot of work. The pieces for me are my family, my work, and my relationship to God. Family is a relationship, right here, right now. My journaling is about my relationship to God, but there's another piece: my relationship to myself. I work part-time by choice, so that I have time for these other pieces. I have really tried to live simply. I do volunteer things with my faith community. And I put a lot of effort into my family and their well-being and environment.

Anna was interviewed by Andrew Cousins in November of 2001.
She is a white Quaker woman in her 60's.

He Leadeth Me Beside the Still Waters
−Nora Bradford

I had a bout with colon problems and polyps. To keep from having cancer, I had quite a few colonoscopies to remove the polyps. I was praying that God would heal me. At the time, I was also going to a particular church. The pastor had what she called a "Pool of Bethesda." It is in the Bible: with the Pool of Bethesda, you walk into it and are healed. She used her granddaughter's little swimming pool, brought it to church, and put water and anointing oil in it. All of us prayed over the holy oil. We lined up, and everybody stepped into the water. It was about nine inches high, enough to get your feet wet. So I stepped in; she anointed me on the head with that holy oil and started praying for me. The Spirit went all over me, and I was shaking like a leaf on a tree. God healed me of my colon right then, completely. I knew it was healed. I felt the Lord all over me. It makes you feel so wonderful, you don't ever want it to stop. You feel like a different person. It is a wonderful, wonderful feeling. God works in mysterious ways, and He assured me I was healed. God is able to do anything but fail.

Then I went to the doctor, and I didn't tell him anything. He did the exam, and then he walked over to the bed where I was recovering. He looked down into my face, and he said, "Ms. Bradford, wake up! Wake up, Ms. Bradford! I have some good news. Wake up!" I opened my eyes, and he had his head hanging down over the rail, staring me in the face. I looked at him and said, "What's the matter?" He said, "Good news! Good news! I went into you, and I couldn't find a thing. I couldn't even tell where it was. I decided to go back again because I didn't even see a scar. I couldn't find one. I couldn't find a polyp. It was clean, like nothing had ever been there."

I said, "Oooh, oooh! Praise God! Thank You, Jesus!" He looked at me with them big brown eyes so wide, I thought they were going to pop out of his head. He didn't understand what I was saying. He backed off from the bed, and I said, "Isn't that wonderful?" He said, "I don't know what I did, but it is clear and clean as if nothing had ever been there." I said, "You didn't do it. God did that for me. God healed me. I know when He did it, but I didn't tell you. I wanted you to see for yourself." He looked at me so strange and said, "Well, Ms. Bradford, I don't think I'm going to call you anymore. If you want to come back, you call me, okay?" and out the door he went, down the hall. Then he stopped in the lounge and talked with my daughter. He told her what he told me and, in the process, she did the same thing. She raised her hand and said, "Praise God! Thank You, Jesus!" She said that he looked at her the same way, with his big old brown eyes stretched wide open, and he said, "I told your mother that she can call me if she needs me," and down the hall he went.

God has healed me, and I know He has healed me. When He does it, He does it right. I am doing fine. He healed my colon, and I haven't been bothered anymore. I don't feel like I need to go back for another checkup. If the doctor wants me to come, to prove to him that it is still healed, that would be my source of going, not that I doubt. Because when God heals you, you are healed. I praise God and praise Jesus; I praise God the Holy Spirit. It is such a wonderful feeling, to know the Lord. It gives you peace that passes all understanding to know that you belong to the Lord.

Last year in January, I had a mammogram. When the radiologist called me into his office, I could tell that something was wrong, and it was. He found four white spots in one breast. The largest one was a little smaller than a dime. There were three other under that, to the right side, about a quarter of an inch in size. I saw the larger one on the x-ray. He explained to me that we needed to watch it, to keep having the mammograms, and for me to do self-examinations at home. I was really concerned about it, but I knew that God was going to heal me. The doctor said, "I would like for you to come in for another mammogram next year. If you need to come before then, don't hesitate." I said, "All right."

I had some prayer, a good bit of prayer. I had prayer in my churches. Two or three months after the first mammogram, I got to thinking about it. I thought, "I don't believe there's anything in there." I was not satisfied with his findings and what he had told me. I wanted to confirm it if it was true. So I told my daughter, "I'm going to get my x-rays, and I'm going to take them to another doctor for a second opinion." I did. He examined me, and he said, "I can't find a thing." He put the x-rays up, looked at them, and said, "I want to let you see the x-rays. See if you can show me where it was." I did, but it wasn't there. It was gone. All of the spots were gone! I had a mammogram again recently and got a letter from the hospital, and it says, "Your mammogram does not show any sign of cancer." God has healed me again.

All through my childhood, I would pray to God and talk to the Lord; I would feel His presence and know that He was there for me. I always pray at night, before I go to bed. It gives me great peace and satisfaction. I wish everybody knew the Lord and everybody had the feeling of the Holy Spirit. God is so good. He can do anything but fail. He created us. So if He created us, He can heal us. He is a wonderful, wonderful God. I am praising Him, and I am grateful. I praise His Holy Name. When you know the Lord, you start a different life, a life of love, patience, and understanding—and faith and faith and faith and more faith! Love and faith are what get you on the right road and keep you there. God is your guide. God has been so good to me. I praise Him with all my heart. I cannot give Him enough praise or enough glory. There is nothing like knowing the Lord. He is just wonderful, wonderful!

Nora was interviewed by Andrew Cousins and Puja Verma in July of 2002. She is a white woman in her 50's who attends a Pentecostal Holiness congregation.

He Restoreth My Soul
–Evan Scott

I was healed from an addiction, and faith was the foundation of it. Before my healing, I was a churchgoer and knew some of the Word, but I never really understood it until I began the process of recovery. Once I began to understand the Word, I began to believe more, and my faith got stronger. The faith was there, but the understanding of faith was what began to make me see the healing process and believe I could be healed.

There are different types of programs, and God has different ways of healing each individual. Some people may go through the healing of addiction and never set foot in a treatment center or support group, so it is whatever road God needs to take that individual down to get what he needs. Addiction is a very hard illness to get under control; as with any illness, some treatments work on some people, and some don't. I do believe that you have to have some spiritual foundation, and some type of Twelve-Step Program. You are not going to get healed from addiction until you deal with God.

I was in a spiritual-based program, a Twelve-Step one, with constant early morning devotional services, and each day I prayed for understanding and knowledge. One morning, about sixty days into my recovery program, a light came on. I felt God's presence, and everything began to make sense. It was like a whole ton of weight just flew away. Everything started to come together, as far as what I needed to do in my faith and what I needed to let God do. I began to make sense of what I had learned those previous sixty days: like being patient and tolerant and understanding that I can't change me; I have to let God change me. I have to do what I need to do, what I am empowered to do, but I also have to let God do it the way He chooses to do it.

Today when a problem arises, I know that somewhere there is an answer and a solution; I either have to wait it out or keep my eyes open to see the opportunities for the solution to get solved. I keep my faith strong and my spiritual eye open, so that when the particular door opens to escape from the situation, I walk through it. In essence, my strong belief is that everything is going to turn out for the best.

I have been in this healing process for eight years, working on nine. There are a lot of character defects that come from being in addiction, but a lot of my character defects had nothing to do with addiction at all. Though I have come a long way, I have a much farther road to go. I have faith and belief that if I continue to do what I need to do, those things, too, will be healed and will go away in their time. I am not a person who is apt to pray to God, "Please remove this character defect," as quickly as it sounds because I have to be ready to accept how He decides to get rid of it. I try not to ask for something outright, unless I am truly ready for the results I am going to receive. There will be results! Now do I really want them? If I am not ready to let Him do it, then I do not ask. It is a process of getting to that wanting. Sometimes I can slow down my healing process by not being ready to do the things I need to do.

As I heal, I am constantly making changes; first, the quite obvious changes: people, places, and things. I also had to change my reasons for going to worship. As opposed to it becoming a habit, now I am able to go into worship and receive something for it, some sense of growth, of satisfaction, of salvation and freedom. There is constant change to maintain the healing, as well as constant change to prepare myself for future healing. It is an ongoing and gradual process for me.

Over time, I have learned many helpful things. The only requirement to being saved is to accept that Jesus died on the cross for you and for your sins. If you believe and allow God to do what He needs to do, then you will get better. I have also learned that it was okay if I failed. Failure did not mean I was less saved or was a lesser child of God. That took a whole lot of burden off, to know that it is okay if you fail. God does not love you any less. I also came to understand, sure, you are going to get clean, but that doesn't mean your life is not going to have trouble. You need to have faith, do the best you can spiritually, and go on because you are going to have troubles. But you do not have to use drugs. There are going to be days when things on the job are not going to be good, and that's okay, or when things at the house are not going to be good. That's okay, too, as long as I don't lose my bearings and decide to hide or medicate to get away from it.

Eight years ago, I was homeless on the streets, hanging out at the Salvation Army. Today, I have a lovely home, a very good job, and a car. I am responsible and I am not broke. I can buy myself a soda—and some! There have been many blessings that have come from the healing, and I know that there are more to come if I continue to have faith and let the healing process go its route.

Evan was interviewed by Vivian Moore in May of 2002.
He is an African American Baptist in his 40's.

He Leadeth Me in the Paths of Righteousness—Tricia Amberly

Throughout my life, there have been instances where I know that it had to be the Lord that provided for me. There was no other explanation. I have learned over the years that God provides things for us financially because He wants us to see Him as a provider. It also builds our faith up. I learned that whatever situation came, God was going to take care of me. God just makes a way for you. He has proven Himself over and over. My father was a Baptist minister, and I was born again about age nine. It is a matter of asking the Lord Jesus to come into your heart and your life and accepting Him, that He died on the cross and rose for our sins, and that you were born again as a result of accepting Him as our Savior.

Around 1985, they found out I had a high level of protein in my urine, and they referred me to a nephrologist. They said, "You have an elevated protein; something is going on with your kidneys." Over the years, they watched my creatinine level. Finally, in 1994, I had a kidney biopsy, and they determined that I had sclerosing glomerulonephritis, which has something to do with the veins or the arteries in the kidneys shriveling. In 1996, I was discovered to be pregnant. I went to a doctor, and he absolutely, unequivocally advised me not to have this baby. I was 35 and overweight, morbidly obese. I had kidney problems and high blood pressure, so he told me I should not go forth with this child. At my first appointment, he said, "You need to go get your husband. You need to talk about this because he needs to know that he could be having two funerals or be raising two children on his own." The doctor had nothing positive to say, and I left the office like I had a ton of bricks on me, feeling devastated. I did want to have a child. After I heard of my pregnancy, I remembered a prayer I had prayed—and this seems crazy for me to have prayed this, but I did—I prayed that the Lord would blow my mind because He has done that so many times, and I felt like my mind had not been blown in a long time. Praise His miraculous works!

I thought, "Oh, my Lord, I didn't know it would be something like this." I really wanted another child, but I would never pray about it. I already knew I had kidney things going on, so I figured this was not going to happen; I didn't ever say anything about it. The Lord reminded me of that prayer, and I thought, "Oh, my goodness, You could have done something else." I was weighing in the balance what to do. My husband and I talked. My husband felt, "Whatever you decide, I am going to stand with you." I talked to my pastor and his wife about what to do, whether or not to go through with this pregnancy, and they felt that they would stand with me whatever decision I made. I came out of discussions with the pastor still not having the answer. Rather, I knew what the answer was, but I was too fearful.

I knew that God would not ever say, "Do not have the baby." I knew that, once I inquired of the Lord, He was going to tell me that I needed to have this child. But I was not convinced, having heard all that I had heard from the doctors. I prayed and I cried, and I finally came to the conclusion that I serve a God that, first of all, has taken care of me throughout my life. Secondly, He has done more miraculous things than I could ever imagine, in terms of bringing somebody back to life, splitting the Red Sea, creating the heavens and putting the sky and the moon up there, and all those wonders of His hands. So I thought, "Either I am going to say He is Lord, King of Kings, Lord of Lords, or He is not." I decided that I was going to allow God to be God, and I felt that even if I died, to be absent in the body is to be present with the Lord. Even though my oldest child and my husband would be left behind, I felt God knows best. That is the resolve I came to. It seemed every time I would try to talk myself out of it, a Scripture would come to my mind, right in the middle of my sentence, to say I was not thinking right and to correct it with what the Word of the Lord said. I got angry with that because even though it was a good thing for me eventually, I could not reason my way out of not having this child. The Word of the Lord kept coming to me, telling me something different. Finally, I decided that I was going to have that baby, and I stood my ground when I went back to the doctor because he said, "What?!? You're going to?"

I thought, "I am not going to sit here and debate with you. My decision is that I am going to go forth." I thought about changing doctors, but I knew not to because I had already prayed for God to send me to the right one. I told God, "Why did you send me to this man who has nothing good to say to me?" But he was so fearful of the outcome that I had an ultrasound every single week, and I was a very compliant patient.

I thank God that I got the best of care under the circumstances, and to make a long story short, my baby was born. She was six pounds and two ounces. The birth went well. My daughter is perfectly healthy. I am doing well, even though a year later my kidneys finally went kerplop. They stopped working, and I am on dialysis three days a week.

I am on the machine for four and a half hours, but by the time I get processed, I am usually there five or six hours. In a dialysis clinic, you are lined up in chairs, some in front, some behind you, and some beside you. The man in front of me died. The lady to the right of me died. And the lady to the right of her died. Then my little buddy who sits to the left of me was in ICU in a coma, very ill. She had had a hysterectomy, but she was also a dialysis patient, and something went very wrong. She was out for weeks. She was a believer, and God hung in there with her. She had lost a tremendous amount of weight when I last talked with her, but her appetite was back. She was gaining weight and doing well. So it's the Lord who helps me with the depression part and not dwelling on death. Even though I have downfalls from time to time, I don't stay there. I know that there are things I do that are pleasing to God. He is keeping me alive, and there is much more He desires for me to do, especially in the area of helping people.

I am looking for a miraculous healing, and my thinking is, if God restored Lazarus . . . ! Lazarus was dead, three or four days, and He restored every system in his body, and I said, "Lord, if you can restore Lazarus with everything he got going, You can at least give me two kidneys."

Nobody can quite do you like the Lord in terms of dealing with your heart; only God can do that. I pray every day. One goal I have is to have a quiet time with the Lord. The Christian faith would have you have a designated time where you pull out from everything and spend it with Him, and I do that. A lot of times I do it in the car. I do it in dialysis. I do it late at night. My desire is to have a quiet time with the Lord every day consistently.

Tricia was interviewed by Jane Teas in September of 2001.
She is a non-denominational African American woman in her 40's.

I Will Fear No Evil
—Carter Boone

I was kidnapped at gun-point when I came home from work back in January. I didn't make it into my apartment. They approached me as I was rounding the corner after I had parked, and I didn't see them until I was right on them, so there wasn't much I could do. Normal instinct would be to react or overreact; however, I was very calm, and part of that is my nature, to be relaxed and calm. I feel like God used that to my advantage. I didn't intimidate them, and it kept them from being overly aggressive with me and prevented some injuries later on. They ordered me into the trunk of my car and drove me around for a half an hour to an hour. They stopped a couple of times, and then we ended up at a park.

The music was turned up really loud, but I did hear that the gun was loaded. So I knew that I wouldn't try anything ridiculously stupid. While I was in the trunk, I prayed; I was very scared and tense. All these thoughts flashed through my mind. First of all, "Is this really happening?" You go through a whole string of things in your mind when your life is in jeopardy. Thoughts of my family started zipping through, and "How long is this going to last?" and then, "Where are we going to end up?" I did not expect good things to happen.

I thought, "This is quite a situation I have gotten myself into." I was thankful for the time in the trunk because it was enough for me to get the initial panic and feelings to settle down. I got to a place where I could think at a conscious level and not overreact, not do things on adrenaline or fear. I panicked for a while, but after a good five to ten minutes passed, I thought, "I am just going to settle down and relax." I prayed more for my family than myself. I come from a close family, and I thought this would be a devastating thing. I also asked for forgiveness for any sins I had committed. I felt like my life was going to end, and I had had wrongs in the past; I didn't want to go with those left out there.

The part that I have had nightmares about more than any other was when the car stopped, and I knew we were getting close. They trashed the inside of it while I was in the trunk; they were looking for money and anything of value. I could hear them going through everything. Then they got out, and I didn't hear anything. It was pretty quiet, but I was going to make sure they were gone. I thought I would give it five or six minutes of silence; if it ended up being that long, then I would make a break. I made that as a pact with God: if it is clear, I will trust You for that. Then I heard noise, so I knew that it wasn't safe. They stuck the key in the trunk, and I will hear that disturbing sound for the rest of my life. Just the key going into the trunk is a pretty simple thing, but I know the sound of it more than any other sound. That was the point of realization to me: this is big; I am either going to be there, or it is going to be the end.

They opened the trunk, and as they did, the gun went to my head, and then another guy came over with a steel pipe. I was thinking, "This is unbelievable. This is a bad deal." They demanded my money, so they were a little tough with me, but considering what could have happened, that was nothing. They got my wallet, and I didn't have cash. That aggravated them. The third guy had a flashlight, and when he shone it on me, he recognized me, which is quite amazing. When they recognized me, that confused them and aggravated them: "Oh my, what do we do?" I told them, "Look, I don't have any cash in my wallet." I offered my credit cards, anything to save my life. They didn't go for that; they didn't want credit cards. They wanted cash, so I offered, "If it is just money you want, let's go. I have an ATM card; I can get cash for you." I did that thinking they wouldn't fall for it.

Because one of them recognized me as the television weatherman, they allowed me to drive. We went to an ATM and I got $500.00; that was all it would allow. Then they wanted to try for more, so we went to one across the street, but it wouldn't give me anything. We managed to get another $100.00 at another location. The fact that I tried and got another $100.00 was the key, because I didn't aggravate them. They knew I was trying to give them money; "Here is some more. It is all I can get out of it." These were teenagers; one was quite young. The other two were older, but it was a gang initiation for drug deal money. I know that now in retrospect; I didn't know it then. Along the way one of the individuals asked, "Why would I do this? Why would I offer to get them any cash or money?" and I said, "If it is my time to go, it is my time to go. I am a Christian, and if my number is up, my number is up."

After the third ATM machine gave me another $100.00, they let me go. Then one of them was touched by what I had said about being a Christian, and he came back. As I have learned now, he was raised in a very strong Christian family, and that had an impact on his life. He came back, returned my cellular phone that they had taken, shook my hand, and apologized for anything that had happened. I can see God working in his life at some point in the future. Then they let me go one way, and they went the other. Not to lessen the crime and what happened, but I pray for them, all of them.

A Christian sheriff's deputy prayed with me that night. He looked at me and said, "You're a miracle. I know that there were two other people before you. This is a string. You're the third victim." He said that this started on a Sunday night and there was another on Monday. Mine was on Wednesday. The other two had overreacted, and one was left for dead. The other guy had been pistol-whipped and had serious head wounds. The first victim had managed to get out of the trunk somehow, but he had broken ribs, and then I was left untouched. He just couldn't believe it. He said, "I am looking at you, and I know what happened before, these other two. God saved your life tonight, young man." He even gave me a card and wrote on it, "I knew you were my Christian brother. I saw a true miracle by God on this date." It was obvious that God was trying to tell me things.

I prayed a lot in the car, and I feel God gave me everything I needed. God took over every situation; not that He organized it in any way against me, but He allowed it to happen for a purpose. The kidnapping was a bad experience to go through, but it is also one of the better things in my life. It has taken me to a point where my level of appreciation of life and walking in faith is much stronger. I like to consider it walking in the spirit. I am not worried about things that used to worry me. I feel comfortable, and if I have any worries or any qualms about things, I go home and discuss it openly with Him in prayer. It is not just in prayer; it is sharing a relationship with Christ instead of drawing on Him when I need Him. God allowed that to happen for that reason. He went to the trouble of preserving my life that night, and there is a reason for it. The whole purpose of the story was to give God the glory.

There was a night somewhere in the spring when I asked myself the question, "What if I had died that night?" I considered where I was in my life, wondering what questions God would have asked me. If He had asked me what I had done for Him, how would I have answered? I thought, "I have done a lot of things for people." I was a very community-driven individual, did a lot in schools, and knew a lot of people, but I really hadn't done much for Him. That bothered me. The major difference now is that He is included in everything I do, start to finish, including waking up, when I do a little Bible study. Whatever it is, I trust He is going to have something for me. I encourage Him to challenge me daily for His work and not my own.

Because of what happened, I have a testimony that I can share with people for the rest of my life. For as long as it is important and serves Him, I believe that He will provide the situation: to serve, to be involved in ministry, to stick with it, to stay faithful. I don't know exactly what each day will bring, but I trust Him enough to know that it is going to be something that He wants. For the rest of my life, I am going to let Him take care of everything. When everything happened, when I gave my life to Him totally, He preserved it. Whenever I live my life like that, including Him in everything I do, everything works out so much better.

I feel very much at peace, and I feel like each day is a blessing. I am already living extra days in my life that may not have happened before January 25th. I tell people, "I effectively was killed that night in the spiritual sense. My old self definitely passed away, and it is gone." God has a purpose for each and every one of us, no matter what age we are or where we are in our walk. Trusting Him is the key. If it is my time to go, I am already on borrowed time; I am different now because I embrace that. If I were to be taken out of this world now, I am more relaxed, at ease, and at peace with that possibility.

By really letting Christ in my life, the healing occurred at an emotional level. He calmed my anxiety, my fear. Faith and my healing have been an emotional experience for me. I made a commitment to serve Him and not to sit back and do my own thing. If it is His will for me to do something, then fine. If not, I ask Him to stop me in my tracks, turn me the other way, whatever it may be, and I listen. Emotionally, that healed everything. It took away so many things: a lot of worry and anxiety, a lot of depression, everything that had been bothering me. This is the first time I have felt like I have been at peace in my life. I know that whatever God's will or plan is from here, I will be at peace. I am not going to get anxious about that. I put a little thing on my computer, in various places in my apartment, in my car, or wherever I am to remind me, "This is an extra day. You had another extra day today." I feel blessed by that alone.

Carter, a white man in his 30's, was interviewed by Andrew Cousins in November of 2001.

Thou Preparest a Table Before Me
–Derrick Yoder

On August 27th, I was lying in bed, reading through my Bible, and doing devotions before I went to bed. I had my hand up against my neck, and I felt something rub across the palm of my hand. At first I didn't think anything about it. Then I felt it rub against me again—it felt like a golf ball—and I thought, "Oh, my gosh, what is this?" So I took my shirt off and started feeling around and noticed that if I put any pressure on my neck, I could feel this golf ball coming out, and I thought, "This is crazy!" I went and looked in the mirror and decided I was just going to finish with my devotions and go to bed and sleep on it and wake up the next morning and pray that it has gone. I didn't sleep at all that night; I lived at home and didn't tell my parents. I got up the next morning and went and had a job cutting grass and then came back home, and it was still there. It wasn't sore; it wasn't hurting. I told my mom; this was on Monday. So I waited that day and went to see my general physician. He looked at it and thought that it was nothing more than a few infected lymph nodes, but as a precaution, they took an x-ray of my chest, and when they did, they saw a little bit of white; it is supposed to be all dark in your chest, and there was a little bit of white in this area.

He started naming the different things it could be: it could be a reaction from a sore throat that I had a month ago, it could be leukemia, or it could be Hodgkin's lymphoma; only two of them were cancer. Never being around cancer, I didn't realize the magnitude of what was about to happen. They ran some blood tests and ruled out leukemia. My doctor called a surgeon to see me on Wednesday. I went to see him, and the surgeon said that there was a nerve running behind it, and they were not going to be able to do a needle biopsy; they would need to go in and do surgery. They scheduled it for Thursday at twelve o'clock. He had had someone cancel and had an opening in his schedule. I was still attending school, going between doctor's appointments that were scheduled around school. On Thursday morning, I went to my auditing class and my other class, and then I came home to get ready to go back to the doctor for surgery.

I had been elected as co-president of the Fellowship of Christian Athletes (FCA) the previous year, and I spent all summer planning for this year with Neil, who was the other co-president. We had spent a lot of time, I can't tell you how much time, in prayer that somehow God would use this year, use us because we felt that God wanted us to give people coming to FCA a reason to see how a real relationship with Jesus Christ is. That was our prayer. We didn't know how it was going to happen, but we prayed all summer long, and we kept thinking that something was going to happen. So many people who come to FCA—and I do it too—you are just so faithful to your faith, and you might call yourself a Christian, but you don't look like it, and you don't put enough faith in God. You don't rely on Him for strength and for daily stuff. A big thing about FCA is that we want to reach out to college students where they are, with school going on, and all the peer pressure of life. We wanted to do something that was going to make it real.

My surgery was scheduled for Thursday at noon, which happened to be the night of the first FCA meeting. I love FCA; I did music there for three years. I love the praise and worship, and I just love what FCA is about, reaching people where they are. I called Neil and told him I couldn't be there, and I told him what was going on. I had told the leadership, so there were six people who knew what was going on with my neck. I didn't get into surgery until about 3:30, and the long and the short of it is that I woke up with cancer. They took the lymph node that was about a 4-mm circle out of my neck, and they got one of the other lymph nodes out. There were still other lymph nodes swollen at this time, and the surgeon knew from the stains that it was cancer. That devastated my family because my family, my fiancée, and some people from church were there. I went in thinking it was nothing, and the doctor came out and said, "He's got cancer."

The college minister was at the hospital, and he told the leadership of FCA. They were devastated—not to put myself on a pedestal, but if you find out that anybody gets cancer, especially one of your friends, then you think, "Oh, my gosh!" I knew just about everybody at FCA. They told leadership, and then toward the end of the meeting, Neil said he could not get up and talk about it. The minister got up instead and told everybody, and from what they tell me, everybody broke down. It was an experience; people realized, "Oh, my gosh, life is real; we are not invincible. Things can happen to us." They all broke up into groups of four and prayed out loud—everybody did—for me. That means the world to know that people prayed for me and cared about me enough to do that. They all got together and prayed as a group.

At FCA, first meetings run about 300 people, so we are talking about a ton of people. My family tells me to this day that it was the craziest thing; I was the only one with a good attitude going out of the hospital; I was laughing, I was joking, and I was telling them, "Hey, I should get free tee-shirts for having cancer." I know that was the joy of God in me, the peace He gave me, because it was from people praying. It is the strength that God gave me through it all. The next week, I played at FCA, sitting on a stool; I could hardly move my neck, playing. But that's just where I wanted to be. I had to rely on God's strength to get me through it, and that's what I did. I was really fine; people would come over, and I was laughing and talking with them.

Going back to the doctor appointments . . . This was a Thursday, and the next Monday they did a knees-to-head CAT scan, and they found that I had about a 6" by 2" by 3" mass in my chest, along with more swelling. Hodgkin's lymphoma on the left side of your body goes from your chest to your neck to your underarms to your back. I went to see the oncologist on Wednesday, and she told us the prognosis, but they didn't know how severe it was going to be; I had to have a PET scan, which was a totally different scan. She said I would probably need eight chemotherapies, four rounds. They found out that it was pretty extensive in my chest, so I would have to start chemotherapy pretty quickly.

A month later, I started the chemo. The amazing thing is that I never once felt down. Obviously there are points where you are going to feel down, like at the hospital, but I never felt like I was losing the battle; I was just more scared of what was to come. The first one was really good—and the first eight; God blessed me so much because I never lost all my hair. There are so many things they told me: you are going to do this, this is going to happen; and none of it ever happened. I didn't ever lose my hair. You are going to be a little bit sick from the chemicals put in your body, but I never got too sick.

It was an amazing experience. There are a lot of reasons, and I believe that FCA is one of the huge reasons because so many people wrote me letters from FCA, saying that they rededicated their lives to Christ or got saved because of what was going on. They were able to see how God used me, to have such an uplifting spirit because I was able to get up in front of FCA and be honest. I wasn't lying. I said, "Hey, I can't complain. God is taking care of me; He is doing it. He is the one doing all this; I'm just an innocent bystander."

I went through my eight chemotherapies, but the mass hadn't shrunk at all in my chest. That was pretty devastating because you don't want to go through another eight. My last eight were a lot worse because chemo is something that is cumulative. It wears your body down. They told me I was going to have to have eight more. I ended up doing sixteen in all, and about this point I started getting a little sicker. By the end I had lost about thirty pounds. I didn't feel good and eventually had to stop doing FCA, which broke my heart. It was through this time, the second half, that I became okay with the thought of dying. It was so comforting to know that I know where I'm going. I knew that I was in God's hands, and He was in control; it was just a peace, a peace that passes all. I know that might be cheesy, but it really was; it was just a peace. I finally felt like the burdens were off of me.

I ended up going for the sixteen, came back, and took another CAT scan, and it had only shrunk a little bit. They were really worried, and this is another cool thing that I attribute to God: I went to have another PET scan, and it came back negative. They were really confused how the CAT scan could show that I still had this mass, while my PET scan showed nothing. It so happened that they were doing a symposium at the hospital with one of the premiere doctors who could read PET scans, and he said that he fully believed it was all gone, which might have saved me more chemo or more treatment because my doctor was really confused on the variations. After that, I went on and did eighteen radiations to this area in my body.

There are so many things that I attribute to God; first of all, I didn't stop doing school through it all. I took twelve hours both semesters. First semester, I had a 3.9 GPA, and the second semester I had a 4.0. I made straight A's the second semester, and that is with missing tons of classes. My professors did not curve my grades at all; they were flat-out A's. I took an advanced class and had 100% averages; I made 100% on every test, every quiz I took. My professor would pull me in the office and say, "I don't know how you are doing this." I would come in and sleep through class because I couldn't keep my eyes open, and then wake up and take the quiz after class and make 100% on it.

I attribute it to God, all the strength and knowledge. He provided for me; there is no other way I could have done it. I would have the chemo on a Friday and take the test the next Monday and make an A on it. Here I was sitting there dying, I had lost all this weight, my tongue was white, I couldn't taste anything, and He gave me that much focus. God was telling me, "Slow down, I'm going to take care of you; this is your time to realize that I'm in control of your life." I felt like God was telling me, "You have no control over your life. I am totally in control, and if you let me take control, things will be so much better."

I was twenty-one when I went through it. I got to speak at a senior night at FCA, the last one. It was the coolest thing because I got up there, and I was telling them how it was crazy sitting there in the hospital. There were ninety- and eighty-year-old people waiting in line to get their blood drawn, and I walked up. I always try to make a point to say hey to everybody, shake everybody's hands because there were people there who looked like death. I didn't want to do that; I wanted to be different. I wanted to have an uplifting spirit because I have something to live for. When we left, my nurse said that she had never seen someone go through that with that much joy; she said she knew it was Jesus Christ in my life. She said there was no other way to explain it. My life is a blessing; every step is a blessing and a learning experience.

I have gone through something; God has helped me through it, and I give Him all the credit. I don't take any credit for the grades I made, for my health now, for anything. I give Him all the glory, and I believe that He is going to use it one day for His kingdom to reach out to someone, to help someone realize, "My gosh, if he can go through cancer and still have that kind of faith and not be angry at God, there has got to be some kind of truth there." No one can take away the fact that I had cancer, that I had a terminal disease and, through it all, I knew God was going to take care of me. That is faith. You can't see God, but you can see the effects of God. You don't see the wind, but you know the wind is there.

My life is testimony of God, His strength through me, and no one can take that away from me. No one can say that God did not help me through this. Because my response to them is, then what did? What gave me that joy? And no one can answer that. There is no other answer than what I know, and I know it was Jesus Christ in my life. I know it was the prayers of people. It is not by accident that I would receive letters when I needed them. It is not by accident that God helped me through school like that. I had never had a 4.0 in a semester since I had been in college, so what is the coincidence of it being during my last four rounds of chemo that I got it? I believe God had a plan for me to go through this for His glory, and I give Him the glory. This experience has helped me realize the compassion that He has for me, and how real He is, and how much He loves people. We are His creation, and He knows better than us, what is best for our lives. I am a lot more thankful for the little things. I am thankful for life. God gave me the strength to be able to live out joy in my life.

One day at my church, they started singing a song: "You alone are Father, You alone are God, You alone, and where He goes, I'm alive." Everybody was sitting down, and when we started singing, I just stood up because I knew. I didn't know it for my own glory, but I knew God was with me. What other confirmation do I need? I am alive; God is with me. He is God, He was God before today, and He is going to be it after. He never left me; why would He leave me all of a sudden? It is a tremendous feeling. I have told plenty of people, I don't see how you go through cancer without God on your side. Without my relationship with Jesus Christ, I don't know where I would have been.

Derrick was interviewed by Andrew Cousins in November of 2001.
He is a white Baptist in his 20's.

Surely Goodness and Mercy Shall Follow Me—Joyce Ridley

My daughter, Jessica, is a fraternal twin, and at birth they noticed a difference between Jessica and Jennifer. Jessica was stuck under my ribs, and when they removed her, her head was slightly enlarged. They rushed her off to do a CAT scan and found that pieces of her brain were missing; the holes were randomly scattered across her brain. They sent her home with us and said, "We'll have to wait and see which parts will develop and which will not, as far as what you can expect out of this child, we have no idea." So that left things really open-ended.

She was born in March of 1987. A few years after that, I became a professional clown: red nose, big shoes, the whole nine yards. At clown school, I met clowns from all over the United States. I met other Christian clowns, so I asked them to put Jessica on their prayer list. I had clowns in Texas, California, New Jersey, and South Carolina—clowns everywhere had Jessica on their prayer lists, praying for her.

In 1994 we noticed some changes in Jessica over the period of that year, and it just so happened that Jennifer, her twin, started having migraines. We went to the neurologist, and while we were there for Jennifer, I said, "Hey, can we go ahead and do a new scan on Jessica?" The doctor said, "It will be interesting, but I don't think there will be any change. It was severe enough that I'm not looking for any change." She was very developmentally delayed. In motor skills, she was at least six to eight months behind Jennifer as a toddler, and as she reached on into childhood, the gap became larger.

She can move; that's not a problem, but her fine motor skills are still very slow. Her speech is broken. She comprehends more than she can say. Her verbal expression is limited: mostly a single words or a couple of words together; every now and then she can get a complete train of thought out, but it is very difficult for her. She knows what she wants to say, but she cannot get the words together. Instead of, "I want something to drink," she would say, "Drink." After three or four words, she gets lost and cannot get out complete thoughts. We started teaching her sign language when she was little to help bridge that gap, so she would not get overly frustrated. Now that she has more words to a point where people can understand her, some of the signing has dropped off.

It just so happened that I was able to get the scans from her birth. That was surprising; usually they get rid of them, but we were very fortunate. They still had them, so I took them to the doctor. He looked at them again and showed me the pieces that were missing; he said, "It's like Swiss cheese." Then we pulled out the new scans, and he got real quiet for a moment. I said, "What's going on?" He said, "It's completely normal now." All the pieces were there. He didn't have an explanation and just said, "Go home, and keep doing whatever you were doing," and I said, "It was lots of prayer." He said, "Something had to intervene because this is remarkable." He told me to keep the film because this is one for the books. He said it would depend on how many windows of opportunity still existed, as far as how far she could progress in educational skills.

She can comprehend an awful lot and is making small strides. She is beginning to read some, she can count, and she can do some writing. She has progressed, and now we have a normal brain to work with. We marked this one down as a miracle, for her brain to be completely normal. The doctor said that if he had looked at the last scan and not at the first, he would not have known that there were any problems. That was definitely a miracle, and we attribute it to all the collective prayers. When she was born, she had been like a rag doll. She was so limp, with no muscle tone, and it would have been very easy for somebody to have pushed and said, "Institutionalize her, and forget it." If we had done that, I don't think she would have developed. I don't think she would have had the intense prayer.

Jessica believes in prayer. And that's an abstract concept! She very much believes, and she asked Jesus into her heart herself; she can tell you she did. She sees people at church, and she will go up and lay hands on them, and she will pray. She will see people in restaurants and make us get up from the table and go and pray for them. That takes a lot of boldness of your faith to go up and say, "My daughter wants to pray for you," in the middle of a restaurant. We haven't had anybody say no, and it has happened numerous times; it has been remarkable watching her.

In October, I had a mammogram done, and they found a cyst, so they set up an appointment a week later for me to go in to have it aspirated. They were going to do that first, to try to drain it, but they couldn't get it done. They found the cyst on the ultrasound to pinpoint where it was, but they could not get the needle through it. The doctor said, "We're going to have to get a biopsy." He left me to collect myself because the other procedure had been painful enough. He wasn't gone but five minutes. While he was out, I prayed, and I said, "Lord, I don't want to go through this. Please remove it; I know You can." When the doctor came back in to do it, he said, "I'm going to numb you up." He started numbing the whole area, and then he looked at the ultrasound. He said, "Oh, my goodness!" and I said "What?" and he said, "It's gone. It's gone." He said, "Go home and be happy." He was very surprised. He said, "I don't have to do a biopsy. There is nothing to biopsy; it's gone."

My husband has poly-glandular autoimmune deficiency. The doctors have said his body has turned on itself and is fighting itself. It is a rare disease; he has seven glands that are malfunctioning. At one point, he started sliding downhill, more so than usual, and we got very, very concerned. He even started getting what they call the "death mask," where you get real gray in your look. I knew that unless something intervened, I was going to lose him by Christmas. This was the first of November. In the past, we had been to the Mayo Clinic in Florida for his treatment, so my father and I put my husband in the car, and we drove to the clinic. They did a blood work-up and saw that his potassium and sodium were all out of whack; they didn't know how he was walking around, and they put him in the hospital. Within two hours of admission, he flat-lined. While he was flat-lined, he said that he heard the voice of God, telling him that his time was not over and for him to go back. Before they could even put the paddles on him, he came back. He said he saw a bright light, and there was a real sense of peace. He almost hated to come back, but God told him that he wasn't through.

When he came to, there were seven doctors and nurses around his bed, and he opened his eyes, and they thought, "Whoa! You're back." We had kept a book of all my husband's medicals, and I had the book with me. The doctor took time to glance over it, and he said, "I know what is wrong." They immediately started giving him this other hormone, and it was like a light switch; by the next morning, he was rosy red-cheeked and bright-colored. He drove home from Jacksonville. It really was a miracle. At that time I had asked seven in my church if they would pray daily for my husband and cover him in prayers, and we believe that is what it was; they broke through the heavens.

He has been sick now for fourteen years. We have had to learn how to balance life; we have had to learn how to keep precious what is precious in life, and that is our family and our relationship with God. Other trivial things, like little fusses and fights, forget it. We don't do it; there is just not time. Life is too precious. Laughter therapy has helped an awful lot. At one point, he was in the hospital for thirty days with a yeast infection that went septic. One night, I asked if we could have a VCR, and I went out and I rented three or four funny movies and spent the night with him. We put a "Do not disturb" sign on the door and watched funny movies. I attached balloons on his IV; I put a face with long balloons for the arms, and that was Fred, and Fred had to go with him every place he went. We did things like that to break it, anything to bring the laughter.

We have three children, so we have had to figure out, "How do we balance all of these life-and-death situations with the children, so that they come out with a normal lifestyle?" We plan movie nights to watch funny movies when things are rough. The clowning helps a lot. When you clown, you give up yourself for other people, in that you are willing for somebody to laugh at you. It is one thing if you are in a group, and you are laughing together; that's laughing with you, but for you to be the object of the laughter, that takes a servant heart. I draw on that laughter therapy. Even if I am not in makeup, I have learned to use the same skills that I learned as a clown. My children have a very positive attitude; it is because of our faith and also the laughter. God gives us the laughter, with the endorphins and all, to help us through.

I talked with a doctor out in California who works with laughter therapy, and he said, "Don't ever underestimate what the laughter has done for your family." We have a church that is very supportive, even with the laughter. They understand that if they come here, we will be doing some unusual things, like the balloons on the IV. They realize it is to keep the momentum going. With all that we have had to deal with, we realize how precious every day is. It has given us a positive outlook. Only my close inner friends know the day-to-day stress that we are under with a special-needs child and with my husband being so sick. As a whole, the rest of them don't have a clue because we have the strength through our faith to keep on going. We have had God's hand of protection.

My mother taught me about Jesus on her lap from the time I was just a wee little thing. I feel the Lord's presence constantly; it doesn't matter where I am. I know He is there, and we talk constantly. I am not talking about the "Now I lay me down to sleep" prayer. Things happen, and I say, "Hey, Lord, that was fun, wasn't it?" He is right with me constantly, and if things are rough I say, "Lord, I need extra strength," and it is there. I can feel somebody lifting and strengthening me, as if somebody was standing right beside me.

Joyce was interviewed by Andrew Cousins in January of 2002. She is a white woman in her 40's who attends a Pentecostal Holiness congregation.

Chapter 4

PRAYER AND ANOINTING

Are any among you suffering? They should pray. Are any cheerful? They should sing songs of praise. Are any among you sick? They should call for the elders of the church and have them pray over them, anointing them with oil in the name of the Lord. The prayer of faith will save the sick, and the Lord will raise them up; and anyone who has committed sins will be forgiven. Therefore confess your sins to one another, and pray for one another, so that you may be healed. The prayer of the righteous is powerful and effective.

James 5:13-16

God Only Wants to Love You
–Doris O'Malley

I grew up in the inner-city of St. Louis. I had a very violent upbringing. There was a lot of drinking and an extreme amount of abuse. I grew up a very abused child in every way, physically, sexually, and emotionally. I didn't feel that God loved me very much because my life was terrible. I tried to survive, tried to make my life have more pleasure and less pain. My parents divorced when I was three, and I was thrown around from then on to different places. As soon as I could get away from people who were bent on hurting me, I took to the streets and found family there, people who were in gang life. The bigger part of my growing up years was spent without having much personal family connection. My family was the kids in the street. I got mixed up in drugs and drinking. I ended up living in an old derelict car in the slum and cleaning up in the filling station down the block; it was a really weird, warped life.

Finally, I got a job in a factory, and I met this lady; she, her husband, and two kids were from Arkansas. I was twenty-one, maybe younger than that, my upper teens. Even though she tried to befriend me, I didn't want to be befriended because I didn't think people cared. By then, I was very walled off and emotionally damaged. But she continued to reach out to me, and that was a key part of my transition to becoming a Christian, in that I saw God's love acted out. I didn't know that's what it was, but I knew for some reason, as much as I tried to turn this person off, she would say, "Don't get high or get drunk." That's exactly what I would do, a continual testing to put her in a position to go ahead and do to me what had already been done all my life, which was walk away from me, but she would never do that. Later, she became more like a mother figure in my life. It was through her influence that I ended up in Arkansas. It took me out of the wild inner-city life to a more pristine place. If you were looking for a God kind of environment, that would have been it, rural backwoods northern Arkansas, where people were very genuine and down-to-earth. I believe that God revealed Himself in another dimension there, which is to say, there is something other than concrete jungle and inner-city ugly; He showed me another dimension of Himself.

All this time in my heart, I was very bitter; I was very angry. I was just trying to survive life; I wasn't really searching. As it turns out, I was dating a man whose parents put pressure on him to go to church. He asked me if I would go with him, and I did because my attitude at the time was, "Sure, I'll give God a break. If He wants us to show up in His little house, then I'll make an appearance." Also, my attitude was, you never know. I was working under the point system, which I don't believe in now. It's against what the Bible teaches, but at the time my theology came off the streets. I thought that if you did more good than bad, then in the end, you're in—the heaven thing. I knew I needed points because I wasn't doing anything that could have been described as moral. I was living with men, using drugs, partying, anything you could think of to bring any pleasure or numb any pain from my life.

I went to a little backwoods country church, and while I was there, I can just say that something happened. I didn't know how to define it at the time, but something happened that made me have to find out what it was. I didn't think the man I was with was very spiritual because I never saw him do anything spiritual; I had him take me to someone else I knew. She went to church twice a year, so I figured she had this hotline to God. All I can tell you was that it was a "God thing," so I needed to find somebody who knew "God things." I didn't go to Rachael, the woman I came down with because I had never seen her in church. What I came to know later is that she absolutely was a Christian, but she had had a very bad experience in church, which caused her not to go. In my limited understanding, you were either church people or you weren't. I didn't understand about a salvation experience, so I didn't see her as religious, even though she was exuding God's unconditional love to me every day.

I ended up going to Elaina; she was the one who went to church twice a year, Christmas and Easter. I said to her, "I have forty pounds of pressure right here," and pointed to my chest, "Telling me to do something, and I don't know what to do. I feel like I'm that close," and I held my thumb and forefinger about an inch apart, "To what I have been looking for all of my life, and I don't know what it is." For the first time in my life, somebody explained to me what the Bible talks about, a personal relationship with Jesus Christ. She explained that God created us to be like Him, and He is life. Life gives life; life is love, the fullness of love. That's why He created me, to have this love, this shared love experience with Him; and then, like every other person of the human race, I separated myself from God to go my own way, to find what I thought would bring life. That caused the separation between me and God, the penalty of which, since God is life, was death. In order for God to bring me back to Him, someone had to pay the debt; so He had the essence of Himself, His offspring in His son, Jesus, come live a life that didn't gain Him the penalty, so He was without sin. He lived a life totally in sync and connected with God, so He was guilty of nothing; and then He took on my guilt, so I could have eternal life. She explained that to me, that the debt was paid; the gift was made, and it was up to me to receive the gift, to ask God to come live in my heart, guide my life, and forgive me of turning away from Him. She told me all of this in a very child-like way where I could understand it. At that point, I had tried and tasted every other avenue in life that I could think of, and nothing gave me that sense of peace and fullness.

I said, "God, if you want my life, I want you to take it because I am so tired of living." I had seen death; my best friend took a shotgun and put it up against her chest and blew herself away. My next best friend, three months later, took a massive overdose and ended up in a mental hospital. There was no hope in my neighborhood. Now, when this was explained to me, I understood what she told me that drawing was, those forty pounds of pressure. She said that's the Holy Spirit drawing me to God. Then she quoted the verse that says, "Nobody comes to God except God draws them." She explained that to me, and I understood that God wanted my life. As the turning point in her explanation, she said, "Doris, God only wants to love you," and it made sense. I understood that it made sense because the Spirit who was drawing me caused me to understand. Prior to that, I didn't understand because it is impossible for natural man to understand spiritual things apart from God. God drew me, and He gave me understanding. I surrendered my life and had an immediate turn-around. I got off drugs, drinking, everything. I wasn't a perfect person and never will be; I am a child in the process of growing up, but my life took an immediate turn-around, and I had an insatiable appetite to know God.

In baptism, when you go under water, you surrender your life; you are dead to self, just like Jesus gave His life for us, and you identify with that belief. When you come out of the water, that is the demonstration that, just as God raised Jesus from the dead, so in like manner when our time here on earth is done, He will raise us up, like Jesus, to a renewed life. Baptism is the identification, the outward showing of what we believe. I understood at a very basic level that this was supposed to happen after I gave my life to Christ, so that I could show the world that I had made this choice, and now align myself with those who call themselves Christians.

During the early days, while I was in Arkansas, I was in a car accident. I was going down the highway at about sixty miles per hour and a car pulled out in front of us; we ran right smack dab into him. My back was broken, and three vertebrae were crushed. The doctor said I would never walk again. I was in a wheelchair. One day, a friend took me to a place where they were baptizing out in a creek, and when they put me in the water, the pain went away, came out of my back, and I could walk! Everything was restored, after having been in a wheelchair for about six months. It was a miraculous healing; God let me know that morning in my spirit. I prayed for God to enable me to walk because there was a lot of pain, and I wanted to be healed of that. I was saying, "God, help. I can't help myself on this." That is how He chose to respond.

God put a retired preacher into my life, a 74-year-old man, and he and I studied fourteen hours a day. I just couldn't get enough of knowing about God because, for the first time in my life, there was a sense of truth that I could believe in; I embraced God and everything about the Bible I could. God left me in that small town for a number of years to find peace. I had such emotional healing that had to happen, to restore me to where I was a normal person and not an inner-city slum kid. Then He led me to college. I graduated from there, and He led me to be a missionary in inner-city Chicago, to work on the streets and to start a campus ministry. I worked at an uptown church and did singles ministry. I went from there to seminary for four years and got a Divinity degree because I never wanted someone to keep me in ignorance again. One of the things that made me so mad was, "Why didn't anybody tell me about this?"

I had heard the words God, Jesus, the Holy Spirit; I knew the Christmas thing, I knew some of the basic stories, but I never heard that God designed you to have a personal relationship with Him, much less how to get into that. I didn't think God liked me because my life was a disaster, and if He liked me, why did that happen? I didn't understand about God giving me a choice, and our choices affect other people. I was very much a product of some huge wrong choices that caused me to be very beat up and wounded through most of my life. Once I became a Christian, I started seeing things from a different light. I wanted to know Greek and Hebrew, so I could know the Bible and so that I could find the truth out for myself.

I have sensed the Lord's miraculous intervention in my life on a number of occasions. Two years ago, I was diagnosed with ovarian cancer. I was out riding my bike with a friend, and then I came in and threw my hands on my abdomen area, and it seemed very hard. The doctor did an ultrasound and other tests, and he determined that I had a mass that they later diagnosed as ovarian cancer. I had a tumor about the size of a softball on one ovary and one the size of a lemon on the other. I had never had any symptoms. The lymph nodes were full, and they took a cancer antigen test they call CA-125; it was ranked at 133. They told me that normal was below 30. My life has always been hard and tough, so I just thought, here's one more bad thing. They set up the surgery.

According to the Bible, "If there are sick among you, let them call the elders of the church, and let them anoint them with oil," so I called my pastor and asked him to anoint me with oil. I asked him, "Have you ever anointed anybody with oil?" He is a new pastor, and he said, "No," and I said, "Well, I've never had it done, so why don't you do it?" He and I and the minister of music met at my house the morning right before the surgery, and they anointed me with oil. So I went in, and the last thing I remember them saying to me as they were putting me under was that they were going to make a large incision, way up above my belly button and all the way down. They said, "This cancer often will spread into the colon, so we need to make a larger incision," in the event that they would have to take some of that out. I went under, and the next thing I knew, I woke up, and the doctor was telling me, "There is no cancer."

The next day when I was a little clearer-headed, my doctor, the one that had found the tumors, called me up; I was in the hospital, and he said, "Have you seen the pathology report?" He talked very seriously because he was expecting this to be cancer, and he knew it was going to be bad. I said, "No I haven't, but I just talked to the surgeon; he left here about five minutes ago and said there is no cancer. He said it was clean; there was nothing." My doctor was blown away; he said, "Girl, do you know what kind of miracle that was? I would have bet my life that that was cancer." Those were his exact words. He was a Christian physician. Later, I was at a graduation of the medical school students because they wanted me to come and speak, and my doctor was there. There were a couple of other doctors with him, and I walked up, and he said, "Gentlemen, I want you to meet this girl; this is an absolute miracle." He told them what my symptoms were, and he said, "Her cancer antigen was 133." They all crooked their necks around at me, and then just looked at me: "Wow." It was such a miracle.

I always believe that it comes back to God being the healer. God gives us faith steps that He desires that we take. It all has to do with trusting God, which is faith. I don't believe that we control healing. God's goal is that people come to know Him and embrace everything that is of Him. We have to understand that this is a very tainted world. Jesus said, "I am going to prepare a place for you." In that world, there is no disease, there is no death, there is no distortion. It is perfection, which is what was designed. In the meantime, here in this world, God's goal is that we know Him, and with God comes the fullness of wholeness. His goal is not to rescue me out of every situation. His goal is that we seek Him and are drawn to Him. It is not what He does, it is who He is.

There are steps God wants us to take to demonstrate our trust, and there are times, like in that instance with my broken back, where I knew I was His child; I didn't even understand it very much, but I knew I was. It was me coming to my Dad and saying, "I'm in pain, and I'm debilitated, and I hate this, and help." That's what it was, a little child talking to Dad. The Bible talks about God, and when Jesus taught us how to pray to Him, He referenced the word "Abba," which is "Daddy," very personal. I very personally talked to my Dad. When I needed help, and I was in pain, I asked my Dad, and that's what He did. God knew that I had lived a life that gave me good reason not to trust anyone, and that I needed to learn to trust. Some of the things that He did for me were to give me great evidence of His supernatural power. He knew that I would one day go and be used in a very powerful, public way to proclaim Him. I have traveled all over the country to share my testimony and have been a speaker and conference leader.

God knew His plan, and He says in His Word, "I know the plans that I have for you." He told Jeremiah, "Before you were in your mother's womb, I ordained plans for your life." God has a plan of how He wants to use each of us as individuals who come to know Him, how He is going to use us to help others know Him. For the way He was going to use me, I believe that it was helpful for Him to demonstrate very strongly to me why I could trust Him.

He is a God who can equip you to do whatever it is within His design for you to do. God was in the process of restoring me, so He showed me—physically, emotionally, intellectually—that there is nothing that is beyond His touch. God is most interested in us finding wholeness in Him. That's what this life at this point is all about, as well as God demonstrating who He is, so that people can see Him, know Him, and surrender their lives to Him.

Doris was interviewed by Georgianna Jackson in June of 2002.
She is a white Baptist in her 50's.

Wait on the Lord
—Lois Bremmerton

In 1985, I was playing on our ladies' softball team and got knocked down. I was the second baseman, and I cracked my head on the infield. I went down headfirst. I got up and continued playing. That was on a Saturday, and I felt light-headed off and on for about five days, but nothing that I thought was any more abnormal than when you have a little bump on the head. That Wednesday night following our choir practice, I was leaving the church. My daughters were approximately eleven and eight, and I had them with me. I got in the car to leave and pulled out of the church parking lot. Midway between the two entryways, I had a severe and sudden headache that was just blinding. It was night, and I could see oncoming lights, so I stopped the car. I looked for the reflectors on the entryways, the best I could to keep my mind and attention on what I was doing, and I was able somehow to get the car back through the two reflectors into the lot. I believe that was a miracle in itself.

Then I lost it. I got the car turned off, or at least it was in idle or park. When my oldest daughter realized there was a problem, she jumped out and ran into the building. She got one of the parishioners who was there locking the building, along with some of the other choir members who had not left yet. When he checked me, he said I had no pulse. While he called for help, he sent some people out to stay with me and a lady to get the girls out of the car and to be with them. Another lady came, and when she saw how bad I was, she began praying. There were several people who stood there and prayed with her. It seems to me that I recall hearing someone pray; I was so sick I did not know who or where it was coming from, but it must have been this woman.

They admitted me to the hospital, kept me for a day and a night in intensive care, and transferred me to another facility. Over a period of time, they determined I had had some type of hemorrhage or stroke. They knew something drastic had happened because of the testing. I lost the use of my left arm and leg temporarily and had difficulty speaking. While this was happening, the entire church was in prayer. With my being the pastor's wife and a mother of young children, they were very concerned. I know of one gentleman who went to the church and literally stayed there that night, praying for me. When he heard about it, he drove into town from his farm. He was a deacon, and he unlocked the church and went into the sanctuary and prayed that night, which I know helped keep me alive.

I gradually got to where I was strong enough to walk on a right-sided walker, a one-sided walker. They dismissed me with therapy, saying that they did not know if I would ever regain the use of my leg or arm, but they would do everything in therapy that they could do. I worked real hard with them, and all of this took place over a period of about a year. I regained the use of my left arm. I would put my hand on the keyboard and take my right hand and press my fingers down, trying to get the strength in my left arm to hit the keyboard. I worked hard and prayed a lot, and it was tough because I had young children. When I was not using the walker, I was in a wheelchair. My left leg was very slow. It was mainly the ankle joint: if I would bear weight, it would give way. It lost its strength during those months. When you have this kind of a brain happening, it takes the muscle-bearing strength out of your limbs, and that is what had happened to my leg.

The real miracle came when it was getting quite discouraging. I had pretty well got the use of my arm back, but I was still on the walker and still had to go in a wheelchair everywhere because I could not walk and did not have the strength to fight crutches. At that time, we had a Tuesday morning ladies' prayer group. There were about five of them, and they met regularly at the church around ten o'clock to pray in the sanctuary for general church needs, for our missionaries, for the pastor, and for the church in general. This was about eight months into my situation, and they were in prayer for me when one of the ladies said that she felt led by the Holy Spirit and by the Lord that they should come over to my house and have prayer for me and lay hands. In our church, it is common for the Holy Spirit to speak to someone, like a revelation from the Lord. I am not saying she heard a literal voice, but in her spirit she felt that she should pray and that would be the day to do it. The other ladies all agreed that they would take the extra time and do that. It was spring break; we had just opened the above-ground pool at our home, and my children were out there for one of the first times of the year. I had an adult friend out there with them when the ladies came over.

I came in out of my bedroom on the walker; they were in the living room, and we sat down. This one lady came over and told me what the Lord had told her, and I said, "That's fine." She said, "Can we pray?" I said, "Sure." They had anointing oil; it was a little bottle of olive oil. In the book of James, there is Scripture about calling for the elders of the church and having them anoint with oil and pray. She said, "I know other people have prayed for you repeatedly. Our prayers are not any greater than theirs. But for some reason, I feel like this is what the Lord wants to do today, so I want to anoint you with oil and pray." I said, "That's fine." And they did; they prayed. They touched my head; she touched my forehead with a little oil, and I felt a warmth that I do not know how to explain. My whole body was warm all over, like if you walked into a sauna and suddenly felt the heat of it. It was a really strong warmth, and it was amazing. I have felt the Lord's presence before, but never like that. That was a special time.

I got up on my good right foot, and I began to test the left one just a little bit. I was still holding onto the walker, but it felt stronger, and I tried a step, and it worked. I felt wonderful and very excited! I cried, "Hey, I can walk!" I wanted to walk and show everybody, and I did. They were excited with me. At that time, we had a deck on the back of the house; it was an older house, and you had to take steps to go up on the deck from the back door. I went up those steps and walked to the deck. The deck adjoined the pool. When the girls saw me walking, they came flying out of the pool and said, "Momma, what are you doing up there?!" They were so excited because they had seen how I struggled. They knew how great that was because they had not seen me walk for almost a year. The other ladies were out there with us, and I explained to them what had happened, how the ladies had prayed for me, and I was able to walk. After the girls came out of the pool, I called my husband. Then I was in a church service the next night, and I shared with the people who were there what had happened.

My whole body was still weak; that happens when you have been in bed. But it felt strong enough that I could bear weight. I could walk without my ankle collapsing, and as I did more, then I was able to do more. To say I went out and ran laps—no, I didn't. But I was able to walk and not have to stay in a wheelchair. And I have been walking since. I know at one time my doctor said, "You might someday get that leg back, and when you do, you are probably going to drag it." But I don't.

Had it not been for God, I do not know how long it would have been before I got the use of my foot back. But I feel the first miracle was that I survived that initial night and then passed through all the tiring stress of the therapy and getting well. If anyone has ever been down that road, it is very long and arduous. It takes you out of your normal lifestyle and really dismantles the family at times. The whole time I was ill, there was much prayer. They had come into the hospital room and prayed when I was in intensive care. I also go back to the man who prayed the original night, that he felt led to do that. I do not think that it was just those women. It was a combined effort of a group of people who really sought the Lord on my behalf because I was too ill to do that. And my husband, of course, prayed for me many times.

I do go to doctors, and they are very helpful; I have a great admiration and appreciation for my physician. I do not hesitate to believe that God heals through doctors; I do know that He does that. But I also know that He can do something when doctors can't, and I am proof of that.

The Lord can heal in many ways. The thing that I learned more than anything was waiting and patience and knowing that things come in time. I learned to wait and to wait on the Lord. It was a growing time for me. As a minister's wife, when I am put in situations to try to help people who are going through long experiences, I can understand better. This has helped me with my counseling, with the patience to listen and to encourage people that with time, things do get better. When you are going through something ongoing and are sick like that, especially if you are a younger person, it is good to have someone who has been there and gone through a similar episode. So I have been able to help people in that regard.

I know that it was also a real witness to my children. They are very devout Christians, and they have a level of faith that they might not have developed had they not seen that and lived through it with us. God was faithful. It helped my faith tremendously—and my girls' faith. It was not my faith that brought me through this. I am not saying that I did not have faith, but I do not know that I had the faith that the other people did who prayed for me. I did not doubt my faith; I just did not understand. And there is a difference. I have enough faith from these experiences to know that all things are possible. I feel like that was just a wonderful thing that God did for me.

Lois was interviewed by Andrew Cousins in November of 2001. She is a white woman in her 50's who attends an Assembly of God congregation.

He Says It, I Believe It
– Alicia Thomas

At the time my daughter, Kristina, was diagnosed with ALL, a type of leukemia, she was three and a half years old. She had a cold and was running a very high fever at night. We kept taking her to the doctors, and in the course of a two-week time period, she was on three or four different antibiotics. After the third antibiotic, the doctor said we needed to go further and do chest x-rays. They weren't good, so he had us take her to the hospital. After some tests, the doctor gave me the news. He said, "You know your little girl is sick." Being a mom, I knew it wasn't a regular cold. I said, "What's wrong? Quit beating around the bush." He was trying to walk me through it very slowly. He told me, "We did a blood test." I said, "What's the problem? Get to the point." He said, "She has cancer." I didn't get anything after that. The doctor was saying that it was very important for them to do a procedure to draw fluid out of her back to find out the diagnosis, but her body was rejecting everything. They couldn't get the fluid that they needed.

But the Father is faithful. They scheduled the procedure again for the next morning. At this point the doctor told me, "She is dying." The cancer was eating her up really, really fast. He said, "We have got to get this fluid because that is the only way we are going to be able to diagnosis her, to try to help her." So the next day came; she was still very, very sick, running a fever of 104 or 105. They were giving her ice, trying to keep the fever under control. They were finally able to do the procedure, but they had a terrible,

terrible time. The doctors were crying and the nurses were crying because they could not get the fluid. The marrow was so compacted in her bones that the fluid would not flow; it would not come out. After the doctor told me what the problem was, I started praying because we already knew that she was dying. My husband was holding her hand, crying. I just walked out. I told the doctor, "I have to go outside."

So I started walking the halls, praying out loud. I didn't care who heard or who saw me at this point. My baby's life was on the line. I did not care. I started crying and praying in my heavenly language, and that is when the fluids started coming. I was praying, and I heard them screaming, and I came back in the room. The fluid shot so hard, it shot the needle out of the bag. They were screaming, "Get another needle; get another needle!" But they were able to catch enough to do what they needed to do.

They got the diagnosis and started the treatment. She was in there a whole week, seven or eight days, before her body started responding to any kind of treatment. At this time the only thing in my mind is, my baby is dying.

One of my friends got in touch with our pastor and let him know what was going on. Right then they started a 24/7 prayer chain. They kept it going the whole time, even after she came home. They kept it going until she got out of the woods. There were a lot of prayers. She stayed in the hospital a few days shy of three weeks. Finally they got her stable where the medicine started kicking in, so we were grateful for that.

At this point, I would just pray when she would go to sleep because she was sleeping in intervals of ten to fifteen minutes. When she was awake, I did a lot of things; I played with her, and we would color. When she would take a little ten- or fifteen-minute nap, I would sit there and pray. I would take that time to clear my spirit. That is pretty much what I did the whole time she was in the hospital. When you are born again, it tells you in Acts that He will leave you with a comforting, that you will be filled with the Spirit. It is a gift from the Father, not to do with anything that you have to earn. It is the Spirit, the Father's Spirit. It is the Father's Spirit that will pray through you when you don't know how to pray. He is our prayer teacher; He is our helper. We don't know what to say or how to say it. So you pray to the Spirit, and you won't mess it up because the Spirit knows what you are trying to say, or what you want to say, or what you need to say. He is there to guide you and to help you through good and bad times. And I use that a lot—a lot!

Kristina did lose all of her hair like the doctor said she would. They told me that she would be like that for about a year. When I would give her a bath, I would wash her scalp and anoint her hair and her head. The same way that you apply lotion, I would put a little bit in the palm of my hand, and I would pray the whole time that I would scrub her scalp. I have a bottle of regular olive oil that I bought at the store. I fasted and prayed for that oil, asking that whatever I need for it to do, agreeable with the Spirit, will be done. That is a powerful little bottle of oil. In a month's time, the hair started growing back. She was still on the powerful chemotherapy. They would say, "What are you doing? This doesn't happen. Hair doesn't grow back for at least nine to ten months." But in a month's time, she had peach fuzz, and within two months, she had enough hair that I could braid. I am a big believer in anointing because it works for me.

I would anoint Kristina's whole body, the same as I did for her scalp. I would put a little bit in my hand, mix it with some lotion, and rub her whole body because her skin went through some amazing changes. I would do her whole body just like I did on the scalp. I did it every single day. I had to apply lotion anyway, so I just added a little bit to it, and I prayed while I was dressing her and oiling her down. She would be laughing and playing like a normal 3-1/2-year-old. Throughout the course of her illness, I could see the Father working in certain areas. She was on the real hard chemotherapy for a year. After that, she grew stable, but she still had so many pills to take. At some point, she was on two liquids and maybe six or seven pills, two or three times a day. They told me that she was going to fuss and fight with me, but she took those pills like an old woman. I would lay them out, and we would talk about them, and I would tell her, "We have to take these, but we still believe in the Father." She would take them, and as soon she was finished, she was ready to go and play. I don't take it lightly because I know this was the Father.

Her healing was a gradual process. You could see little things, not every day, but I would notice little things here and there. She was into her second year of chemotherapy when they couldn't trace the cancer. I asked them if they could stop the chemo, and they said no because it would do more damage. They had to wean her down instead of stopping it cold turkey. But they weaned her way down, even less than half of what she would have taken. I don't even call it remission because when they can't trace it, to me that is a total cure. The doctor told me remission is just lying dormant, where the cancer is not active, but with Kristina, they can't even trace it lying dormant. She is twelve now—and not even as much as a head cold. She is doing great. She only goes once a year. She just went for her once-a-year checkup, and they still can't trace it. Her system is very strong, very strong. The second or third time they told me that they couldn't trace the cancer, that's when it set in my spirit that He did it, that the Father healed her. When they told me the first time, my mind messed with it, but the second time I thought it, and the third time I knew it had worked. I remember that Sunday when I told them in church; we prayed, the whole Sunday.

It really solidified things in my spiritual life. You can't sway me when it comes to healing. Things He has done for us over the years have solidified a lot of things in my spirit that I have read in the Word that He has promised us. They will come to pass if you have the faith to believe it and receive it. It will happen. It may not happen when you think it is going to happen, but it will happen. He tells us the work is already done; all we have to do is to have the faith to receive it. We, as humans, want to go by what we see and what we hear, but spiritual is just what it is, spiritual. For me, it is simple now; it wasn't when I was going through it. If we believe what He says and have faith that He has already done the work, He has already promised us that we can receive it.

You wouldn't expect a three-and-a-half-year-old to have the faith that a thirty- or forty-year-old person would have. But I would encourage her to speak: you speak your faith; Mommy is praying and believing, and you speak it, too. We are both going to watch it manifest. That's how we handled that. If He says we can do it, and we have sense and faith enough to believe that we can do it, then why not do it? That is my attitude. He says it, I believe it, and we're going for it.

My church family was most important because they were here with me. It made me feel good to know that I was part of an affiliation that was willing to pray 24/7 because I was sleeping at 3 o'clock in the morning. You have to be really dedicated. You have to want it just as much as the parent wants it, just as much as the child wants it.

Sometimes the presence of the Lord was so real. Sometimes I would cry. Kristina would say, "Mommy, your head hurt?" She didn't understand. Because when you cry, you put your hand on your head. She thought my head had to hurt. I was so happy on the inside to know that He could care that much. When I gave her a bath He would come and visit us. You could feel His presence. I would get this new burst of energy. I was always so tired, but when I would work with her, my body would get a second wind. You can do this; we can do this together. That is why I know it was the Father who kept me all of that time because I was physically and mentally drained; but when I would work with her and spend time with Him, I would get this second burst of energy. I would have the people in church tell me that I didn't look like I had been through anything; "You're just glowing." I know it was the Father because I was so tired. I had to go to church, so I could be in the presence of the Father.

The Father is also using Kristina in the area of healing. During the time that she was on chemotherapy, one Sunday, our pastor had her come up and pray for another little girl who had very bad nosebleeds. All she did was say, "Father, in the Name of Jesus, I thank you that her nose won't bleed no more." At this time she must have been five, and we saw her mama at the fair two years ago, and that little girl has not had a nosebleed from that day to this. He has also used Kristina many, many times this past school term. A little boy had a disorder; he would get the hiccups, and he would have them so bad that he would pass out. She said it looked like he was choking on something. When she came to tell me about it, she was so excited; she was screaming, running down the road. "Something happened today!" I purposely get home before my children get home, so I saw her coming down the road. She was running and screaming, "Something happened today! Mommy, Mommy, we were on the playground today, and he was choking." She called his name, and she said, "I didn't get scared. All I did was put my hand on his chest, and I said, 'Stop.'" She said that she didn't say anything; she just put her hands on his chest and spread her fingers. She just touched him. When the EMT's got there, they went back, and he went on back to playing. He was fine.

It excited her to see what the Father did. She knows He is doing it. But every time He does it, she gets crazy with excitement. I tell her, "You are a special person." I say, "He'll do it for a three-year-old, four-year-old, ten-year-old, fifty, and sixty." I try to drill that into both of my children; if you are a respectful person, He will do it for you. It solidifies your faith, even as a child. I told them that we have got to have wisdom, so we do what the doctor says, but we also line it up with the Word. Everything that we do, I try to line it up with the Word, so they can see that the Word does work. I was trying to help them understand that the Word works. That's what grace is for, but your heart has got to be in the right place, and you have got to have that intimate relationship with Him. I get my private time with Him; you have to have that relationship with Him. Once you have that relationship, and you are striving to live a holy life, and you are striving to do the things that He wants us to do, then He will heal you. Not in your time either, but in His time. The Word works.

Alicia was interviewed by Vivian Moore in July of 2002.
She is a non-denominational African American woman in her 30's.

Divinely Healed!
Deanna and Patrick Murphy

Deanna begins the story . . .

Eighteen years ago, on April 4th, we gave birth to our second child, Sarah Ann. The doctors announced that she had ten toes, she had ten fingers, and everything was great; at least that's what they thought. However, three days after we brought her home, Patrick and I had to take her back to the hospital where she was born. She had a really high fever and was lethargic and unresponsive to any type of stimuli. The doctors told us that she had an ear infection. That was the beginning of many, many trips back and forth to the doctor with many rounds of different antibiotics. Finally, when she was between nine and ten months of age, one of the pediatricians advised Patrick and me that we needed to have a hearing test done, which is called a tympanogram, to determine the severity of the damage done to Sarah Ann's ears because of infection.

As a result of this, the physicians told Patrick and me that our daughter had been deaf since birth and that the scar tissue that had built up on her eardrums and in her ear canals had made it much worse. I knew from a very early point in her infancy, having a three-year-old son, that there could be a loud sound coming from him, and nothing would faze her: no clapping, no singing. It wouldn't startle her like it would most children. From very early on in her development, something just wasn't right, but being a mom for only three years, and having had a boy, I thought girls were stubborn to begin with, that they moved when they wanted to move. I thought this was normal behavior. After her fevers and through the medications, she would get better for a little bit of time while the antibodies in her system were built up, but then they would deplete themselves, and it would start all over again. Each time, this infection within her ears progressively worsened. We were advised by our pediatrician to take Sarah Ann to an ear specialist in a large city nearby.

Patrick and I went into this glass tower of a building where the ear specialist practiced. Since it was March, it was very, very cold that day. With our baby bundled in her daddy's arms, we signed in, and the receptionist had us fill out all the needed paperwork. We sat for close to an hour before they called us back. Sarah Ann was still in her daddy's arms. When we got back to the doctor's office, he didn't disrobe our child, he didn't take a pulse; none of this was done prior to the visit in his office. He did not listen to her lung sounds, and he was on the phone when we got into his office. You would think that he would have hung up, but he didn't. He propped the phone receiver between his ear and shoulder and pulled our daughter's earlobe just enough—without looking with an otoscope—to say that he had touched her physically. He said, as he lowered the receiver under his chin, "Yes, your daughter needs tubes; she's deaf for the rest of her life," and he continued his conversation on the telephone.

My husband looks at me with this "I don't think I like this doctor" look, and I look back at him, and I have this look of, "When is the examination going to begin?" As we are sitting there in the office, the doctor reminds us that, on our way out, we need to make the surgical appointment with his receptionist. Patrick doesn't stop at the receptionist; we are now on the elevator going down to our car. I am a Christian woman, and the wife of a pastor, and I usually don't let unwholesome things come out of my mouth; but on the way down in the elevator, I didn't say Sunday School words to my husband. I wanted to know why he would let our daughter be deaf the rest of her life? She didn't know how to communicate. Sarah was very content just to lie there. She was in a very low percentile in birth weight for her age, low in everything for an eleven-month-old baby. She was at the bottom. I could not understand why he was so insistent on getting our baby out of that man's office and not making an appointment. It was ludicrous, it was crazy. Our baby was going to be deaf, and we needed to make an appointment to get tubes in her ears and begin the process of getting her fitted for hearing aids, learning sign language . . . and he was bypassing all of this. I could not for the life of me understand why he would do that to our baby.

Patrick continues . . .

I am a believer in the Lord Jesus Christ. What my wife didn't understand at that moment, and what I didn't feel like saying in the doctor's office, was that I had an impression from His Holy Spirit in my heart that we didn't need to be there any longer. Somehow, He was going to take care of it, although I didn't know how at the time.

We knew this acquaintance through babysitting his child, and his name was Eric. So I called Eric that night when I got home and said, "I need for you to come over and bring another friend." I don't remember his friend's name, but those two came over to the house and I said, "We need to pray and anoint Sarah with oil." At that time, I had never done such a thing and didn't even know how strongly I believed in faith healing, but we went into the bedroom where Sarah was asleep in her crib. We put some oil on her head and laid our hands on her, all three of us, and began to pray for her. We prayed for several minutes, committed the situation to God, and trusted what He would do. The next morning when we awoke, I didn't get a chance to tell Deanna what had transpired, so she didn't know anything, except that she got up and began to notice some differences in Sarah.

Deanna reflects . . .

I believe within my heart that the healing took place the minute that those men laid hands and prayed for that baby. That's when I believe that she was healed, instantly. The next morning, this child was standing in her crib, making sounds that I had never heard in my life. I thought it was her brother on the floor, playing with Legos, because I was in the kitchen. The only thing that Sarah had ever really enjoyed eating was bananas with tapioca pudding and rice cereal. That morning, she ate a full Tupperware bowl and drank almost a full cup of apple juice. I knew that something just wasn't normal as I knew it. Her little brother came in and dropped his bucket of Legos right at the base of the high chair, behind her, and for the first time ever, I heard our baby scream. It just scared her to death. Before that morning, a bomb could have gone off, and this child would have shown no emotion.

I did not understand what was going on with Sarah. It was more what was wrong with my baby, rather than what was right. I did not know what had taken place the night before, but in my mind, my baby was making sounds and doing things that I thought were abnormal. Looking back on it now, it was very, very normal; this is what she should have been doing all along. I spent the whole morning staring at our baby, who was making sounds that I had never heard, doing things that I had never seen.

All along—I don't know what the connection is with children relating to children—but whenever Sarah was fretful, the sight of her brother would calm her. He could go in, and I would tell him, "Rub Sissy's hand; just rub Sissy's hand," and he would rub it in his three-year-old way. He would jabber, talk, and dress her up; they were pilots, they were doctors. They were something all the time. But this time, it seemed like she was corresponding with him. She would make sounds as if to say, "Okay, let's play pilot, or let's build blocks," and whatever it was that he wanted her to do, she did it. When my husband came home that afternoon, I looked at him and said, "Patrick, something is very desperately wrong with our baby. We have got to get her to a doctor." I remember that he got a look on his face that was almost angelic. There was an aura that formed around it that was just indescribable. My first reaction was that I wanted to know why he was not showing any more response to me and the fact that something was wrong with our baby. But then he sat me down on the couch and told me about the healing, about what happened Thursday night with the anointing of oil and those three men praying for her.

He told me that, during the healing, she had become fretful, and it was Eric who spoke against the demons and spoke directly to them. He told them to "uncup the ears of this baby," that they had no control, they had no power, and they had to leave. It was at that time that Sarah became very, very fretful, almost to the point of screaming. Eric prayed for the spirit of peace to overcome this child, and she just fell asleep in her daddy's arms.

The weekend continued, and we were on cloud nine rejoicing. For the very first time that afternoon, Sarah heard the splash of the water as her hands hit it, and it was the most fun thing for this child to hear water splash. It was even more fun when she poured it out of the cup from the distance of her high chair onto the floor. She loved that sound too; that wasn't a good thing, but that's okay. I admit there was still some skepticism with me, but with Patrick being the spiritual leader in our household, he carried the faith that I didn't think I had at that time, that our daughter was healed.

We called the pediatrician's office on Monday morning, and that Monday afternoon they ran the same test that I had seen with my own eyes before, a tympanogram. It measures the vibrations of your eardrum. If there is a remote amount of sound that your eardrums are receiving, it looks like a miniature lie detector test; it has this little needle. I saw before Friday that needle unscathed on the piece of paper; it never moved. The further she turned the dial, there may have been somewhere around three or four frequency, a little flick on the piece of paper where the needle had moved. That day when she put the earphones on our daughter, I don't even remember the red dial coming off the outer edge of the zero when that needle went off of the piece of paper with the amount of vibrations that our child was receiving. It wasn't just one ear; it was both ears because she plugged one and did one, and then she unplugged it and did the other, and then she did both. The pediatrician began to cry, and we thought, "Dear gosh, what is going on with this woman?" Come to find out she was a Christian, and she asked us, "Where have you had your baby? What have you done?" Patrick told her the same story. She looked at Patrick, and he told her with a little bit more detail, and she said, "I know that you took this baby to the throne of Christ, and the Great Physician Himself healed her, not partially but completely, and that is what is going in her chart." She put, "Divinely or miraculously healed!" and signed her name on the chart. Since then, Sarah has never, ever had ear infections; never have we been to a doctor because of her ears.

Deanna and Patrick were interviewed by Georgianna Jackson in June of 2002. They are white Baptists in their 40's.

Chapter 5

FOLK HEALING

*Jesus . . . said to them, " . . . Truly I tell you, if you
have faith the size of a mustard seed, you will say to this
mountain, 'Move from here to there,' and it will move; and
nothing will be impossible for you."*

Matthew 17:20

You've Got to Be a Believer

—Foster Graves

It has been both hard and easy. It came down from my mother, and she taught me. When the pilgrims landed, there were four Graves on the boat. They came over as laborers and medicine men. I suppose the teaching came from them. Lord, have mercy! I was about 14 or 15 when I learned, and I have done the work ever since. You strictly have to be a believer. If you don't believe what you are saying and what you are doing, you might as well sweep it out the porch because it won't do one bit of good.

Another month from now, when the weather starts getting hot, we will get as many as eight long-distance telephone calls from Myrtle Beach to take the fire out of people if they have been sunburned. That's the last we hear of them because it takes it out. It works. Out at Six Mile, this man calls about every third week to get the poison oak cured on him. The poison oak is exactly the same thing as the burn. You use the same words, and poison oak just blisters up like a big burn blister.

A man can teach a woman, or a woman can teach a man, and you can teach taking out fire, curing the blood, stopping blood, and thrash. A woman can't teach a woman. In order to cure the thrash, or for me to teach it to anybody else, they have to be the seventh child in the family. You can teach it to the first one, but they can't do it. They can't cure the thrash. It came out of the Bible that way, that the seventh child would be the only one who could cure the thrash, and I'm the seventh son.

Lord, have mercy! I have had them come in here three and four at a time. Every year it's that way. They will call from their homes. I like for them, if they need the thrash cured on the inside, to come walking in here and sit down; I take the baby and go in the back room. They don't see what I do, and I don't tell them what I do. That's the way it's taught. That's been going on ever since I was a pup.

Sometimes it will take two or three times over the telephone, but you can get it if you just stay in there with it and have enough faith. You've got to be a believer. If I wasn't a believer, we wouldn't be sitting here talking. We were talking to one of my wife's nieces. She called and said, "Please have Uncle Foster stop the blood on Trevor." She said his nose was bleeding furiously, and by the time I got through saying the words on the telephone, it slowed down a little. She said, "Tell Uncle Foster that the blood has already stopped." That was last week. It's somebody at least once a week. It just beats all you ever saw. People just pass the word along. It used to be so many around did this that you didn't notice how many have problems, on account of somebody else doing the work.

There are a lot of things you are not supposed to tell. To tell you the truth, I have just about covered everything that's legal. Also, they are not supposed to thank you. They just more or less take up the conversation they had before they started on the curing part. And there's no payment. I kind of wish there was. But no, that's never mentioned.

They have to believe also. It has to come from both ends. If you believe, why, there's no way in the world you can keep it from stopping. It's an amazing thing. You don't know why it does it, or how it does it. It tells you in the Bible why it does it, but it doesn't tell you how, because it doesn't want you to be as smart as it is. You can understand why too. They wouldn't call if they didn't believe, like a man doesn't stop to get a drink of water unless he's thirsty.

Not over two months ago, I had a preacher call me who was going to move a patient from one hospital across town to another hospital; the patient was having a serious nose bleed, and they could not get the blood stopped. The preacher called me and asked me if I would see if I could stop the blood. It was 1:30 in the morning, and I went ahead. I didn't think anything else about it because I knew if it was deep down, then it would stop. He let it slip his mind and never did call me back to say whether or not the blood stopped that night. Later I saw his brother-in-law at the flea market, and we were talking. He said, "Foster, my brother-in-law called you about that lady whose nose was bleeding," and I said, "I've been laying off to call him and see if I did any good that night." He said, "You needn't worry about it. You did." He said, "It stopped real good."

It's just a thing that you do so many times, till you don't think about it when a person forgets to call and say everything is okay. Once you are through with it, it's just like sweeping the floor. You're done. The verses come from the Bible. It will be consistent, and it will also be different, but it's still the same words, put down on the page it's on. It's amazing how many different ways you can skin a cat.

Foster, an 84-year-old white man, was interviewed by
Sue Heiney in July of 2002.

The Good Lord Does It All
–Janelle Wright & Elaine Duker

Janelle shares her story . . .

Momma taught me about the blood. My husband's cousin taught me about talking out the fire. I have seen it done ever since I was a kid. A woman who lived over on the Mill Hill told me that the same verse that does poison oak also does the thrash, warts, and shingles. With poison oak, you have to say the verse nine times; with the others, you just say it one time: fire, psoriasis, blood, shingles. Momma and I work together, every time somebody calls me or somebody calls her. We call the other, so we can do it together. We feel like we do better with both of us doing it.

Last week, we went to church, and they told us that a man had shingles. Most of the time, we have to know the whole name before it works, so I asked the preacher's wife for his name. She gave me his phone number, and I called him. Then I called Momma, and we both said the verse. He came back to church on Sunday, and I asked him how he was doing. He said that he could tell the difference that night, after we hung up.

I work at the Dollarama store, and you hear people talking, standing in the grocery line. If I hear people talking about an ailment, I will just say, "I know how to do this. If you give me your name, I will do it." Sometimes people call us, and we don't even know who they are. My brother-in-law didn't believe in it. He always said, "That stuff doesn't work; it isn't real," but one day, he was at work, and his nose started bleeding. That night, he called me and said his nose had been bleeding for hours; it just wouldn't stop. I said, "You really have to believe, or it's not going to work." He said, "I believe." It wasn't long before he called me back and said, "Elaine, it quit." Now he will call me when his nose starts bleeding.

My sister was doing fireworks one night. That is when I found out that it worked without being with the person. She was burned by the fireworks, and she called and said, "Please take it out." I said, "If you meet me halfway, then we will do it." She said, "Just do it now; it's burning." I said, "Okay." I said the verse, and she said, "I can feel it," because when you are having the fire taken out, you can feel it coming out of you. You can tell when it is working; the one who is being healed can actually feel it burning a little more as I am saying the verse. Afterward, the skin may feel a little rough, but it doesn't leave scars.

Whenever we say it and people say thank you, we always tell them not to thank us. We are not the ones who do it; the Lord does it. I was at Dollarama talking with a man, and I told him I could talk out his poison oak. He told me that if it had anything to do with the devil, he didn't want to have anything to do with it. I told him, "If it had anything to do with the devil, I would have nothing to do with it." I told him it was the Lord's doing. People get mad at you for not telling them the verses. They try to get you to do it, and they say, "If it's in the Bible, then why can't you tell us?" People don't understand that you don't want to tell everybody.

Janelle's mother, Elaine, continues . . .

My stepdaddy was the one who told me. He was the only daddy I ever knew. I have been doing this since before my daughter was born. My daddy told me, "You can't tell another woman; you have to tell a man. You can't tell but three people." He said if you didn't tell three people, then you couldn't do it. Instead of telling my daughter, I just wrote the verse down on a piece of paper, and she found it. I didn't give it to her. As for my son-in-law, some woman left it in his mailbox, and he found it. He just left it lying on the table, and I found it. It is more or less like you are stealing it. You have to say it many times. For talking out shingles, thrash, or warts, there are three different verses. We don't give them to anybody. But they will get mad at you if you don't. I have a friend in North Carolina; she wanted me to tell her because she has grandkids. When she moved up there, I told her, "You can call me." She got mad at me because I wouldn't tell her.

We don't do it; the good Lord does it all. We just say a verse. I always like to know afterwards if it has helped them. It is also good for the sunburn; it takes the burning out of it. Sometimes it doesn't blister either. Some people think it is the devil's work; I don't know why, unless they think it is witchcraft. But if it is witchcraft, it would not be coming from the Bible.

I have always believed in it. I was raised up on stuff like that at home. Prayer and home remedies, I reckon, are what brought us all through. All of us were just raised up in it. I have always believed in prayer. I am living proof. Three doctors told Momma she would never raise me. When I was just a baby, I had broken out in big water blisters. Wherever someone would touch me, it would leave a big blister. Somebody told Momma, "If you take her to Ms. Reynolds, she'll be all right." Momma had already sat up twenty-one days and nights with me, looking for me to die at any time. She took me over to Ms. Reynolds, and she prayed for me and gave me a little bit of something in a spoon. Momma didn't know what it was, but she said I went to sleep. When I woke up, I was about to starve to death. I was hungry because I hadn't had food in so long, so Ms. Reynolds fixed some dinner. Momma said I ate so much, she was ashamed of me. I have been all right since then. I am living proof that prayer works. I always believe in prayer.

Janelle and Elaine, both white women, were interviewed by
Sue Heiney in July of 2002.
Janelle is in her 30's and Elaine is in her 60's.

Nothing Without the Power of Jesus
—Eric Jennings & Randolph Meyers

Eric remembers his father-in-law . . .

My name is Eric Jennings, and I am sixty years old. I'm a former chemistry and physics teacher. I taught at the local high school for thirty years. I am Baptist, and at my church, I am currently on the Board of Deacons and on the Property Committee, and I have assisted the Sunday School teacher.

During our first or second year of marriage, around 1967, my wife and I went over to visit her mother and daddy one day. I was sitting in the den, and she and her mother went shopping. Her daddy was in the back room napping. All of a sudden, I heard this awful commotion out in the yard, and I went out to see what was going on. My wife's first cousin, Celia, from next door, was running toward our house with her little girl in her arms. The little girl was between one and two years old. Celia was screaming, and the little girl was screaming at the top of her lungs. I asked Celia what was wrong, and she said, "Where's Uncle Graham? Where's Uncle Graham? Find Uncle Graham, quick!" The little girl had tipped a pot of boiling water over on herself, and it went from her face all the way down to her toes on the front of her body. She was red as a beet all over. I wondered why Celia wanted Uncle Graham, but I thought maybe she wanted him to carry her to the doctor.

She said, "I've got to find him. I've got to find him! I want him to talk the fire out of Alicia." At that point, I was saying, "What have I married into?" I had never heard of it before, and I said, "You want him to do what?" She said, "Talk the fire out of her." So I went running to the back room and woke him up, and he came running. All this time, the little girl was screaming like you wouldn't believe, just screaming for all she was worth. He took the little girl, picked her up, and put her on the couch. He squatted down in front of her like he was praying for her. He took his index finger and next finger and just touched his mouth with them; then he reached over and touched her and said some words I didn't quite understand. He said something for twenty or thirty seconds, and all of a sudden, the little child quit crying, like someone turning a radio off. She just stopped completely. She instantly stopped yelling and screaming, though she was sniffing and still crying a little. To this day, she doesn't have any scars, and a lot of the pink coloration, where she had been pink from the burn, went away. It started getting better and better; I could physically see it get better and better. After a while, Celia took the little child back home, and that is the last I've heard of it. I just happened to be there that particular day.

As a science teacher, I was very skeptical at first. But then—it worked, so what can I say? I saw it. This is what I physically observed with my eyes, so it had to be real. After he touched her with the tips of his fingers, he touched his mouth. Then he touched her and said this Scripture, and the baby stopped crying instantly. It was just like instead of touching her, he had touched a radio knob and cut her off. I do not have a problem believing that the Lord heals people because I know He can do it. If you believe, He can do it.

His brother-in-law, Randolph, continues . . .

My father's name was Graham Meyers. He was extremely strong in his faith. He believed that if things were going bad, the best way to solve them was to pray. I can remember daddy reading the Bible; he read it almost every night. He believed that you should read your Bible and study it to know what Jesus wanted you to do. At a very young age, I found out that daddy talked the fire out of burn victims. I remember one or two adults and numerous children who were brought to him; they had been burned by grease, by scalding hot water, or by falling in the fire while they were burning brush. Sometimes I saw blisters on the children when they came; a blister would be a third-degree burn.

Inevitably, daddy would take the child and step into the living room. Daddy had a calming effect on children, and he loved them. If a burn victim came in or was brought by a parent, daddy would take them to a place where there was quietness. Sometimes the parents would go too. I have seen the mother hold the child, as daddy prayed over it. He would take spittle and rub. It was strange because a mother could touch it, and the child would holler; it would hurt, and the child would cry out in pain. But daddy would be able to take the child, especially the little ones, and pray. He had a calming effect, and he had this God-given ability.

Daddy accepted Christ in his early twenties. After that, he was the superintendent of the Sunday School or the church secretary for twenty-five or thirty years. He was extremely influential there. He appeared to get the ability to talk the fire out of a burn from uncle Luke. The Mantle of Healing was passed from uncle Luke to daddy; Daddy was his favorite nephew. It was not a mystical thing, but we never talked about it. I remember people coming fairly often, thirty, forty, or fifty people through the years. People trusted daddy. It appeared to them to do good, and the ones I knew, they never had scar tissue. Folks would bring their children to daddy rather than go to the doctor.

Once I got burned at the tobacco barn and daddy talked the fire out of it, but it wasn't a third-degree burn. Daddy knew that I knew that he could do that, so he did it to me. I remember which arm, but I can't even remember how I got burnt. It was when I was little, because we still had old tobacco benches, where they cropped it by hand, before the mechanical harvesting of tobacco took place. I would go with daddy and we would sit down there and talk during the curing of the tobacco.

Daddy never did healing in a group. He almost always went into the next room, where there was privacy for the healing event. Most of the time, he took a parent with him. These people knew who Mr. Graham was from church, so the children knew he would take care of them. I don't know whether it was because he was an adult or because they believed in him. I don't know what he said to talk the fire out. I once heard my uncle say, "I believe I would get better if only Graham was here to pray for me." He believed strongly that daddy's prayers had a healing power. It may have been just a sick man wishing, twenty-five or thirty years after his brother had died, but I heard him say, "I believe I could get better if Graham was here to pray for me."

He never received money for praying for people; daddy would never have done that. He felt strongly that you had to have faith that Jesus would do this for you. He had the faith that was necessary to believe that the healing power of the Lord would take place. He was pointed about that: it was the power of the Lord doing it. He never thought it was his power, but the Lord Jesus working through him. Daddy would often say, "We are nothing without the power of Jesus." Anything that came to you, he saw it as a gift. He never said the gift of healing; he said the gift of talking the fire out. So talking the fire out of a burn was something that he thought that Jesus used him to do. He was an extremely humble and gentle man and never very pushy. He never thought of himself as anything except an instrument of doing what Jesus asked; he gave everything to the power of the Lord. He saw himself as being an instrument of that power. I remember him telling me one day, "Don't be afraid to listen to the voice of the Lord."

I broke my neck about thirty-five years ago. I broke it in the afternoon, and as it bled, it put pressure on the spinal column. It hurt real bad: on a scale of one to ten, a ten. That night I lay in my bed, trying to wait through the night to go to the doctor the next day. My momma sat by my bedroom; she sat there and prayed all night. I know she did it out of love, but it irritated me to death that she sat there praying aloud, trying to get me to go to the doctor. I was going to go when daybreak came, and this was at three or four in the morning. My mother literally prayed all night until finally the pain got so bad; I laughed and said it was in aggravation of her sitting out there praying. I finally got up and got daddy up, and I said, "Daddy, we have to go to the hospital. It hurts so bad, I can't stand it any more."

We got to the hospital about five o'clock, and Dr. Williams was there on call. I was the most frightened I have been in my adult life because he had me x-rayed and came back and said, "There are bones pushing against the sheath of your spinal column. I don't want you to move. If those slivers of bone cut into it, for every nerve they cut, something below your neck will go numb." They put me in traction. I stayed in traction for at least three weeks, and I never had any ill effects. I had an officially broken neck, but the Lord blessed me: I have never had any trouble with my neck, never had any paralysis, never even had nerve tingling. I could say it was momma's praying and daddy's praying.

Eric and Randolph, both white males, were interviewed by Georgianna Jackson in May of 2002. Eric is a Baptist and Randolph is a Methodist.

Chapter 6

HEALERS

One day Peter and John were going up to the temple at the hour of prayer, at three o'clock in the afternoon. And a man lame from birth was being carried in. People would lay him daily at the gate of the temple called the Beautiful Gate so that he could ask for alms from those entering the temple. When he saw Peter and John about to go into the temple, he asked them for alms. Peter looked intently at him, as did John, and said, "Look at us." And he fixed his attention on them, expecting to receive something from them.

But Peter said, "I have no silver or gold, but what I have I give you; in the name of Jesus Christ of Nazareth, stand up and walk." And he took him by the right hand and raised him up; and immediately his feet and ankles were made strong. Jumping up, he stood and began to walk, and he entered the temple with them, walking and leaping and praising God. All the people saw him walking and praising God, and they recognized him as the one who used to sit and ask for alms at the Beautiful Gate of the temple; and they were filled with wonder and amazement at what had happened to him.

Acts 3:1-10

Healing is the Bread of the Children
–Santosh Rajdani

I grew up in India. I had read the Bible through seven times in my teens, but it was in my head and not in my heart. After high school, I thought that there was no God, that God is dead; who cares? I was twenty years old, and I had lost everything in my life. I had lived my life too fast. I went hungry for seven days and weighed about 90 pounds. Nobody cared for me. Nobody loved me. Where was I going? So I decided to kill myself under a train. While I was waiting for the train, I wrote a seventeen-page letter saying that nobody was responsible for my suicide. I thought I had a master's degree in failures, so I decided to kill myself. The train comes from Bangalore to Hyderabad. I was waiting, waiting . . . but the train was delayed and delayed.

At last, I said I was going to pray. I said, "God, I don't know whether I am going to hell or heaven,"—I knew I was a sinner—"But do something." Suddenly, I was not sleeping, and I was not dreaming, but I saw a light come from the western horizon. In the light there appeared a figure, and the figure became like a man; it was Jesus. Jesus began to speak to me in English, and He said: "Santosh, you don't have to die. I have died for your sins, and I am alive. If you would only ask me, I will forgive your sins, and I will give you a new life and a new beginning." I said, "I know I am a sinner. How can You love me?" He said, "I know that you have read My Word. I have loved you, and I am alive now." So I said, "Forgive me! Forgive me! Forgive me!" Great peace began to come into my heart. It lasted for about fifteen or twenty minutes; then it vanished. Then I said, "Something has happened. What has happened is not real. I am going to commit suicide." This happened six times, and with the train that day there was a big delay. Six times it happened; it was so real! It was not a dream.

Then I went back to my home. My room cost twenty rupees a month, and I had not paid for three months. I used to leave at four o'clock in the morning, so the landlady wouldn't ask for the rent, and I would get home at ten or eleven o'clock. That day at two o'clock I was not afraid. I said, "Thank You, Jesus; thank You, Jesus." Then there was a knock on the door. I opened the door, and there was a postman, and he brought me enough money to pay the rent. That day, I gave my heart to Jesus.

I began to see healings in the lives of other people. John Wesley said many years ago that God is limited because of our prayers. When we pray, His power is unleashed. I prayed for two people; one was a Muslim and one was a Catholic lady. God gave an abundance to them in three days' time. Then there was a young man; he had boils over his head, and he had to take a lot of medication. For three weeks he suffered. I said: "Praying is free; it doesn't cost to pray," and I prayed in the evening. The next day at six o'clock he came round, and everything had gone. I showed all my neighbors. When I prayed for these people, they were so blessed; they were healed and said, "You are a man of God."

I said, "Me? A man of God?" How I got here, I don't know. Since that time, I came to the ministry. I would not call myself a healer. I believe that everybody who believes in Jesus, God gives them power to heal. I am not the healer; Jesus is the healer. If you want anything, God says, "Ask, and I will give." I am not anything special. But I have seen some fantastic things. Faith doesn't come by prayer, faith doesn't come by fasting; faith comes by hearing the Word of God. One of the names of God is the Spirit of Faith. Faith is produced when my ears hear the Word of God.

About twenty years ago, in my city of Nagpur, we had invited an evangelist from Canada. He was coming to the city, so I bought the front pages of newspapers in our region, and in the newspaper we put something like this: "The blind will see, the deaf will hear, the dumb will speak, the lame will walk. What can't be handled by doctors, come and let's pray for you, and God will do the healing." One of the ministers called me and said, "Pastor Santosh, why did you print lies in the newspapers?" I said, "What do you mean?" He said, "You wrote that the blind will see, the dumb will speak, and the lame will walk. Don't you know that the days of miracles are over?" I said, "Pastor, they are over for you because the Bible says, be it unto you as you believe." I like to be very kind in saying things, but sometimes things need to be said boldly. So I said to this preacher, "Sir, if you don't believe in miracles, you are not going to get them." He said, "Why don't you preach for salvation; why do you want to preach on healing?"

I said, "The word salvation means not only forgiveness of sins, not only soundness of mind, not only deliverance from evil; it also means healing for the body. The Bible says, by the stripes Jesus received, we are healed. He went to the cross and poured His blood for the forgiveness of my sins. But Jesus did something for my body also." So I said to this priest: "Sir, the days of miracles are not over. The word salvation includes physical healing and spiritual healing." He says, "I will prove that you are wrong." I said: "You can prove that I am wrong, but how can you prove that God is wrong?" He said, "I know a bunch of lame people; I am going to bring them to your crusade. What are you going to do if they don't get healed?" I said, "Sir, what are you going to do when they do get healed?" He got somebody's truck. No one even prayed; they parked as our praise and worship were going on. There were a lot of people in the truck, and they were healed; they jumped and came running towards the pulpit, and I interviewed some of them. God has called us to pray impossible prayers, especially for impossible situations.

My wife is allergic to penicillin. We were in India, and a small splinter went into her finger; it became septic. When it became too painful, we went to a medical college hospital. There is always a big line. At last, at four o'clock we reached the doctor, and he said it must be incised and the pus taken out, and he wrote something. He said, "Go to the next room and get injections." We went to the next room, and I said to the nurse, "Sister, what are you giving?" She said, "I have to give penicillin," and I said, "Sister, don't give her penicillin; she is allergic to penicillin." She said, "Do you know more than the doctor?" I said, "No, but I will go to the doctor and change the medication because she is allergic to penicillin." By the time I came back, she had already given her the penicillin.

My wife was shaking all over; her eyes became big, and her whole body was shuddering. I got upset. Medicine is God's medicine; it is God's agency to give us healthier bodies. I said to the doctor, "You have no cure now." I said to myself, through my prayer, God will do something because the Bible tells me why should you die before your time? I picked up my wife. The doctor shouted, "Do you know what you are doing?" and I said, "Doctor, do *you* know? Can you do something?" He said, "No," so I said, "I am doing something."

I picked her up, put her in my car, and came home praying in tongues. I said, "My wife is a gift to me, a gift of God." I repeated, "Spirit of death, be gone!" The Bible says by signs people shall believe; I am a believer, not a doctor, and it says they shall lay hands on the sick, and the sick shall recover. I got to my house, and then the neighbors gathered. Some of my neighbors are nurses, and they said to me, "Pastor, you are a priest; you do spiritual things. We are nurses. We know what is happening: she is dying." I said, "Thanks for your sympathy, but I don't need that kind of sympathy right now. I am going to pray. The best thing you can do for me is pray." I began to pray. The more I prayed, the worse she became—she got spasms—one hour, two hours, her whole body was swelling; after that, I thought I was going to lose her. I was praying in tongues, "Thank You, Lord; thank You, Lord." There was not even one person who joined me in prayer. All I did was pray. At midnight the spasms were so bad, her teeth had locked. Around three o'clock she began to relax. I kept praying in tongues the whole time; at six o'clock she completely relaxed, and all the swelling was gone.

Six or seven years later we had gone to Delaru, and somebody had put something in our well. Because of whatever was in the well, my wife became very ill. The doctors came and gave her penicillin. That afternoon I arrived by train. Some people came to see me, and they had very sad faces. I said, "What happened? What happened?" They said, "She is dying; maybe she has half an hour." "Where is she?" "She is in the hospital." I said, "Drive the van there." So they drove the half-mile to the hospital; it is near the railway station. I got to the third floor, and the nurses were working on her. I saw death upon her. I said, "Lord, You have used me to minister, to heal so many; I ask for a gift of life. Satan, you cannot have my wife."

Then I began to pray, and my body began to shake. I believe that the divine power of God was flowing through me. As I began to pray, a couple of nurses agreed to come and pray with me. The bed began to shake, and I knew it was the power of God that was flowing. I said, "Spirit of death, be gone! Poison, be gone!" I prayed for about twenty minutes, and in twenty minutes she relaxed. I said, "How are you?" and she said, "Fine," and tried to get up. The doctors said, "You can't get up." So I said, "I'll take care of that. I am taking her." So she walked from the third floor of the hospital without a stretcher, and I took her home.

In healing, I cannot have an attitude of *que sera, sera*, what will be, will be. God has shown that healing is the bread of the children. God wants to see healing. Always God gives you insight how to overcome. Jesus never said in the Bible that you will never get sick; He said, if you get sick, I will heal you.

Santosh was interviewed by Andrew Cousins and Puja Verma in March of 2002. He is a non-denominational Indian man in his 50's.

We are All Spiritual Beings
—Larry Conners

When I was younger, I had a case of osteochrondroma that was not malignant. It was on the head of my humerus, a bone sticking out off my arm. It was underneath the skin, like the tongue in your cheek; you could see it clearly on x-ray. It was bone; it was not cancerous. It had been a pain; the tendons snapped over it and locked my shoulder up. My mom was praying it would go away. One day, in the shower, I had an intense jabbing pain in my shoulder, and I reached up, and it was gone. I was in high school when we first noticed the problem, and I was in medical residency, which would be in the late 1980's, when it went away. I cannot explain it any other way.

Another time, I hurt my knee. An MRI showed that it was a torn meniscus. I ended up having arthroscopy on my knee. It had been an evident tear on the MRI, according to both orthopedics and radiology. When I had my arthroscopy to fix it, it wasn't there! To quote the surgeon, I had "the knee of a sixteen-year-old," and the knee was "pristine." Others could argue that the MRI was wrong; it is not perfect. But something happened because my knee had hurt. Between the MRI and the surgery, my whole family had been praying about it.

I do not have a denomination. I believe it is not a religion, but a personal faith, a personal relationship with Jesus. I believe we are all spiritual beings; we have a soul and a spirit. If you fail to recognize or refuse to recognize that there is a spiritual component to your patient, you might be missing some things. I don't try to proselytize them into my way of thinking, but I may share with them. I am honest, and I tell people how I believe. I am not going to hide my beliefs or deny my beliefs. But you have to know the patient, and you have to be sensitive to the patient, see where they are, and go from there; you have to be perceptive.

Most of the time, in my family practice, the topic of faith comes up on its own. There are a few patients who are unreceptive, and I don't preach at them. Oftentimes patients are very receptive and want you to pray for them. With the patients whom I have known for years, I know them well enough to know that I can ask if they want me to, but some of them know me well enough that they just ask me to pray with them. After you get to know somebody pretty well, you know where they are and what they want. How they believe affects where they are and how well they are going to do. I had a lady the other night—she has a mass on her kidney—and I called and told her to hang in there and try not to let it bug her. She said, "Oh, no, you and I both know Who is still in control." They bring it up all the time. It has an impact on how they approach the problem.

Does faith have a role in the recovery process? Yes, I believe this; I definitely do. I believe that there is a two-part thing: one is motivation and attitude, and that definitely makes a difference—people who have a better attitude and approach make things better—but there is also a faith outside that person. There is an outside power that is bigger than their disease. I have seen people healed by a miracle that cannot be explained otherwise. People have gotten better, and they may have been under treatment, but the treatment would not have been expected to work that well; that is with actual cancers. I have seen other people improve where the reason is inexplicable, such as people with heart problems or people with bony abnormalities. I have seen folks who really should not have lived: people who had taken ten times the *lethal* dose of a medication—walk out of the hospital. But they had a lot of people praying for them. Would that have happened without prayer? Statistically, it would not have ever happened without something outside.

Larry was interviewed by Puja Verma in March of 2003.
He is a non-denominational white male in his 40's.

Speak It and Believe It
–Odessa Short

When I was twelve, I wanted to be saved, and I prayed. Way back in the older days, you had to get on your knees and pray, and you had to feel something before they would know you were saved. I went down on my knees. I don't remember getting up. All I remember is shouting and praising God. I look at people now who are getting saved, and it is different. It is like back then, we had pumps, and now they have spigots. We had washboards, and now they have washing machines. It's an easy way, but it is about knowing that God is God, that God said we must be born again, about believing and having faith.

Years ago, there were a lot of children having dysentery. A lot of children died, and my little girl got it. I took her to the doctor, and the medicine wasn't helping, so I carried her to another doctor. I took her there, and he said, "Why did you bring this dead child here? She's too far gone, and I can't help her. I can't help you." I kept saying in my mind all the time while he was talking, "You can say what you want to. My child is going to live because God is going to let my child live a while. God is going to help me, and I am going to praise God."

We left, and God told me to give her some soda crackers and a banana. I got in the car, and my daddy brought me on back. It looked to me like Satan wanted to take her in spite of all things. I told my daddy, "Stop the car. Her lips are turning blue, and it looks like she is gasping for the last." In my mind, I heard, "You know how to pray. You pray, and this child is not going to die." I said, "God, you said it. This child has got to live." When I got home, I was so glad when night came, so I could get off by myself and pray and cry to God and let Him do what He had to do. She got better, and she's here today—over 50 now. God is so good.

One day, my oldest daughter was sick; she was in the hospital with a high fever. In my mind, I said, "God, if I can get up there, that fever is going to leave. I am going to trust in Your Name, God." You have to have faith, and you have to believe. I believed, I prayed, and that is what happened: her fever went away. Speak it and believe it. After I prayed for my daughter, I saw another lady there who was really sick. It felt like a heater was coming from her bed. I touched her in the Name of Jesus, knowing that God was going to heal her fever too. I walked over to the window and looked out, and when I walked back, it was cool. Instead of the hot heat, it was like a fan being on, and her fever was gone, just like that. They let her go home the next day. I'll never forget things like that. I thank God because He is a healer.

Those healings were sudden. I prayed over them, and it just happened. I always feel the presence of the Lord. Every time you think about it, you want to praise Him. Thank You, Lord. Sometimes I praise Him all by myself in the midnight hour. I will be praising and singing all I want, and I go to bed, and I praise the Lord all I want. I don't have to wait to get to church to praise God because I know where He has brought me, and I praise Him.

I always pray for all my kids and grandkids. I pray with them when they come to my house; I will say, "Y'all, let's pray. Let's pray." One day I said, "The other day some children got burned up in a house, not too far from where we live." I said, "Y'all, let's pray. 'God, don't let nothing happen to them. Don't let this happen.'" I told them, "Y'all pray with me." They prayed with me and went on home. They lived two or three doors down from me. At that time, I was working at a factory, and my boss told me when I went to work the next day, "We want you to come in an hour earlier tomorrow." I said to myself, "How am I going to get there?" My husband was working at night and coming home in the morning, and he wasn't going to be there to take me to work. I said, "Lord, tomorrow morning, let me get up earlier and go to my daughter's house. Let me ask my son-in-law to take me." That had to have been God's plan. Why did my boss tell me to come to work earlier? He doesn't know why he said it either.

The next morning, I got up early to go wake my daughter and my son-in-law, so they could take me to work. Their next-door neighbor's house adjoined theirs. When I got up, went to their house, and knocked on the door to get him to take me to work, I heard the people next door, running up and down, saying, "Tommy, Tommy, go get the kids!" He ran back up toward the kids, but he said, "I can't make it." They had left the kids up there with an open flame, and one of them knocked it over, and it started a fire. I said, "Oh, my God." I ran up against my daughter's door and knocked it open, and I hollered and told my grandkids, "Fire! Fire!" They jumped up and came running down. I could feel the heat upstairs, coming from the neighbor's house, and my grandkids ran down, every one of them.

My kids, all of them, would have burned up if it wasn't for God. That was God. If the man hadn't told me to get up early to come to work, all of us could have been burned because all of us live in the same row. I went down that line of houses, waking everybody up: "Fire! Fire! Get up! Get up!" That was God; you know that was God. I am telling you the truth. God is good, and God is real. I want to give all honor to God. I say, "Thank You, Jesus." People don't have to be worrying about how they are going to be healed. God is going to heal you. God is good. He is good. I am as happy as I want to be in Jesus.

Odessa was interviewed by Vivian Moore in August of 2002.
She is an African American Baptist in her 80's.

We Expect God to Do Things
—Oliver Mathews

I am studying for the priesthood in the Charismatic Episcopal Church. I felt like I did not have enough experience working with sick people. When I grew up, I didn't like hospitals at all. I had never visited a sick person in the hospital; I felt like that was something I had to confront. I decided to join the Clinical Pastoral Education program, to see if I could figure out where I was as far as dealing with people who are sick, who are dying, who died, and how to deal with the family trauma involved.

I started about a year ago November, and dealing with sick people was a lot more stressful than I thought. I remember my first death call: it was late at night; it must have been one o'clock in the morning. There were thirteen people in the room, and they were all screaming at the same time. Other people would come in, and they would start screaming, and the people who were there were trying to calm them down. I felt like I was on the periphery, just watching because I didn't know what to do. I thought, "How do you deal with that kind of situation?"

For an Evangelical, as a chaplain, you are thrust into a pluralistic environment; it is almost like fighting with one hand behind your back because you are operating in two realms of truth. The one truth is, the patient is suffering, and you have to try to comfort that patient. The other realm is as a person who believes that the Bible is true and that Christ rose from the dead. The kinds of comfort that I offer I do not feel are sufficient for a lot of the people who are suffering, especially the people who are dying. I deal with the mentally ill, and that makes it doubly difficult because they don't necessarily understand what you are saying. In my tradition, mental illness is often looked at either as demonic possession or demonic activity. That puts me in a bind as a Charismatic. If I think this person is suffering from demonic activity that is not categorizable. I can't write that on a chart. You have to write whatever it is you think people want to hear, almost like you are operating in two worlds.

Chaplaincy seems overly humanistic for a discipline that is supposed to be religious. It is almost like religion is an afterthought or a tool that you use, a "feel good" tool. I have a person who wants you to pray, so let's pray. I don't know if there is a whole lot of belief that goes on with the prayer, and this has troubled me in my own life. As a Charismatic Episcopalian, when we pray, we expect God to do things. Experiences like healings, like praying for God to miraculously intervene, are things that we expect. When someone is sick, sometimes they don't get better, so that is a conflict.

The problem in a chaplain setting is that it is very neutered. While most officials who run chaplaincy programs say, "We do not discriminate against anyone," it is expected that certain behavior is not permitted. For example, if I were in a patient's room, I would be told not to proselytize. On the other hand, my tradition is very evangelical. Often the first, last, and only reason you are talking to a person is to find out where they are spiritually. That doesn't mean if you find out they are not Christian, then you don't become their friend, but there is no true comfort if there is no spiritual healing. Spiritual healing is not necessarily as important in the chaplaincy program as emotional healing, which, to me, is not the province of a pastor, but more of a social worker or a counselor.

As a chaplain, you are supposed to provide comfort to this person through your religious tradition. The only problem is if your religious tradition feels the only real comfort a person gets is in spiritual healing and connectedness with God, then you are not providing them a service. You are just being a religious counselor; what you are trying to do, in my opinion, is to paint a picture of God that is as accepting as possible and that anybody can plug in to. That can be problematic if you are in a confessional tradition. Part of our tradition is confessing your sins to a priest; if that person has not taken that first step, then where are we going at that point except spiritual assessment? Or trying to make a connection to get to that deep-rooted sin that needs to be confessed? I have found myself modifying my approach to patients, trying to associate both parts of me—and being quite unsuccessful at it.

If your theology is liberal, your conflicts are different because then your conflicts take the form of, "God can't be this way; therefore, I am going to change how I view God." As an Evangelical, you don't have that luxury. If you are in a historic tradition like mine, things don't change that much. That brings up a lot of conflict; even as an intern, you are supposed to talk your way through these things. The problem is you can't talk to a person who has a liberal faith about being conservative. It is like asking a voodoo priest about Christianity. They will have a knowledge of it, they will kind of understand it, but in the end—and I found this over and over again—they just won't understand what the hang-up is. When I tell them, for example, that I believe in a literal hell, then that is very problematic when you are dealing with people who are dying. I had an interesting discussion with another chaplain and asked him, "If someone is dying, do you make an effort to evangelize them?" He said, "Oh, no, I'm just there for them," and I said, "What service exactly are you providing them if you believe? Aren't we called to sound an alarm to people?"

I have considered resigning more than once. All my supervisors talk about how good this is toward pastoral training, but I disagree. You are almost choosing to opt out of the game. You can't be yourself, and you have to hide part of yourself somewhere until you get a chance to do it. It is true that I have become more comfortable ministering to sick people, but I think that is just from experience. My conflict, as an Evangelical, is that I am not evangelical enough. I am this pseudo-person who goes to visit people. It is almost like hiding who you really are.

I was with a patient, just a few months ago, whose heartbeat was slowing. You could tell the pulse was going down and down and down. All the doctors were working on them; you could tell they were about to give up because they had worked on this patient for a while. I came on the scene, stretched out my hand, and prayed for the person. The doctor stopped working, so I could pray. The person's heartbeat started going up, and the patient finally stabilized. In that instance, I felt like I was doing what I was supposed to do.

Oliver was interviewed by Sue Heiney in December of 2002. He is an African American in his 30's who belongs to the Charismatic Episcopal Church

My Place is to Be a Vessel
–James Watts

One of my strengths is the ability to believe that God is able to do anything, no matter what. Part of that faith comes from seeing people healed. When I was in junior high, our church had what we call a "Dial-A-Miracle Prayer Line." Somebody from the church manned the phones and stayed there from one o'clock to three o'clock every day. We would just have prayer if nobody called, and if somebody called, we prayed for them. One day, in school, I broke out with a rash under my chin. When I went to the nurse, she told me that I needed to go home; I needed to see a doctor. I went home, and I remembered we had the Prayer Line. It was after lunch, so I went straight to the phone, and I called Dial-A-Miracle. Our Sunday School superintendent was manning the phones. She prayed for me and said, "You are going to be healed in Jesus' Name." I never went to the doctor, and the rash underneath my chin started healing up right then. So I knew that God could do anything. I can speak from experience.

Two years ago, a young lady from our church came to me. The doctors had discovered hepatitis in her bloodstream. She said, "Pastor, I don't know what to do. I have never had to deal with this type of thing before." I told her, "We're going to touch and agree, and we're going to believe God will bring forth your healing. I don't want you to fear because God is able to do anything. There is nothing too hard that God can't handle it." I build them up in the Word of God. I give them the Scriptures: "He was wounded by our transgressions, bruised for our iniquities; chastisement of our peace was upon Him; with His stripes, we are healed . . ."

After a while, you begin to receive what you begin to believe. You take the Word, and you say it; once you hear it, it begins to internalize. The Scripture lets us know that we are snared by the words of our mouth, so we try to teach how to have a positive confession about our lives. I prayed for her that day, prayed what we call the prayer of faith: "Lord, she is in Your hands. You made our bodies; You know all about her. And so we ask that You would heal her." We prayed for her, and she continued to pray. When she had a doctor's appointment, if it was on Wednesday, she would stop by for noon-day prayer. We continued to pray for her, and she continued to confess the Scriptures. One day, about a year later, she came back and said, "Pastor, I got a report from the doctor. It's gone." She was healed by the power of God, and it was an exciting time! She gave testimony in church how the Lord had healed her. It is always good to see people come to that place of healing.

There are times when we have healing services; we pray for people who have sicknesses and believe God for their healing. The Bible says in James, the fifth chapter, "If there are any sick among you, let them call for the elders." In this particular Scripture, the first part says, "Let them pray . . ." We tell them that the first line of command is to pray. We tell the saints, "Pray for your healing. Pray that God would heal you." A lot of times we use oil. We know that the healing is not in the oil, but the oil symbolizes healing. We pray with anointed oil, as the Lord instructs us, and we expect God to do what the Scripture says. When we are praying for people, we are led by the Lord how to pray, what to pray, and what means to use. We encourage them that no matter what they are going through, keep on taking God at His word, and their healing will be manifested.

The gift of healing is like any other skill. The more you use it, the sharper it becomes. It is the gift of God that uses me to pray for people and to build people's faith up for their healing. My position and my place is to be a vessel. God has to do the work. I believe that my job is always to build, to pray in faith, and to believe God. It is up to God to bring the healing. We tell our members how to be led by the Lord and how to deal with their sickness. We believe that doctors and healing work together. It is teaching and building in faith, and it brings stability; it is not up to us to do the healing, but there is a part that we play.

We build their faith up and look for God to give the increase. We look for God to bring the results. I don't believe that healing is in our power to give or to take; it is in God's power. There is absolutely nothing too hard for Him. To me it is exciting and rewarding to see people's lives change: to see people go from one level to another and receive what God has for them, to see people move in the area that they were born to move in.

A lot of times when people hear about a sickness, one of the first responses is fear. Fear is one of the things that causes a sickness to run its course, so we preach faith instead of fear. We try to show people, "Don't be scared of it, no matter what." We try to dispel the spirit of fear that hovers over people. A lot of times their sickness begins to progress because they are so afraid. I have had members come in who had reports that were false, but they moved in a spirit of fear. They started feeling symptoms and the whole nine yards, and then come to find out that what they thought was there wasn't there anyway! God has not given us the spirit of fear, but of power and of love and of a sound mind. We try to get our members to walk in that type of faith.

We cannot look at the problem or the situation and take it at face value. Fear is an instrument that the enemy uses to accomplish his task. The most important element for someone to be healed is faith. It is believing that no matter what, God can fix it: all I have to do is apply faith. Being led by the Lord is part of what we do. God knows everything; there is nothing hidden from Him. He already knows: He knows if that person is getting up out of that sick bed; He knows if that person is getting up out of that wheelchair. He knows if that person is going to be healed from cancer, diabetes, or whatever ailment they have. All I can do is pray for His will to be done.

James was interviewed by Vivian Moore in August of 2002.
He is a non-denominational African American in his 40's.

Pierced by the Spirit of God
—Sarah Williams

Twenty-three years ago, my husband and I went to a large Lutheran Conference of Renewal regarding the Holy Spirit. During Holy Communion, at that service, I had a vision from the Lord. It was so real, more real than what I was observing outside. In this vision, I saw a ditch, and it was dirty. There were all of these bodies that had just been burned in the ditch. They were little, and they had been discarded. I saw the heavens open, and the Lord's hands came down and lifted a body up out of the ditch and put it on the road. He gently wiped off all the grime, wiped off the tears, and got that little person started on the road. That was repeated; it was so beautiful. Then the Lord's hands reached toward me, and I knew in that moment that God was saying that that is what I needed to be doing. That was what He wanted me specifically to do: to pick up those little broken people, just as He was showing me. That really touched my spirit. In the Bible, the Lord would speak specifically to His servants, and He would say, "Do this; you are called to that. Do this; do that." I knew it was God's hand on me saying, "This is what I want you to do."

When we came back from the conference, my husband said, "You need to do your work in pastoral care and counseling." I believe that when God wants you to go in a certain place, He opens the door. So I got into the university's program on pastoral care and counseling. For eight years, I worked with an agency, which was very good training. Now, for fourteen years, I have been in private practice, working full-time, and I love it. What

I have attempted to do is to bring together good training with the Holy Spirit and the power of prayer. If we are looking at complete healing in people, we need to have that combination, especially if we are working with deep hurts or difficult, very complex situations. I value training; but only using training, without the gifting and the leading of the Holy Spirit, brings some limits.

Sometimes people have more gifting for physical healing, and that's a blessing. Some people have more of a gifting for inner healing. God has worked both of those to be in my life, and there is certainly a unity in that, but two-thirds of my time I am working with inner healing: emotional healing, healing of past hurts, very delicate inner healing. I work a lot with women who have been abused, both as children and as adults. I work with couples who have destructive patterns. I know that God can heal every situation. I know that God can, will, and has the heart to heal every marriage. I know He has the heart to heal everything. I know that God has the power to heal everyone who comes in the door when my husband and I are doing a healing service. There is in me an optimism and a joy when I hear people's problems. I hear the hurt; I need to hear it, but I know, beyond that, that God can heal it.

One of the things I train myself to do is that if I am listening to someone and I am hearing what they are saying, I am also hearing what God is speaking into my spirit. He is giving me clues and keys that I try to mesh and integrate with what I have learned and what I am hearing.

It gives me discernment into things. Most of the training of the Word of the Lord will show the real problems and the real issues before they are spoken. So there is discerning of the Spirit and discernment of specific words of knowledge. One of the things that is a necessity for me is that every morning I clear my mind. I have quiet time before the Lord, so that I am empty of all of my stuff. Then when I come to meet people in the course of the day, God can really flow, and my mind is clear.

When I was twenty-four years old, I was in a terrible automobile accident in which I broke my neck. At first, I did not have feeling in my leg. My vertebrae were out of place, and I was told I might have very limited walking. On the sixth night that I was in traction, I was praying. The neurosurgeon was going to make a decision the next day if they were going to do surgery. That night as I was praying, an angelic presence came by my bed, and said, "I heard your prayers; I see your tears. If you give Me the rest of your walk, you will walk out of here tomorrow," and I said, "Lord, I give You my whole life. My walk is Yours." In the morning when the neurosurgeons and everybody came, they were amazed because I had regained feeling in my leg. They did not have to do surgery. They put me in a half-body cast. It took a long time, but I walked out of the hospital. Because of that experience, I was made aware of the connection between our physical body and our emotional life.

I have been healed miraculously by the Lord in many ways. I was at a healing service with Mr. John Wineburg eleven years ago. In that service he said, "Tonight I am healing spines. Everyone in here, raise your hand if you have spinal or back problems." My hand went up because my neck was very restricted, and I had problems with mobility. A man I did not know put his hand on my neck. My husband was there, and some very good friends put their hands on me also; I felt like molten lava was flowing through my body. I felt bones and everything moving; I could hear it and feel it. In my neck, I could feel it. The man who did not know me at all said, "Her bones and everything are moving in her neck. Praise the Lord!" Within five minutes I could move my neck, almost like when I was twenty-four, before that accident. I went running around, saying, "Look at me move my neck!" I am a miracle; I, myself, am a miracle. If God can heal me on every level, touch my spirit, open doors, and direct me, He can do it for anyone. And He wants to. The Lord speaks and touches your spirit, and you are pierced by the Spirit of God.

I do not know God's will. In every situation, I have to see what God wants to do. Sometimes God may feel that there needs to be spiritual or emotional healing before physical healing. It is different with everyone. The key is not to limit God, but to come before God humbly. Healing is a process, and we do not know what piece of us God wants to heal at a given time. It is important to work at a speed each person is willing to go, to let the healing process take the amount of time that is needed, and to do the work of listening, of reaching out. Unless it is out of the dark, the light of the Lord, cannot shine on it, and it is not really dealt with. After it is, they will be able to move into greater balance and a fruitful life.

My husband and I do healing services, healing ministries. We have been blessed to be able to see the movement of the Holy Spirit; we have seen incredible, miraculous works of God.

It is so different for everyone. There is no formula for healing. It is important that each person be heard and listened to in those deep places, and that what they need for them is what comes forth. I caution people against a quick or simple formula, for every person is different. God's Word is the key. It has to be put together with what we hear, what we pray, and what we are receiving, but it is the foundation and the undergirding of what we do.

Many people have been afflicted in the realm of the demonic, and if there are open doors from inner hurt or wounding, it makes them an easy prey. Even if only 10% of the people are struggling with demons, they need to get help in that area. I do think those who are working to help people with demons need to have training. They need to be protected, and they need to know what they are doing.

God's heart is for everyone to live the abundant life. His heart is for all of His children to be in a place of safety, security, and well-being. It is a tremendous responsibility and a very humbling experience for someone to trust you with the healing process. That's how I feel. It is a sacred thing, a very awesome thing. Someone says, "I trust you to journey back to my painful places, to the hurt places, to the darker places." You develop this tremendous trust and responsibility. I pray every day, "Oh, God, please make me a responsible person," so that I may be trustworthy. It is a great responsibility for someone to entrust us with turning back into pain and to say, "Share this with me; now walk with me." Every day, my prayer is, "Oh, God, please let me be responsible for these lives and these couples who are coming."

Sarah was interviewed by Georgianna Jackson in June of 2002.
She is a white woman in her 60's who is a Charismatic Lutheran.

We Have Power in Jesus' Name
–Kevin Jansen

I was born and raised in the Baptist Church and became a Christian when I was a young lad of eleven. I have felt the call to be in full-time ministry all my life. That is what the Lord wanted me to do. In 1987 or 1988, I attended an evangelism conference in Washington, D.C. I was downtown studying overnight. I got up the next morning and went to the breakfast table. In those days, I had had serious migraine headaches from time to time. I sat down at the table with men I didn't really know because I was the only one there from my church. We were talking, and a man there says, "I was really praying this morning, and the Lord told me I was going to meet somebody by the name of Kevin, Kevin Johnson . . . Kevin J—?" I said, "Kevin Jansen?" He said, "Well, yeah. That sounds right. The Lord tells me you are having a lot of headaches, and that God is going to heal you of those headaches." It amazed me. I can honestly say, for eight, nine months, or a year, I did not have a headache. I did not know this man at all. I believe that was an experience with God, where God was really real and working. That's a powerful thing, to know that God knows your struggles, and God knows your pain. God knows where you are. That floored me. "Kevin J—" . . . and I am sitting beside him! Chill bumps run down your legs. It is awesome that God can do that, and I believe we need to be filled with the Spirit of God.

My wife had cancer in 1982 and was in the hospital with choriocarcinoma, a pregnancy-related cancer that began after our second daughter was born, due to the afterbirth that was left. We did not know what it was until September of that year, and by then the cancer had metastasized to her lungs. She had a brain tumor before we found out what it was. She spent five months at the hospital, and it was a poor prognosis. In my Baptist upbringing, it was, "If the Lord wills." That is true, but when my wife was dying of cancer, I didn't say to the Lord, "If You will." You know why? Because I didn't want it. I didn't want there to be a funeral; I wanted her to live. It is okay for me to say, "God, I want my wife to live. I do not know what Your will is, but I want my wife to live." Certainly, I am not trying to twist God's arm, yet in prayer, I am trying to get some results. "God, I need Your attention here. I need some help." Prayer and intercession are about being active, being proactive. Let's believe God; let's ask God. Peradventure, God will move. The more you believe, the more you will pray. After five months, my wife was free from cancer and has been ever since.

We know that God's hand was really upon her life, and we got His grace and healing. We did chemotherapy and radiation and those things the doctors wanted to do, but we know that ultimately God gave us the victory. Subsequent to that, she developed blindness and is legally blind. We know God heals, but she doesn't have her sight. So you get caught in that tension between the fact that God heals you—you have seen God heal, you have seen miracles—but yet you live in expectation of something that is unfulfilled.

Three Sundays ago, a man came up for prayer after service. He said he had hurt his back; it had been bothering him all week, and he asked me to pray for him. I followed the Scripture in James, Chapter 5, to anoint him, and I asked God to touch him and heal him. I didn't feel anything happen; I just said a prayer of believing that God would do it, asking God to do it. He came back the next Sunday and said, "Pastor, I want to tell you that that next morning my back was better, and it has been better all week." A lot of people feel a hot sensation on their back during healing. He said, "I didn't feel a hot sensation; I felt a cool sensation. But the next morning my back was much better, and it has been better all week." He had been having trouble with it for a week or two. He did not say anything about it to me on that day that I prayed, but the next week he came back and gave that report. Did I feel anything? I didn't feel anything. Did I do anything? I would say, "Not really; God was the one who did the healing. I just obeyed His Word, and God did that." Was I surprised? Somewhat because you are always surprised when God does miracles, even though you know God can do it.

I don't think God is the author of sickness. I do not think God makes us sick. Our sicknesses and illnesses are a result of living in a fallen world. We have floods and disease and tornadoes and sickness, and all that is part of this world. If I get sick, it is not because God made me sick; it is because I live in this world. When miracles do happen, it is God's divine intervention in a system that has fallen. There are times when God intervenes, and I believe the reason we pray and the reason we believe is we ask God to intervene, and sometimes He does. That is the reason I pray for the sick and encourage people to believe and have faith in God. Perchance God might grant a miracle. But if He doesn't, that doesn't mean He is not God. We pray, we beseech Him, we ask. If God heals, praise God. We've got a miracle! If He does not, He is still God. We have to trust Him. As far as why some are healed and why some are not, we don't know. Our finite minds are not able to understand the infinite wisdom of God.

There was a young woman who had come to church a couple of times. We began talking with her and realized there was a lot of stuff going on in her life. Her father was very much involved in a satanic cult, and she had been promised to Satan and all kind of things. At some point, you wonder, "Is this person fabricating this story or are these things true?" Nonetheless, we continued our relationship and built in her a trust, such that this person would come and talk with me. One time, I asked her if we might lift her up in prayer, and she agreed. We began to pray for her, and as we began to pray, I could sense more and more an evil power, an evil presence in her life. In talking with her, she said, "Mason didn't want me to come here." Someone asked her, "Tell me who Mason is?" And she said, "I won't tell you." I picked up that Mason was not somebody sitting in the car, but Mason was this presence in her life that had come to be true. That's what she called him, this power in her life. A couple of the pastors came, and one rebuked the devil and the presence of evil power. I could see in her eyes, at times when I was praying for her, that there was this real cold, steely eye. You could sense an evil presence there. I would read from the Bible, "Ye shall live," and she would draw back. I took the Bible and went to place it on her head, and she put her hands up and knocked that Bible away and would not let me touch her with it. We prayed for her for quite a while. It was literally an hour that we really engaged. At the end, I believe there was a real degree of release in her life because we followed up with her. I believe those powers are real. As believers, we do have power over them in Jesus' name.

We need to encourage people that God does heal. Let's ask Him. Let's believe. I am not a faith healer, but I am the pastor of some of those people that God can heal, so I need to pray for people that I am encouraging to believe God. Peradventure, God will intervene and save their lives. My heart is for the pastors on the front lines dealing with people when things don't happen, when miracles don't come true. Yet we pray, and we believe all the time. We ask God to heal people because we know He can, and we want him to, and God is okay with that. We always say at the end of the service as people are leaving, "If you need a special healing prayer, you can come forward. Someone will be here to pray for you." Or, "If you need an encouraging touch in your life today, then come forward to the worship of this song today, and we'll pray for you." Many times, people will come because of something going on in their lives, or because they need a physical healing, and we will anoint them with oil and pray for them. We don't do it all the time, but as we feel led.

I believe healing is part of the covenant, and the right way for us to pray for healing is in the benefits of Christ. When Jesus died on the cross, He made a covenant with us. These benefits that Christ left us are forgiveness of sin, peace of mind, and healing of my body. God was not intended to be studied. He was intended to be experienced. In America we have mindsets that say, "I have to understand it to believe it." I believe that is why there are not as many miracles in Western culture because, in general, we don't care about experiencing God. It's about understanding, information, knowledge, and pride. But God is real. He is alive. He is about experience, and God wants us to experience reality and who He is and not just study Him in our theology schools and on Sunday morning. People are beginning to want more in their experiences with God. They want to know God in a personal way, and they are realizing that that is available. God is real, and He really does make a difference. The power of God is real, and we need to embrace it.

Kevin was interviewed by Jane Teas in July of 2002.
He is a non-denominational white man in his 50's.

Jesus is in the Healing Business
–Karen and Carl Simmering

Karen and Carl share the stories of their daughter and son . . .

There is a certain degree of obligation to Christians, to believers, to open themselves up to the possibility of unusual, miraculous healings taking place in their lives and in the lives of others. It is possible that there are healings. Some healings are attributed to the individual's faith, and some are just miraculous, and everybody wonders exactly why they took place. We have had quite a few instances of healings in our own lives, our own family, and in praying for other people.

Our daughter was diagnosed with a heart murmur when she was nine months old. They showed us where she had a hole in her heart. The right ventricle was enlarged. We took her to a pediatrician who sent us to the hospital to do x-rays. They took the x-rays, and they did a cardiogram on her; everything was abnormal. We picked up the x-rays at the hospital and took them back to the doctor, and he showed us the shadow on her heart where she had a hole. He showed us the part that was enlarged and said they couldn't do anything until she was a year old.

During the interim, we prayed that God would heal the hole in her heart and heal the part that was enlarged. We took her to the hospital when she was a year old. They did a cardiogram and x-rays, and everything came out normal. She went back for several years, and they checked on her, and finally, they told us not to even mention it to insurance or the school. They referred to it as an innocent murmur. So she went from a hole in her heart, with the right ventricle enlarged, to an innocent murmur.

I had told the first doctor from the moment they told us, "She will be healed." They said, "No, you don't understand. This is not the kind of thing that she would grow out of." I said, "No, but she will be healed." I knew in my heart, I knew beyond the shadow of a doubt that she would be healed. I refused to accept anything like that. If somebody comes to my door with a package that I don't want, I am going to refuse to receive it. It wasn't that I was denying that this was happening, that she had this heart defect; what I was denying was that she was going to keep it. I would not receive that. I knew she would be healed, and as it turned out, she was healed of those things. That was thirty years ago. It was like faith was dropped in my spirit, and I just knew that she would be healed.

We believe, according to what we see in the Bible, that there is a gift of faith, and that was what was operating. In this particular instance, there was that gift of faith that I knew that I knew that she would be healed. A lot of times when you talk to people about having faith, what they are trying to have faith for is for something to happen—their faith is that they will be healed—when their faith should be in God. If your faith is in God, it gives you a trust and a confidence. You believe His Word, and you believe God is a good God. You expect good things from God. We don't expect bad things. When a bad thing comes, then we believe that this is not of God, and we are not going to receive it. It is a matter of putting your foot down and saying, this postman is bringing something to my door that I will not have. That is not God's will for my life, and I refuse to accept it. We have faced this not just in the area of the healing, but in other areas. When the impossible was standing in front of us, we refused to believe the impossible.

There have been quite a few instances where our lives were threatened, but God has protected us. Our son was in a boating accident one time; he was way out in the boondocks. Normally, there wouldn't be anybody around. It wasn't a normal boating place. He was accidentally thrown out of the boat. The propeller hit him; he tried to dive away from it, and it hit his foot. He and his friend were both teenagers and, of course, scared silly. It just about completely severed his heel, which was hanging by a thread. When they got him to the dock, there just happened to be two paramedics there. If they had not been there . . . They were a long way from the hospital, but the paramedics were able to start treating him immediately, to keep him from going into shock. They called an ambulance and had the ambulance meet them halfway and got him to the hospital. We have had all these coincidences, and if you are a Christian and you are expecting good things, then you don't see that as coincidence; you see that as God intervening and protecting. You see this sort of thing over and over again.

Carl continues . . .

I believe that faith is available; God wants us to see wonderful things accomplished through faith, not just in Him, but through faith in His Word, through faith in what He says you will be able to accomplish. A man came into my office several years ago. He would come by once a year. This may have been the third or fourth time I had seen him in my life. He was a salesman, and he would try to sell me a certain product. I told him as I had told him the previous years, "No, thank you; I appreciate it," and we talked for a few minutes. It was five o'clock, I was ready to go home, and I was letting him out the front door. He said he was going to Florida. As I let him go, I had an unusual impression—that's the only way I can say it—and the impression was to pray for him before he left. I stopped the man and said, "If you don't mind, I'd like to pray for you before you go." He looked kind of strange, but he said, "Okay, sure."

I said, "Come on back in here with me," and he stepped in the office, and as I went to pray, I had what I consider a most unusual impression. It had never happened before in my life. I was supposed to ask him to take out his billfold and hold it in his hand, and I was to put my hand on top of it and pray for him for financial reasons. I said, "This may sound strange to you, but do you mind taking out your billfold and holding it in your hand?" I would have been thinking, "I'm going to hang onto this billfold; this man is trying to get some money," but he had this strange look on his face. He quietly reached in his pocket, pulled out his billfold, and laid it in his hand. I said, "Now I'm going to put my hand on it, and I'm going to pray. This is what I believe we are supposed to do," so I put my hand on it and began to pray. Three things came to me specifically. One was that I was supposed to pray for a financial blessing for him, and I did. I was also supposed to pray that he was to go back and fire somebody who worked for him. I didn't want to word it that way, so I prayed that he would go back and do what was right by that employee for whom he had been avoiding doing what he knew he should do. Then I prayed that the next day, when he got up, he would be full of joy, encouraged, and excited about life. When I got through, he thanked me, and his eyes were real big. He said,

"I have an employee I am supposed to fire," and I didn't use those words at all. "He's been causing a problem for a long time; I knew I should have fired him, and I have been putting it off, so I know that is what I have to do now." This man and I had never had any conversation related to faith. I said, "Well, good to see you," and he thanked me for praying for him.

The next day, to my surprise, right before noon he showed up in the office. I am sure I had a strange look on my face. I wondered, "What in the world is he doing here?" He was grinning from ear to ear. He said, "I want to tell you what! When I got back to the motel last night, I called my boss because I wanted to tell him about you praying for me. When I called him, he said, 'I'm glad you called because I've been trying to get in touch with you. I wanted to let you know that you have just consummated the biggest sale in the history of our company. I want to take you and your wife out to lunch.'" So the boss took them out to lunch.

Karen shares her own story . . .

One time, I spoke at a women's conference. One of the ladies was in the last stages of Crohn's disease. She had already had surgery several times on her intestines, and she was in severe pain. They told her she needed to have surgery again, and she had told them that she couldn't go through that; she was preparing to die. She was in constant pain. She had small children. It was very frustrating because she couldn't keep up with the housework and take care of her kids. She was already requiring help to do basic things, and she felt the Lord spoke to her and said, "If you go to this conference, I will heal you." It was a two-day conference, and at the end of it, we had not prayed for her to be healed. Nobody had told me anything about it. At the very end of the conference, they told me about her situation and asked that we pray for this lady. I got some of the women to come stand around her and lay hands on her, and we prayed for her, and instantly, the pain left. She went home and began cleaning up her house. After she cleaned her house, she started painting it. She was up until one o'clock in the morning, painting her house, and the next morning at church, her husband stood up and gave the testimony because she was in the nursery keeping the children. He stood up immediately and said, "I want to say something," and began crying. He told the story, with tears running down his cheeks, of what had happened when his wife came home the night before, and he told about how she was up most of the night painting. Before the conference, she had had no energy. She was almost completely incapacitated and was getting worse and worse, but she has not had any symptoms since that time—and no pain.

Carl shares other incidents . . .

We have been to India. We spent a month in India praying for people and speaking and teaching. Imagine a really crude building, everything even less than sparse, with dusty and uneven floors. There were thirty people there, and I spoke and then offered to pray for people, and people came up for prayer. One man came up, and I asked the translator to tell me what he wanted prayer for, and he said he had pain in his back that had been there for years. He could not sit down because of the pain, so he wanted prayer for healing. I said, "Sure, I'd be glad to pray," so I reached out, as I do to everybody, and put my hands on him, a natural reflex. But when I touched him, his eyes started getting really big, and he started to bend backwards at the waist. He looked like he was scared to death. You might call it a word of knowledge, but it came into my mind, for whatever reason, that this man's problem was demonic. When I saw that, instead of praying for healing like the man asked me to, I began to say, "In the Name of Jesus, come out!" and the man bent further and further, and his eyes got bigger and bigger. I kept saying, "In the Name of Jesus, come out! In the Name of Jesus, release this man; let him go!" I kept saying that until the man started to straighten back up. His face relaxed, and he seemed to have a much more peaceful demeanor.

When he seemed to be normal, or relaxed and at peace, we asked him—through the translator—how he felt, and he said he felt better. We asked if he was in any pain; he said, "No, there is no pain." We asked him to bend down and touch his toes, and he immediately did so. We had him do that five times in a row. He said there was no pain; there was joy apparent on his face. There was another man with me, and he said, "Sit down on the floor," and the man sat down immediately; then he got up and said the pain was completely gone. As far as he was concerned, he believes he was completely healed. I didn't pray for him to be healed. I just prayed for a spiritual force that had been present and hindering him for many years to leave, and when that happened, his condition straightened out.

Another time, a woman came up and asked for prayer at work. I was working for an ear, nose, and throat specialist. I had to do some work with her as an audiologist, and she told me that she was going to the doctor. She had had these problems, and they thought something in particular was wrong with her. I asked her to let me pray for her before she left. She said, "Okay," so I prayed that the Lord would heal her. Then I forgot about it, and five years later—we had then opened another office—this woman came in, and as she was leaving, she said, "Do you remember me?" I looked at her, recognized her face, and said, "Well, yeah," meaning that I remember seeing you somewhere. She said, "I'm the one you prayed for five years ago." She said she had been diagnosed with Hodgkin's disease, and after I prayed for her, she went back to the doctor. She said, "I haven't had a symptom from that day to this." As far as they knew, it was completely gone.

An elderly man was in my office one day; I see patients to fit hearing aids on them, to clear wax out of their ears, and to test their hearing. When I got through, he said, "I have to go to the hospital." I said, "What for?" and he said, "I'm having trouble urinating." I said, "Do you mind if I pray for you?" He said, "No, pray for me." I often tell people, "Jesus is still alive and well, and He is in the healing business," so I said, "Jesus can heal you. Let me pray for you." He said, "Okay." I prayed a simple prayer, asking Jesus to heal him. He came back very quickly after that; I don't remember whether it was a week or more, but he came back and said that night, everything started working properly.

One woman had a tumor in her stomach. She was scheduled for surgery on a Monday morning, and we prayed for her at a Full Gospel Businessman's Fellowship Meeting that Saturday night. When she went to the hospital on Monday, they did the x-ray again before surgery, and the tumor had shrunk to the size of a pea. They told her that they didn't need to operate, and they sent her back home. When she told us about that, she told the story about going out on the sidewalk in front of the hospital, jumping up and down, and shouting. She was so thrilled!

Karen concludes . . .

Some of the inner healing experiences are almost more fantastic than the physical healings. The one that keeps coming to my mind happened over twenty years ago. We were at a Full Gospel Businessmen's Meeting, up front praying for people. A lot of people came up for healing. This one young girl came up whom we did not know. We had never met her before, but we began to pray for her. I don't remember what her prayer request was. When we started praying for her, my husband asked me to put my hand on her stomach. He said, "I believe we are supposed to pray for her, something to do with this area." I don't remember what he prayed, but she burst into tears. She had had an abortion years before, and it had been a burden to her and a guilt; she had carried the pain of that for years and had a lot of emotional problems as a result. We ended up doing some counseling with her after that, but whatever he told her in prayer indicated that the Lord knew about it, and she was forgiven. It made such a difference in her life. She had had all kind of emotional problems before, and yet that girl ended up going on the mission field. She got straightened out, she got strong and encouraged, and the last we heard from her, she was still on the mission field.

I like to tell people, when you get saved, when you first make that step, it is a step of faith. You really don't know, and you make that commitment. But after a period of time, it is no longer faith, it is a knowing. After so many coincidences, it is absurd to think it's a coincidence. What is going on? What am I doing? What causes these results? It is praying in the Name of Jesus to God Almighty, and we get results when that happens. After you get results over and over again, it doesn't require a whole lot of faith on your part. You know that He is there and that He hears and that you get results when you pray.

We base our lives on our relationship with the Lord. We took that step of faith, not knowing, and over a period of time, the confirmation has come back to us in so many different ways: things people have said, impressions we have gotten, encouragements we have gotten, and breakthroughs we have had. Over a period of time you get that confirmation, that encouragement, and your confidence and your faith grow. Your tendency is to step out in areas you had not stepped out in before because the Lord has been so good to you. The Lord has heard and answered prayers, and we tell people He still hears and answers. God is still on the throne. Jesus is alive and well, which means something very special to us. It goes back to the book of Deuteronomy. God says, if you obey My Word, all these blessings will come on you. When you get to the point that you acknowledge God knew what He was doing, He wrote the handbook, if you follow the handbook, you are going to be blessed.

Karen and Carl were interviewed by Andrew Cousins in October of 2001. They are a non-denominational white couple in their 50's.

Chapter 7

CASTING OUT DEMONS

As [Jesus] stepped out on land, a man of the city who had demons met him. For a long time he had worn no clothes, and he did not live in a house but in the tombs. When he saw Jesus, he fell down before him and shouted at the top of his voice, "What have you to do with me, Jesus, Son of the Most High God? I beg you, do not torment me"—for Jesus had commanded the unclean spirit to come out of the man. (For many times it had seized him; he was kept under guard and bound with chains and shackles, but he would break the bonds and be driven by the demon into the wilds.) Jesus then asked him, "What is your name?" He said, "Legion"; for many demons had entered him. They begged him not to order them to go back into the abyss.

Now there on the hillside a large herd of swine was feeding; and the demons begged Jesus to let them enter these. So he gave them permission. Then the demons came out of the man and entered the swine, and the herd rushed down the steep bank into the lake and was drowned. When the swineherds saw what had happened, they ran off and told it in the city and in the country. Then people came out to see what had happened, and when they came to Jesus, they found the man from whom the demons had gone sitting at the feet of Jesus, clothed and in his right mind, and they were afraid.

Luke 8:27-35

Healing is a Gift that Drops Upon You
–Drew Hall

As a child, I was given up to die. I was very small, and I had lost a lot of weight. According to the doctors, I was dying, but they did not know what was wrong. My grandmother belonged to a church in Brooklyn, New York, a small storefront church. I was only a few months old, and my grandmother told me later that her pastor called her and said, "Bring me the child." They were going for noonday prayer, and he met her with his wife. She had wrapped me in a bath towel and carried me there. He took me out of my grandmother's arms, walked up to the front where they had the table they used for offering, laid me on the table, pulled up a chair, sat down, and began to pray. Part of his prayer was, "Lord, give me this child. If You give him to me, I will give him back to You, like Hannah gave Samuel." And I lived.

Years later, I ran into a minister by the name of Rev. Stuart in Brooklyn. When I first walked in his office with two friends of mine, he looked at all three of us, and he looked at me, and he said, "Son, God is going to use you to cast out devils." I said, "I always thought I was going to be a preacher," and he said, "Oh, yes, you're going to do that, too, but God is going to use you to cast out devils." I am still amazed and fascinated by what I have seen the Lord do. One day, Pastor Stuart preached a message, "Except they see signs and wonders, they will not believe," and he said, "I'm going to lay hands on you." He laid hands on us, that God would grant signs, wonders, and miracles. When that man laid his hands on me, I walked a couple of yards away from him, and something felt like it dropped, hit me on the top of the head, and went down through me. I said to myself right then, "I got it." I knew that signs and wonders would fall on me in a greater measure.

Shortly after that, I was at a church in Harlem. I will never forget it. I knelt down in prayer before I got up to minister, and I prayed that God would use me. I was sitting in the pulpit, watching people come in. When they walked in, as soon as I saw them, I would hear about them; I would know about them. For instance, a woman walked in on a cane, and the Holy Spirit said in me, "She suffers with her hip, and she is going to be healed." I was a little afraid, so I said, "Is someone here who suffers with . . ." and every person I spoke of came up, and that woman came. When I started calling things out, the people started screaming, saying, "God knows, God knows!" It was something they were seeing as a great sign. Here's a perfect stranger; I had never been there before, and I didn't know anything about them. Yet I was telling them things about themselves that no one could know, except the Holy Spirit revealed it. This woman came up on her cane. I laid hands on her, and she got healed. All the pain left her, and she walked up and down. She gave me the cane, and I took it home as my first souvenir.

Some years later, a woman came up to me after a service and said, "Pastor Hall, I have a friend who has suffered four strokes and five heart attacks. She is in a wheelchair and has not walked in five years." Without thinking, I said, "Get her here. We will get us some faith and get her healed," and she said, "All right." The woman was sitting there in the wheelchair, looking over her friend's shoulder. I said, "Roll her up here," and they pushed the wheelchair up. I took the woman's hands in my hands and closed my eyes to pray. The Holy Ghost spoke in me and said, "Don't hold her hands. Lay your hands on her legs and pray," so I put one hand on each leg. I closed my eyes, and I went to pray. When I laid my hands on her, suddenly I was in the spirit. I was no longer conscious of where I was or what was happening. I saw an evil spirit fly down, hit this woman, bounce off of her, hit her, bounce off of her, hit her . . . I knew by a word of knowledge that this was a spirit of infirmity, and I knew that the pouncing on her represented the repeated attacks that she had had, four strokes and five heart attacks. Still talking to the Lord, I commanded the spirit to leave her in the Name of Jesus. When I finished praying for her, she looked no different, not a bit.

Suddenly that voice spoke up in me, which was the Holy Ghost, and said, "Say again to the spirit, 'Come out of her in the Name of Jesus.'" The first time I didn't address the spirit; I was talking to the Lord about it. I closed my eyes again and put my hands back on her legs, and this time I said, "You foul, unclean spirit, you foul spirit of infirmity, I command you in the Name of Jesus, come out of her!" When I said that, something jumped out of her legs and hit both my hands at the same time, and it felt like it went through my fingers, hitting the palms of both hands simultaneously. At the same time, she started screaming and pushing herself back up the aisle with her own legs. She didn't know what was happening to her. I said, "That's it. Get up. Get up!" And that woman, without anybody helping her, jumped up out of the wheelchair and walked. Her son had come with her. He started doing flips. He was yelling and praising God, and I said, "When was the last time you saw your mother walking?" He was jumping: "Over five years ago, over five years." She was healed, and at the end of the service, when it was time for them to go, that woman pushed her own wheelchair out the door.

Years ago, a woman in her late thirties came to a service; she was bent over and could not straighten up. She had some condition in her back and walked with a cane. In the service, when I approached her, the Lord said to me, "Do not lay hands on her. Tell her to start praising Me that she is healed." Here the woman is bent over, still in pain, not moving. I said, "The Lord told me not to lay my hands on you, just to tell you to praise Him. You are healed. Raise your hands this way, and say hallelujah." She was still bent over. "Say hallelujah; say thank You, Jesus." I had her saying that and praising the Lord. I said, "Amen."

When she finished and put her cane back down, she was still bent over. I said to the congregation, "She doesn't look healed, does she?" Everybody said, "No." I said, "What did the Lord say? She is healed. I say she is healed." Her back and her spine began to burn like they were on fire. The power went into her while she was praising God, but she didn't know it. She didn't know what was going on, so she went home, ran a tub of water, and got in to soak, thinking that it would cause the pain to subside because it was uncomfortable. After it subsided a little bit, she got in bed, laid her cane aside, and fell asleep. She woke up the next morning lying straight, and she sat up, sitting up perfectly straight. She never used her cane again. She was completely healed. She got healed when the Lord said it, but it manifested the next day.

People receive healing, and they come up on the platform and start testifying. So many people receive healing in those services because the atmosphere is charged with faith. That is called a corporate faith;

a corporate faith is greater than individual faith because it is a group believing. Where God sees faith like that, His power is present. Where faith comes alive in people, God manifests Himself. Once when I was preaching, I said, "Anybody who needs healing, come forth." I was praying for people. The strong anointing came on. I didn't even have time to talk or ask anybody anything. I simply had everybody line up, and I went from one end to the other, laying hands on them rapidly. I didn't even pray; I just touched them. Sometimes the moment I touch people, I feel a charge, almost like electricity.

A few moments later, I heard someone screaming, "I'm healed. I'm healed! I'm healed of cancer!" I saw this woman standing with her hands raised, praising God, and people saying, "Praise the Lord." She became a member of that church, and I was able to keep up with her. She had been taking radiation and chemotherapy. She went back to the doctors, and they could not find a trace of cancer anywhere in her body. That's instant remission. Furthermore, it never came back. They tested her every so often. She would go for tests, and they could not find a trace. When I last saw her, it had been ten or twelve years that she had been healed.

When one of my daughters was two years old, she had a high fever and went into convulsions in my arms. I commanded the devil to take his hands off her in the name of Jesus, the name above every name. When I did, her whole body went limp. I thought she had died, and I called her, "Leanna!" and she said, "Huh?" In an instant, the fever was gone. I am not talking about, "She's starting to cool down." In that instant, it was completely gone, completely healed. I never had anything like it before, never had anything like it since. She was completely healed by the supernatural power of God.

Another time, I had a service where I didn't ask anybody any questions; I just laid hands on them. A year later, I went back to the church. A woman walked up to me and said, "Pastor, you don't recognize me, do you?" I said, "Well, no." She said, "Maybe because the last time you saw me, I was wearing a wig." I said, "What's the story?" She said, "I had cancer. I was taking radiation treatments and chemotherapy. When you came last October, I got healed that night; however, the doctors did not release me until April. There is no cancer left in my body." Sometimes the power comes into you by the Holy Spirit, and it begins to drive the disease out of your body gradually. In her case, it took six months, but eventually, it was driven out.

Another time, there was a woman who came to a service in a wheelchair. She told me that she had something wrong with her, including cancer, and she said to me, "I can stand, but I cannot walk." I said, "Stand up." I laid my hands on her. The power of God came on her, and she fell on the floor. I went on ministering to other people, and while I was ministering to those people, the Holy Spirit said, "She is ready." I turned and said, "That woman is ready. Stand up," and she stood up. I said, "Come to me," and she followed me all around the church. Her daughter had brought her to church that night, and when they went home, the ill woman's husband would usually wait on her: run out, get the wheelchair out of the truck, get her in it, and bring her into the house. Her daughter went into the house first. Her father was reading the newspaper. He put it down, started to jump up, and she said, "Daddy, you don't need to get the wheelchair. Mama got healed tonight." The woman walked in behind her a few moments later.

About six weeks later, I went to that same church, and I saw this same woman come in on a walker. I said to her, "What are you doing on this walker?" She said, "Pastor, I know the Lord healed me, but the devil won't leave me alone." If you wait on the devil to have mercy, you are in trouble. That showed me a couple of things. That woman did not get healed by her faith because the same faith that it takes to get you healed, it takes to keep you healed. The woman could not have believed for herself when I first ministered to her because she would have been able to maintain her healing. She had doubts, so the enemy was able to rob her of it, even though she got healed, walked all around, and went home. Within a matter of weeks, the enemy had robbed her. It is like a fire. You start a fire, and there is no question that the fire is in the fireplace and that you have logs burning, but if you don't keep putting logs on there, what happens? It goes out. You have to do what is necessary to maintain it.

There are all kind of reasons why people fail to receive, and all kinds of reasons why people fail to keep their healing. In that same meeting, there was a woman who had a large tumor in her belly. The Lord told me, "Don't even pray for her. Just point to her, and say, 'Jesus Christ makes you whole.'" I did that, and the thing disappeared; it vanished from her instantly. It had been the size of a grapefruit, and it was gone. Some weeks later, that woman called my office, and I spoke to her on the phone. She said, "Pastor, I am the woman who had the tumor that healed that night, when you spoke, and it disappeared instantly." I said, "Yes." She said, "It came back, but I know where I missed it. I know what I did wrong. Pray for me again, and this time I will keep the healing." I prayed for her again on the phone, and it disappeared again.

If the minister who is laying hands or praying for you is in doubt himself, it can hinder you from receiving, even though you believe. I have to be conscious of this. I try not to look at the condition; I stay with what the Word says. I am not the healer. I am a believer and one anointed, but I am not a faith healer because I am not doing any healing. God does the healing; I am a vessel. It is a gift of faith. It is something supernatural that comes upon you, and when that works on you, there is no doubt involved. You cannot doubt. Real faith does not worry. I don't care how much you say you are in faith or what you say you believe, you cannot worry and believe at the same time. Healing is a gift that drops upon you, and it goes into operation as the Spirit of God wills. The Bible says, "They shall recover." It does not say, "They shall be instantly healed," but, "They shall lay hands on the sick, and they shall recover." The recovery may take longer. If one believes, they receive. Believe that you receive. Don't doubt in your heart, but believe. You cannot go by how you feel, but by what you believe.

Drew was interviewed by Vivian Moore in May of 2002.
His a non-denominational African American man in his 40's.

Talk to My People about Me
—Sylvia Wylie

I have had several healing experiences, but the most exciting one for me occurred two years ago. My kidneys had shut down for a year and a half, and I did not know it. I found myself having chills, such severe chills that I would hallucinate or blackout. My husband and I would pray, and I would be all right. For a year and a half, I was experiencing this. I eventually ended up in the hospital, and the doctor told me that my body was poisoned, that my kidneys were functioning at 18%. They said that I would have to be prepared for dialysis and that kidneys never get better. I ended up having surgery eight times. The last time I went to the hospital, I could not dress myself, I could not feed myself; I didn't have control over any body functions. It was a Saturday night, and they were having a Pastor's Appreciation for us; I knew that my members would be upset if I didn't show up. I took a lot of drugs, got myself together as best I could, and went to that function. By the end of that function, I was feeling so bad I could not even stand up very well, and my husband helped me to the podium. I was going to say thank you for what people had done, but instead I found myself saying, "I cannot die because I have to work six more months with you and a year with you and . . ." I kept pointing to different persons I was seeing and saying how long I had with them.

They carried me out and took me home, and the next day, my husband went on to church. As I lay there in my bed not able to get up, not able to do anything, I died. I found myself in the arms of the Lord—in His arms, in so much love that I could not ever think of such a wonderful gift. It's indescribable. It was total love. You feel like you are in a blanket of love. There are no strings attached, no conditions, nothing, pure love, total acceptance. I don't know how long I remained there, but at some point in time, I got the impression that He wanted me to go back, and I said to Him, "I am not going. I want to stay here." And He didn't say anything, but I felt like I was supposed to go back. Then He did a dirty trick; He played the tape of me standing there telling my people, "I have six months to work with you, and this much time to work with you . . ." As I watched the faces of the people and saw myself knowing that I had a job to do, I said, "I will go back, but You have to send me because I am not going to help You get me back." Then I heard a sound, and I looked from where I was, and it was like a veil. I was above that veil, and I saw my body there on my bed. I saw the elders from my church surrounding my body; they were really praying. They were going at it, and I thought to myself, "They think I'm there, and I'm not even there." They were trying so hard, crying and praying, that I started feeling sorry for them, so I told the Lord, "I'll go back." I went back and entered my body, and I told them in a very weak voice, "If you want me to live, you need to pray that I want to live" because I knew that having been where I was, I didn't want to live. It wasn't going to work if they didn't have my help.

They began to pray that I would want to live, and as they prayed that, I began to say, "I need to live. I know why I need to live." I told them, "You better give me a word of prophecy because I remember that the Bible says that you can wage a good warfare if you have prophecy." They began to prophesy, and one girl began to say, "Dislodge, dislodge," and as she said that word, "Dislodge," I saw inside my body, and I saw this black, ugly, furry thing, all intertwined in my organs. Suddenly, I knew that it was the spirit of infirmity, and we began to pray against it, and it slithered out of my body and ran. I thought having seen that, I would be healed, but I was not. I was still just as sick as I was before, and they ended up taking me to the Emergency Room for emergency surgery. My doctor said that when they opened me up, they had never seen that much disease and poison in anybody's body. They did the best they could, and then they took me to a hospital room. They had to call a specialist to come in because the infection that I had was beyond anything that could be treated by normal antibiotics. They told my husband to prepare for my death; they were just going to try to maintain me.

People had to wear gowns when they came into my room, and nobody could touch me. I had four intravenous antibiotics. A member of my church came in, and she said, "The Lord told me to tell you, you've got a bad bug. The Lord said to lay blessed handkerchiefs upon you and to cover you with them." They had prayed over the handkerchiefs and put oil on them. They covered me up with them, and they prayed over me, and I was still sick. The doctors kept telling my husband and me, "You people seem not to understand the severity of this," but we also knew that the spirit of infirmity had gone.

After a while, I wasn't getting any better, and I was getting bored with this situation. I thought, "Come on, God. If You wanted me to die, You should have kept me when I was there. If You don't want me to die, then do something." I got a little feisty with God and said, "Listen, it has come down to this. If I die, You die because You are a liar, and You cannot be a liar. If You lie, then You are no longer God. If I die, You lied, and You are no longer God . . . so the whole universe rests on whether I live or die. Now I am not trying to be smart, and I am not trying to say that I am the most spiritual person in the world, but people have called me from all over the world. People are praying for me. Somebody's prayer has to get through. Somebody's agreement has to be enough. Your Word has to be true, or else that's it."

About ten minutes after that, a pastor called me up. He said, "What is wrong with you? I have seen your face, and I know I have been praying for you. What is going on?" I said, "Look, I don't know. I have done everything, and I don't understand why I am not healed." So he said, "What has happened?" I told him the whole story, and he said, "You said that spirit came out of you and ran, but you never said it was destroyed." I said, "That might be the key." So I got my Bible because I always have the Word, and my tapes, and when I listened and felt that I was ready, I began to pray and to say, "I plead the blood of Jesus against you. The blood of Jesus stands against you." As I prayed that prayer, I saw that thing run again, but this time I saw the blood of Jesus come over it and cover it, and it just disappeared in the air. As that happened, I began to feel my body getting better, and eventually, after about two weeks, I was sent home. My doctor had said that my kidneys had been down to 1% functioning. After I improved, they took some tests, and they discovered my kidneys were functioning at 100%. I said, "You said that kidneys can't get better." He said, "You made a liar out of me." They did not believe it, so both my doctors had me come back after six months, and my kidneys were still all right. I have not had any medication or any treatment, no dialysis and no new kidneys (other than the ones God gave me!) since February 2001. That's a year and a half, and I have not had a problem at all. That's my favorite healing.

I have had friends who have had experiences where they have gone to heaven, and they have seen things. There was a little boy in our church who was three years old, and he drowned. His mother called us when he was in the hospital. They had already pronounced him dead. His body was lying on the bed, and there were about eight of us around him, including his mother. As we prayed, I saw him. His name was Jacob. I saw Jacob in a field of the most beautiful flowers I have ever seen. He was traipsing through the flowers, trying to catch a butterfly, and he seemed so happy. I didn't want to influence his mother, but as we prayed, I said, "Look into the Spirit. Let God show you what is happening in the spirit realm." And suddenly, she said, "I see Jacob with lots of flowers. He's chasing a butterfly." I knew she had seen exactly what I had seen, and she began to call him, to say, "Come here, Jacob. Come here, Jacob." He would run toward her voice, and then he would stop. He would look back, and then he would start again. It was a longing to respond to his mother's voice, but he longed to be where he was. He came all the way to the place where he was hovering over his body. While he hovered over his body, you could still see him looking back; he was in this field of flowers. She kept saying, "Come on, Jacob. Come on, Jacob." Then suddenly, she began to cry, and she said, "You can stay there. God loves you." And we saw him just run.

When we were preparing the bulletin for Jacob's memorial, one of the elders who had been there while we were praying said, "Can I do the picture for the bulletin?" We said, "Yes," and she drew a picture on the bulletin just like what I had seen, Jacob chasing that butterfly. Since that time, Jacob's mother has ministered to several parents whose child was dying or whose child had already died. She has been such an instrument in their healing process. Having seen Jacob, having seen others who were at death's door, and now having died myself, I have a whole different attitude toward death. I am more discriminating in terms of how I pray for people because sometimes death is better. People think death is cessation of life, and it's just not.

Many years ago, through a miracle of God, I was sent to the Philippines as a missionary. I knew no one there, but God had prepared the way. Before I left home, God said, "Go and minister life to My people." At that point I was not even a minister; I was in Bible school and had never preached before, but God said, "You minister life to My people. You take My Word, and you build on their strength. You may say they have no strengths, but I say unto you, 'Hold silent. You take My Word, and you will.'" He said, "You will be assigned to the Director of Social Services. You will talk to My people about Me." When I got to the Philippines, this evangelist came up to me and said, "Would you like to preach in my church?" I said, "I don't know how to preach." Then I remembered God said, "Minister life to my people," so I said, "Okay, I'll do it." That Sunday I went, and I almost turned around because there were people sitting all outside the church. I walked over and said, "What's going on?" They said, "The American evangelist is here!" And I found out that's me. So I went in there, and all these people were so excited. I had written my first sermon, and I was going to teach on righteousness.

When it finally got to be my time to speak, I got up and read my first Scripture, and suddenly it was as though I came outside of my body. I was standing there preaching, and I was looking at myself and hearing myself preach. Then suddenly, I got nervous because I thought, "What am I going to do when I finish?" Everybody was excited about my message, and I was excited, too. Then this pregnant lady walked forward, and she said, "Would you lay hands on me for my healing?" And I said, "I don't lay hands on people." But then I remembered, "I don't preach either," so I said, "Okay." I laid my hands on her, and her stomach went down instantly, like a balloon burst. It was a tumor, and she started screaming, "I'm healed! I'm healed!" Then everybody started coming out and saying, "Lay hands on me; lay hands on me," so I said, "Okay." I was laying hands on people—30, 40, 50 people—and they were screaming, "I'm healed! I'm healed!" All these people got healed, and I was saying, "What is this?" I was exhausted and amazed at what God had done.

When everything started settling down, a little short lady came from the back. She looked at me and said, "Are you a social worker?" I said, "Thank God somebody knows I'm just a social worker. I'm not a healer; I'm just a social worker." She said, "I am the Director of Social Services, and I would like to have you assigned to me so you can go through the provinces and talk to people about God." She said the same words to me that God had said when I was in the U.S. It turned out that she was second in the chain of command to President Marcos, and she had been born again two years before. For two years, she had prayed and asked God to send somebody who knew His Word and also knew social work. I ended up getting assigned to President Marcos's cabinet, and I traveled throughout the Philippines talking to social workers about God.

I was there in 1984 for a few months and in 1985 for about eight months. I saw all kinds of miracles. One time, I emptied a hospital in Andaluz City; I went through the hospital praying for people, and everybody got healed.

I remember one time a young man came up to me, and he said, "Thank you so much for my healing." I said, "Thank God for your healing; I don't remember you." He said, "That's because I don't look the way I did before. I was a leper." He said that he had had boils all over him, that I did not touch him, but I moved my hand over his body. He said as I moved my hand, he felt power and healing, and after I left, all the boils left him. He was totally healed.

Another time, when I was in the Philippines, I was in a region where they are totally anti-Scripture, anti-Bible. They are into voodoo. I prayed and said, "Lord, I don't even know how to preach, let alone how to preach in another language, so I need some help." A man came and asked me to heal his wife. I didn't know what was wrong with this lady. At the time, I had these big high heels on because I had worn out my other shoes. She was way across a field, and I was walking across the field toward her, not knowing what was wrong with her. My heels were getting dug down in the dirt, and I was having difficulty walking. Suddenly, I heard this "skreet"—"Yaha!"—and it sounded demonic. I discovered that his wife was totally demon-possessed. She was running toward me with a long machete. Here she is, with this demonic scream with this machete up, getting ready to stab me or cut my head off. With my heels dug down and with her right there, all I could do was pray. I couldn't move. She was coming at me, so I pointed my finger at her and said, "In the Name of Jesus, stop!" She stopped just short of my finger, and the momentum from her running was such that her heels got dug down in the ground. Her heels somehow would not let her move, and the momentum was so forceful from her running that she fell over on me with that machete. I reached behind me, got the machete from her, laid my hands on her, and got her healed and delivered and set free. At the end, she was in her totally right mind. And I didn't get killed!

I do what I am supposed to do. Many times in a service when I finish preaching, I will say, "Anybody who needs healing, come forward." Then I lay my hands on them and pray for them, and they get healed. So many times, when a person comes to me, I see inside of them: I see hurt, and I see pain, and I see problems. I always thought that was normal. I thought everybody, when they met a person, could see that person's skin pulled back, look inside that person, and know all about the person. I thought everybody did that. I would say things to people that I thought they knew, and that everybody else knew, and people would get angry with me and deny things. One day God told me, "Tell them I said so," so I started saying,

"God said to tell you . . ." and then they would listen. God will work with you to tell you what to do.

Recently, I was talking with a pastor at a luncheon, and he asked me, "How many people that you lay hands on get healed?" And I said, "All of them." He said, "You don't understand. I'm saying, 'How many of the people that you lay hands on get healed?'" I said, "All of them." He got upset with me, but I believe in the Scripture that says, "The believing ones will lay hands on the sick, and they will recover." It does not say they *might* recover, or that 50% will recover. God said, "They will," so I believe they do. Whatever happens after God heals them is none of my business. God does the healing, I do the believing and the laying on of hands. After that, if the person doesn't keep the healing, or if they don't believe, it is not my business. The main ingredient to a person's healing is faith, and so many people are afraid. They are afraid they are going to die or that they are going to have a lot of pain. Some people don't believe the report of the Lord. God says, "You are healed," and they might believe, "Yeah, but I still have this pain," or "Yeah, but I am still sick," or "God said it, but maybe I am too sinful." They have all these contra-indicators that they think cause a nullification of God's healing power, and when they think that, they dilute God's ability to heal them. They have the deciding vote, and whose side they vote on, that is what gets manifested in their lives.

Sylvia was interviewed by Vivian Moore in August of 2002.
She is an African American Baptist in her 50's

The Spirit of God Moves
–Donald Carruthers

When I was thirteen, I had my appendix rupture before they could get me to the hospital. I went in, they cleaned it up, and did the normal appendix thing. Instead of being in and out in three days, they said it was going to take a couple days longer, five days in the hospital. The next day, they were going to release me, and it was weird. That night before I was going to get released, I got really sick, and they said, "What's going on here?" All these toxins and parasites are in your appendix, and they didn't get it all. They didn't clean it all out, and the antibiotics they gave me didn't kill them. The infection started taking over my body, and I was really going downhill big time. It got so bad that my legs, all my extremities turned black because the main core of my body was trying to preserve my life. They brought in this specialist from Denver and told my mom, "Listen, looks like your son is going to die."

This is the honest-to-God truth: I had a dream that there was a wall surrounding me. It was made up of all these stones, and I was standing in the middle of the wall. I can still visualize this, like it was yesterday, and part of the wall had been broken in, but not all the way to the bottom. It looked like a "V," and there were all these rocks lying in the middle of the wall or in the middle of the circle where I was standing. Outside of the wall, I felt this very evil presence. I didn't know what it was. It was like I was being stalked by a tiger. I was kind of afraid, and the wall was serving as a protection for me, and I began to take these stones and put them back into the wall. I knew if

I didn't put them back up in time, I was going to die. In my dream, I knew this, and at the time I didn't have a clue what it all meant. Now I look back and see symbolism in the dream. The wall was God, and He was protecting me, and the devil or whoever was trying to kill me and take my life. He was trying to get to me and take me out before I could be used today like I am being used.

My mom said that these three Catholic nuns heard about me, this young boy who was very sick, and they came and prayed for me, and I came out of it. Even to this day, the doctors don't have a real explanation why I got better. It really drew my mom to Christ, and from that day she really started seeking after God and praying for me. She said, "Wow, God, You really are real. You saved my son, whom I had to beg to go to church."

There is truly a Spirit of God because I have seen Him move. God communes with me through His Spirit living inside of me. As I get filled with Him more and more through His Word, praying, and spending time with Him, I just overflow Jesus wherever I go, all over the world. I have seen some incredible things happen. It wasn't me healing the people or me taking a drug addict and setting him free because I prayed for him, or seeing somebody who was completely miserable come to life and the reality of who God is because of me. It was Jesus in me coming out. I am just a person and a vessel He is using for that moment to touch them Himself. The majority of the miraculous healings are taking place in the nations where He is really on the move. God is really moving.

One time, when I was in Brazil, a lady who had muscular dystrophy (or something like that—who hadn't walked in ages) during the meeting, she walked! I gave a call at the end of the message. I said, "Listen, if what I've said today has touched your heart, the Lord is drawing you to Himself, and if you want to give your life to Christ today, come forward." I'm not into letting people come down front, but I felt that it was what I was to do that Sunday. This lady stepped out and started walking down, and everybody in the church erupted, and people were crying. I found out that the lady hadn't walked in thirty-five years.

Another time, also in Brazil, and I was preaching to this youth meeting. There were eight hundred youth. The pastor there didn't believe that God really could move or had any power to do supernatural things, and I thought, "Wow, what's going on?" He was just a religious guy, just this pastor dude. I was preaching to this crowd; the meeting was fine, everything was good. All of a sudden, this pastor comes running out. It was twenty minutes after the meeting, and I was talking to some of the youth. He comes running out and says, "Pastor, please come help me!" They had been talking to a girl in the back room, and she started to manifest or do something crazy. When I walked in the room, she was throwing these 180-pound and 200-pound guys off of her like they were flies, with a supernatural strength.

I grabbed my translator, and when I walked in the room, she stopped everything she was doing, throwing these guys off, screaming, and looked at me. It was funny because my friend said, "Man, you must be on the devil's 'top ten' list or something," because this lady knew when I walked in the room. She could sense Jesus in me, and she just stopped.

Then she jumped up and came running at me, and when that happened, I wasn't like a mighty man of faith and power. I thought, "Man, this girl's going to kill me." She was throwing these other guys around like puppets, and she is going to pummel me.

Right before she got to me, all I knew to do was say, "In the Name of Jesus," because the Bible says, "At that name every knee is going to bow and every tongue is going to confess that He is Lord." It's a very powerful name. When I said this, she fell to the floor, just like a dead person, and the Lord started speaking to my heart, "There is some stuff in her I want to get out." I started getting these words, like, "promiscuity," very sexual stuff, and I started saying, "You demon of lust, in the Name of Jesus, get out of this girl. You have no authority." I started saying all these names and commanding them to leave. I was saying this in English, and she only spoke Portuguese. But every time I said it, she would convulse. I would say, "In the Name of Jesus, you demon of lust, get out." When I would say that, she would convulse. After I named these seven things, she sat up, looked around, and said, "Wow, what happened?" She didn't even know.

Some people can be totally overcome. That's what had happened to this girl. I found out that her mother was a prostitute and had had her out of prostitution. All those things I was naming sexually, I didn't know why, but things are passed down. I believe there is this scheme and this diabolical realm, and they are causing a lot of the problems that we see in society, in people's lives and what they are struggling with. But I believe God is more powerful. It is very clear that He is.

Donald was interviewed by Andrew Cousins in February of 2002.
He is a non-denominational white man in his 30's.

Call on Him
–David Lions

I have prayed for people who have been ill, and they have gotten well. I have never done this in their presence or when I laid hands on them or anointed them with oil. It did not happen suddenly, but the possibility of their recovery had been very, very slight, and now they are completely well. This happened three times. The funny thing was, in each of those cases, every time I prayed for the person, I was so angry at the disease that had them that it was a fury. I did not feel that way about it except when I was praying. I was just furious. There have been other times when I have prayed for people who have had the same disease, and I have not felt anything in particular. I have said, "Lord, bless Jake. I pray that You would heal him, and I trust him into Your hands in the Name of Jesus." I have some cassette tapes of Oral Roberts, and on one of them he said that one of the ways he could tell when the Spirit was working through him to heal someone was that he would feel an indescribable, almost uncontrollable anger. When I heard that, I thought, "Maybe that is something that other people feel." He said he felt he could see the tumor or the clogged artery, and he was physically attacking it, and that is the way I have felt. It was almost like I was directing God at each infected cell, and it was a funny feeling.

One time, a man came to see me who made an appointment, and I had no idea what it was about. When we sat down in my office, he asked me if we could go back in my inner study, and I said, "Sure." So we went back there, and I said, "How can I help you?" He said, "Well, I bound by the books, and I can't get free." And I said, "What do you mean?" And he said, "I bound by the books, and I can't get free." I said, "I don't know what you are talking about. Tell me what you mean." He said, "I have been a practicing warlock since I was seventeen, and I am now thirty-three. I have books of black magic that contain spells and incantations. I am a member of an olden cult. I have a magic cape, a magic sword, and a magic hat that looks like the Minnesota Vikings, and we get together as a cult and cast black magic spells on people. I have come to the conclusion that it is wrong, but I cannot get free."

I said, "Do you believe that Jesus Christ can free you from the power of the devil?"

"I do, but He won't."

"Well, He can, and He will, if you call on Him."

"I can't."

"Well, you do what I tell you to do."

"I will try."

"Bow your head." So he bowed his head. I said, "Repeat the words that I say, and mean them in your heart." I said, "Kind Heavenly Father," and he said nothing. I said louder, "Kind, Heavenly Father." He still said nothing, and when I looked up he was shaking like a person in an epileptic fit. I looked at him and shouted, "Say it!" He said the words, "Kind, Heavenly Father," and at that moment, I felt the temperature in the room drop by about 50 degrees. That lasted for about a second, maybe two. The hair on the back of my neck stood up in ways that it has never stood up, except when I felt like I was in the presence of evil two other times. Then it was like a spell was broken, and he was able to pray the rest of the prayer of salvation. It was very calm and easy the rest of the time. He called me the next day to say that he had gone home that night and set fire to his books of spells, had broken his magic sword with a hammer, and had burned his cape and his hat. He was free and was ready to be baptized.

That was my one experience with that, and I have been in ministry for twenty-four years. It was a very frightening experience, one that was completely unanticipated. I had always thought that stories like it were fabricated, so it was quite an experience to be there for myself.

David was interviewed by Jane Teas in the summer of 2002.
He is a white Southern Baptist in his 50's.

You Can Be Something Different
—Peter Sands

I was born and grew up in South Africa. I went to a boarding school in a little town and then spent my high school years in Durban. The largest contingency of Asian Indians, outside of India, is in Durban. My parents were missionaries who worked with people who believed in Hinduism, and many times as a young boy and teenager, I would go to their celebrations and festivals. I have been to fire walks where men would take fish hooks, put them in their backs, tie lemons on them, hook carts to that, and then pull the carts across hot coals.

When I was sixteen, I gave my life to Satan. One day, I knelt down and said, "I want all the power that I see in the Hindu gods. I want all the power that I have seen." Inside of man there is the aspect of wanting power. We seek power as human beings. It goes back to Adam and Eve, who ultimately decided we would make our own decisions and select our own power. I did that as a young boy, not understanding what I was doing. At that time, the country of South Africa did not have television, but I was very influenced by the British rock subculture. Most of our music came from a station in Mozambique because South Africa would ban anything that came into the country. My influence was from that world, from sitting many hours listening to music and, in some ways, wanting to be like the Rolling Stones.

I got very involved in drugs and became very corrupt. I would act as a narcotics agent for the police and bust the same person I had just bought the drugs from, and yet I was still using the drugs. I attempted to kill my mother one time. I chased her around the dining room table and wanted to kill her. I tried to drown my brother, to throw him off the end of the pier into the ocean. Psychologically, I went pretty crazy, and that continued all the way through high school.

I really began to struggle. I became very violent. Things began to happen in my life, based on what I had committed to. I threw stuff out of windows onto people's heads just to do that, to be violent, to be crazy. My dad sent me to work on a kibbutz in Israel, on a big communal farm. That lasted only a couple of months, and they asked me to leave. I went to live in a hippie commune. I lived in a cardboard box and slept on the ground.

Going from South Africa to Israel, I thought, "Well, let me try and be good. I'm tired of this mess in my life." Then going from Israel to the United States, I thought again, "Let me try and be good. I'm tired of all this." There was an aspect of trying to do things on my own. I got into trouble. I tried to be good again. It didn't work. I got in a lot of trouble again. When I made that commitment to Satan, when I made that change, drugs became a part of my life.

I lived at a Bible School for a year in Colorado, then came back home. I was still trying to be good, trying to get involved in the church, but I would have struggles and failings—pretty major failings sometimes—and I thought, "I will be a missionary. I'll go to Bible College and study, and maybe that will change." I went to the university for a while, took a lot of different courses, and got involved in psychology as a major. It helped me to begin to look at myself and say, "What is going on?" I thought, "I'll analyze this, and I'll fix it." You end up with a means of control, but you don't end up with a means of freedom. You end up being able to figure out how to get well, but you are not necessarily well.

My wife thought I was nuts. I would get violent and beat on things. The first seven years of our marriage were very difficult. And yet, I had been in a Bible School, I had preached in a church, and I had been a Deacon. In fact, I was a Deacon in the church when this took place in my life; I ended up in an evangelism meeting. I had made a confession to one of the counselors and told him I had given my life to Satan. I had never told anyone that. I thought, "This is good. I have cleaned up now. I have confessed." Then the next day, I confessed to my mom and to my wife. We went out to lunch, and I said, "I need to tell you something that I did many years ago, but it's gone. It's finished. I have confessed it now and made the change. I have laid it out in front of people. I have told God I am sorry about it."

The very next day, I was standing in a worship service. Nobody was near me. Nobody was touching me. They were singing a very simple song; it was, "Let's all go up to Zion. Let's all go up to Zion. There's healing in Zion. There's water in Zion . . ." It was a simple song, just a chorus. There was nothing powerful about it. But as I was standing there, something welled up inside of me and came over me. As I was looking at people around me, there was a young man standing in front of me, and he had his hands raised. He was singing, but it was almost like he was glowing. He was very radiant, and all I could see was the back of him. I could see that he knew something, or he was entered into a presence that I wasn't. There was something in me that was different from where he was. It was incredibly disturbing to me, and I began to say, "God, I need that. I want whatever he has."

Something inside of me began to well up, and I said, "God, I want to know You. Is it possible that I could know who You are, God? God, do You really even exist?" Mentally, I had made these commitments over the years. I had tried to make changes. I had constantly gone from being extremely bad to trying to be good. Now I realized that that wasn't possible; you can't do it on your own. I was very much un-free. I felt like I was a personality within a personality. I knew that there was something there that was not what I was. There had to have been. But I didn't even understand what it was that was welling up inside of me.

I would have to say that it was God who was inside: "Peter, you can be something different." I remembered the story of Samuel, how in the middle of the night, he heard God calling him. I said, "God, if you call me like that, I'm here." I will never forget it. I was watching this young man, and at the same time, I was thinking, "Lord, call me like Samuel, like you called Samuel." I had watched other people in that meeting, falling down, beginning to laugh, doing different things that were strange. It was really shaking me, and all of a sudden, my knees began to knock together. I put my knees together, held them really tight, and tried to stand stiffly. I was in the middle of the aisle, and nobody was standing next to me; I don't know how I ended up there. Everybody was singing this little goofy song, the last song of the meeting. Then my hands began to shake; it was totally involuntary. There is a verse that says, "To this man I will look, to him who is humble and contrite of heart and who trembles at My Word." I looked up "trembles" in the dictionary; it said it's an "involuntary shaking." I thought, "This is nuts." I crossed my arms, held them together. I thought, "No, I'm not falling down. I'm the head guy and strong and don't need to fall down." But inside of me was, "God, what do you want? What do you want, God?"

The next thing I knew, I was on the floor. I was lying on my back on the floor, and a war was taking place inside of me. There were two voices. One was a voice from me, saying, "Jesus, I love You, I love You. Jesus, I love You, I love You." There was another voice that said, "No, you're mine! I own you." It was a war inside of me that was like two swords fighting. I was aware of people praying around me. It was this tremendous battle, and eventually, they picked me up and took me into a back room, and a pastor, a good friend of mine, began to pray with me. He stopped things, and he got me to focus on him, to look at him and open my eyes. The eyes are the window of the soul; there is real light in the eyes. There is real vision in the eyes, and it is the ability of what comes in through the light. The demon of darkness, he can control you in the dark. It is difficult to do in the light. Even though they say he is an angel of light, he is really a demon of darkness.

Then the pastor began to take me through confession, and he asked me questions. "What is there?" I would say, "Lust," or "Stealing. Lying. Cheating," things that we could call sins or nasties. We can call them whatever we want to, but they are not people-honoring or God-honoring. They hurt people. They hurt God. I went through this confession, and yet there was still a struggle. It was, "No. You're mine. I own you. You gave your life to me. You belong to me. You're mine." I could hear it, as plain as anything—and constant. It was tremendous trembling and shaking and screaming and ugliness, and all of a sudden, on the blank wall in the room where I was, I saw a visual picture of Jesus with his arms outstretched. He said, "Peter, I created you. I made you." A light went off inside of me. It was a recognition of, "You are my Creator. You are my God. You made me." When I confessed that, when I said, "My Creator, my God, You made me. I want You," the other presence just left. It couldn't stay. It had no more home. I made a decision inside of me that said, "God, I want this, and I don't want that."

It was explained to my wife. She was in shock. She didn't know what was going on. She had never experienced any of this. She was outside waiting and had said, "What's going on with him?" Somebody said, "He's having open-heart surgery." I did. I had open-heart surgery, and I came out a different man. Everything was different; even making love to my wife was different. I was a different personality. I was no longer bound or controlled that way. There had been fears in my life. We had a cat at home, and it would provoke me. It would do things that would get me so irritated, angry, and upset. When I got home that day, the cat was gone, and we never found it. I don't know if the demon said, "Let me go into the cat." I don't know the conversation that took place between the demon and God. It wasn't Satan. It was a demon I had committed to, a demon of lust, a demon of power. Satan doesn't have time to mess with us that way. He lets his demons do that. In my life, I had had that demonic presence, that demonic stronghold, and that demonic control.

For two years, I thought I was in heaven. It seemed nothing could touch me; I was so pure, so clean. If I made a mistake, if I had a struggle with somebody, it was easy to confess and tell them, "Look, here's the situation. I blew it. I messed up." The Bible talks about us being allowed to have milk for a season. Then it says, "When I was a child, I spoke as a child. I understood as a child, I thought as a child. But when I became a man, I had to put away childish things." When you become a man, there comes a season when God takes you to a greater level. He says, "I protected you. I have kept you clean. I have helped you to walk it out. Now I am going to put you in situations where you can be tempted, and where you can struggle; we will see if you can make it. Where is your faith level? Let's see where the changes are in your life." That became a real reality; it became a walking it out, knowing the healing, the change, the forgiveness, and the grace that took place, knowing that it was a faith issue.

As a child, I had asthma and hay fever and spent three weeks in a hospital. After I was set free from spirits, from the control, and I was healed, God began to show me things. I began to realize that asthma also was a hold and a control, and that it typically would happen when I was nervous. I have learned that whatever is in the nervous system that creates nervousness and triggers the glands, also creates the hay fever, the onslaught, the asthma attack. What is nervousness? Nervousness is fear. What is fear? Fear is a controlling spirit. Fear is something that is produced. It is what initially separated Adam and Eve from God. It was what produced having to cover themselves; they were afraid all of a sudden. They saw the realms of darkness. We do not fight against people; we fight against principalities and powers. We fight against things that are not of this earth. They are spirits. They are the realm of the other world.

I was healed from asthma and hay fever. I have tested it. I went and baled hay one day to see what would happen. It was good as long as I kept believing that I was okay. If I let any kind of fear rise up inside of me, I realized that I was going to get attacked again. I could feel it coming on, so I said, "No. Let's stop this."

Satan has the ability to know and understand how to use properties within the realms of—and the scope and the magnitude of—a created earth that is already existing. Satan knows how to use the properties that make things work and has used them for centuries. We are discoverers, we are not creators, and Satan is not a creator either. He just knows how to use what has been created. He cannot create the heart or the emotions of the heart, but he can stimulate fear. He knows how to take fear and use it to trigger things in us. He knows how to take anger and trigger things in us. He can't create the chemical change that takes place when the fear takes place, but he knows what will happen in the producing of that fear.

My father was a minister for many years. He is up in his seventies now, still ministering. He told me many times, "I believe that ninety percent of the people I minister to in hospital are ill and sick because of their sin because of a broken relationship because of anger because of bitterness because of roots of bitterness and anger, and not for any other reason. They won't let it go. They won't have the faith to believe that God can heal that, and in healing that, He will heal them." In the New Testament, it says for healing, there must be confession and repentance. It says, "Those who are sick, have the elders go and lay hands on them, and pray for them. Let them confess and repent. They will be well." Many people I have prayed for in hospitals and other places get all the way up to, "I want to be well, but I don't want to confess. I don't want to repent. I don't want to change." I believe that there is a piece of confession and repentance that takes place as well. We are created so beautifully. We are created in God's image. We are created not to be sick; we were never created to be sick. We are sick because of sin.

Peter was interviewed by Jane Teas in June of 2002.
He is a non-denominational white man in his 40's.

I Am a Victor in Christ
—Fred Simmons

Casting out demons is not something I looked for and not something I enjoy doing. It is not so much a matter of faith as obedience to what God tells me to do. I love helping people, but it is a grueling experience. Satan was one of the greatest angels God ever made, and he rebelled against God and was cast out of heaven. When Satan fell, he took some of the angels with him. Satan has an army; he is at the top and then has principalities and powers on down. There are different levels of army, and all of them are fallen angels who have become demons and evil spirits. These entities have the goals of perverting us, of keeping us away from becoming Christians, or if we are Christians, of messing our lives up.

I invited Jesus Christ to come into my life at age seventeen. A teenager sat down with me and showed me the Bible, and when I became a Christian, the whole world looked different. It was like putting on polarized glasses; it took away the glare. Things bothered me that hadn't bothered me before. I had inclinations to please God that I never had, and that was the Holy Spirit. It is almost like having a radio and tuning it in every day. I can listen to Him, but I can also turn it off. If I turn it off by sin, then I am not going to listen very well. It is not that He is not talking; it is that I am tuning Him out. I went into Christian work, and my role is to be a representative of Jesus Christ and let His Spirit work in my life to point other people to Him.

I had heard missionaries talk about demons, but I had never thought I would see such a thing. Then in the early 1970's, I was dealing with a kid who was brought to my office by two friends of his. Nothing was mentioned about the demonic; I didn't even think about that. I shared with him how to become a Christian, and he was interested. I said, "Let's pray." I prayed for him, and then when he tried to pray, he started choking, and he couldn't pray. I thought, "That's strange." I asked him, "Have you been involved in cult activity?" He said no. I was surprised. Whatever was there, it was causing him pains in his side and in his head, and I said, "Whatever power is causing this, I command you not to use it," and he was able to choke out a salvation prayer. I saw him about two days later and asked how things were going. He looked at me with a strange look on his face and said, "I feel like I lost my best friend."

After our Campus Life meetings, he would come up and have questions. We would get together and talk, but it was an adversarial relationship. He would attack everything I believe: "What about this?" and "What about that?" One time he said, "You make me so mad!" When I asked him, "Why?" he said, "Every time I think I have you trapped, you give me an answer from the Bible." I said, "Those are the only real answers I have." One night, we were talking together in the car, and he said something, and I turned to him and said, "In the Name of Jesus Christ, come out of him!" As soon as I said it, he started moaning and groaning, going down in his seat and acting weird. It scared me. I thought, "Fred, what have you done?"

I started commanding whatever was there, and this thing talked back to me. I said, "I command you, get out!" and the thing said, "I'm not leaving." I said, "I command you; you have to leave in the Name of Jesus Christ!" It said, "No, I don't. I'm staying here." About that time, I said, "God, wake people up to pray for me because I don't know what I'm doing." When I went to the office the next day, my secretary said, "What was going on last night?" I said, "Why?" He said, "I had to get out of bed and pray for you." Another friend came in an hour later and said, "Hey, what was going on last night?" I said, "Why?" He said, "My wife and I had to pray for you about eleven o'clock; we had this overwhelming urge to pray." Another couple told me later, "Last month we had an overwhelming feeling that we needed to pray for you; what was going on?" This is a spiritual battle.

I worked with the young man for two years before he finally was released. I didn't want to deal with it; I didn't know what I was doing. I had to read and study in the process; the Lord taught me a lot of principles. Over the years, different people have found me. I never asked for them; they just came. Recently, a lady was brought to me. She is married, well-educated, and she gave her life to Christ about ten years ago. She teaches Bible studies, but she is hearing voices. I found out that she has had demons from birth. They came down the family line. The Bible says that the sins of the fathers are visited on the children to the third and fourth generation. When one family member who has demonic powers dies, the demons feel they have a right to go right down the line. That is why some people believe in reincarnation: the demons watch what is going on, and they can mimic anything from that other person's life. With her, there had been rape and murder in her ancestors, all kinds of strange things in her family. One of the demons in her was called Scam, and one was Horny; I probably don't need to say more.

With many of these demonic powers, their names are connected to their function, and when you hear about it from the outside, you say, "You have got to be kidding." I ask them questions to find out how they got in, how I can get them out, and what hold they may have. There are two levels of demonic activity: possession and oppression. Oppression is from the outside, when the demons are on the outside talking to you, but they are not internalized. When they are internal, the word is "possessed," but a more accurate term is "demonized." It is not ownership. Some people say a Christian cannot have demons, but I have been dealing with this lady for six months, and we are continually getting more out. Last week we got two out that were really nasty. Each time they leave, her personality changes a little. Some of the inclinations leave her. She, at first, was having tremendous sexual temptations; she did not act on them, but perverted things were going through her mind all the time. Those are no longer there.

It is a strange world; the best illustration is pulling up a rock, and all the insects scurry for cover. The demonic world is a bunch of insects, a bunch of childish ones. When I talk to this lady and the demons manifest, she takes on a different personality. Her facial features change; some are really cocky, and some are like a little kid. When I cast an evil spirit out, I tell it to go to the place where Jesus Christ sends it. If I suspect that a person has a demon, then I deal with them intellectually first because, usually, they have been told lies. Many have been told that they have committed the unforgivable sin, that they are evil people because of what they are doing. There are all kinds of distortions of the Scripture and of God. They will be feeling that Satan is more powerful than Jesus. The demons will say, "God has let you down. God doesn't like you." They are liars.

I try to teach people that as believers, they can be victors in Christ over this. They have been invaded by a power that can be gotten rid of. It is a process; it may take a short time, or it may take a long time. Then I try to find out what ideas or actions they have taken that need to be confessed and renounced. First, they need to confess to God and acknowledge what they have done wrong. I usually have them take a piece of paper, write such things down, and check them off as they confess them. That frees them from guilt before God. Then I have them talk to the demonic power that is there and say, "Any power I gave you through this action, I cancel in the Name of Jesus Christ," and then go back to the same list. Many times, these demonic powers get power over the person by an action or attitude on their part. Sometimes when you try to cast out, to command a spirit to leave, it will not go. I try to figure out why, and most of the time the person knows what is going on. They may say, "I need to confess this sin." We talk about it, and confession and renunciation take place. Sometimes we have to go back and confess the past sins of the fathers. That came as a surprise to me.

I talked to the first kid I dealt with on the phone about ten years ago. He told me that he had toured the world in a singing group, and he was in another country. A girl in their group fell to the floor and started shaking like crazy. He hadn't told anybody what he had been involved in, and he went down to help her. Her eyes opened and looked up at him, and a voice said, "We remember you." He didn't do anything. It's strange: there is a whole army out there. Jesus gave His disciples authority to cast out evil spirits, and He sent them out to do it. They came back and said, "Lord, even the evil spirits obey us in Your Name," and He said, "Don't rejoice in that, but rejoice that your names are written in heaven."

"Dungeons and Dragons" is one of the greatest introductions to the occult that the world has ever seen. The Bible says have nothing to do with evil spirits, but I come along and say, "God, it's just a game; I'm going to play it," and yet it is something He hates. You cannot play the game unless you cast spells. You are instructed in the procedure used in witchcraft. Let's say you are a young person and you play it. This is a game that is usually very attractive to an intellectual kid. Average kids don't like it because it is too complicated. So you go through it—a lot of them use the names of demonic powers—and then somebody invites you to a special program where they are doing some of these things. Are you going to be interested? Yes. You're not that serious; you are just going to watch it. That is when you get involved. I became aware of these games because the kids involved in them were coming to me and telling me what problems it was causing them. You think that you are "playing" in the demonic world, but that is what you are doing in the demonic world right there. People say, "It is just a game. It is just something that is playing with fear." Satan blinds your mind if you think that because it is dangerous. Those who play are opening themselves to potential demonic invasion.

Satan can do things, but he is not omniscient. He doesn't know everything. He is not omnipresent. He is only in one place at a time. People say, "Satan made me do it." No, unless you are a high-level important person in the world, you will probably never encounter Satan. It will be the demonic powers, his army; they are all over the place, but Satan is only in one place at a time. He is not omniscient. He is not omnipotent or omnipresent. Satan is not creative. None of the attributes of God does he have; he is just a created being, but he is extremely powerful. The Bible says, "Draw nigh to God; resist the devil, and he will flee from you." It is not for me to resist the devil and flee from him; first you have to draw nigh to God.

People say, "How can you do what you do? Aren't you afraid?" I don't have to be afraid; I am a victor in Christ. The demons cannot do a thing to me that God does not allow. But I do not play with demons; I do not mess with them. The only reason I ask them anything is to know how to get rid of them. There is no other way to get rid of them except for Scriptural means. They will try to intimidate you: "I've got power." I say, "I've got more power than you do. I'm not afraid of you. You're serving a loser. Satan hates you." I say to the people, "When you want out, let's talk. You can get out. You have been told that you are trapped; you are not. If you want Christ, you've got Christ. You can have Him." The primary temptation Satan uses is the power of suggestion. He wants to be so much a part of your personality that you don't know the difference. Demons can whisper to you and motivate you to do things, but it is still your choice. You don't have to do it. They have to admit that you have authority over them, and they hate that. If a spirit will not leave, if I am still trying to figure out how to cast it out, I say, "We will get back together later, but right now I am going to command you that you cannot have communication from the outside. You cannot have communication among yourselves. You cannot divide. You cannot gain any strength. I isolate you in the name of Jesus Christ. I have authority to do it." One spirit said, "How did you know to do that?" Sometimes they are funny.

You can recognize whether it is a demon or a part of someone's personality because of a rapid emotional change, switching quickly from personality to personality. Sometimes people have extreme hate or rage in their eyes. You can see the hatred streaming out of their eyes to you. They have a strong aversion to Christian things. Sometimes they have destructive habits, like cutting themselves. They also are attracted to very evil activities. Usually if a person has been very far into drugs, they have demonic problems because they have been playing in a forbidden area and have released control of their emotions to something else. With this one woman, I could see what was happening because of her facial tics; they would take over her face. The demons usually desire to be under medication, like Prozac; they love that because it tunes the person out and gives them more control. They also do not like vitamins because it gives a person more power. It gives them more health.

Going through these experiences, I have seen the extreme power of the Name of Jesus Christ. In the Name of Jesus Christ, the demons have to obey you. You can cancel whatever ground they have. You see the extreme power of the Bible itself. The Bible calls itself a sword, and sometimes when the demons won't talk, I will read the Bible to them until they start talking. They hate that. There are certain passages that they especially hate: Isaiah 53, which is the Old Testament prophecy about Christ and the crucifixion. The spirits hate the crucifixion. They hate the resurrection. They hate anything like that. If you find out their particular leaning toward a particular sin, then read the Scripture verses that are the opposite of it, the positive. If one feeds on lies, read it the truth. They hate passages on love.

One time, a spirit would not talk, no matter what I did, so I started reading the Bible, and the thing said, "Why do you cut me?" I said, "You are not talking," and kept reading. It said, "What do you want to know? Stop reading it. Stop reading it!" They can't stand it. The Bible is a sword of the Spirit.

As Christians, who have given our lives to Christ, we are living behind enemy lines. The world still has the image of God on it because it is His creation, but it has been perverted. Those who have given their lives to Christ are victors in Christ, and it makes the world make sense. Becoming a Christian is a transaction between you and God. It is realizing who He is, what He did for you, and who you are. It is a yielding of yourself. The Bible says, "For whosoever shall call upon the name of the Lord shall be saved." It is so simple. Some people say, "I can't believe in something I can't see, taste, or touch," and I say, think of magnetism. You can't see it, you can't taste it, you can't touch it, and you can't feel it. Yet you see its effect on things. It is there. How else would you prove that a magnetic field is there, other than its effect on other things? It is the same with God. You can demonstrate His effect in the lives of people.

Fred was interviewed by Andrew Cousins in December of 2001.
He is a white man in his 60's who has served with Campus Crusade for Christ.

Chapter 8

AMAZING FAITH

Then Jesus told them a parable about their need to pray always and not to lose heart. He said, "In a certain city there was a judge who neither feared God nor had respect for people. In that city there was a widow who kept coming to him and saying, 'Grant me justice against my opponent.' For a while he refused; but later he said to himself, 'Though I have no fear of God and no respect for anyone, yet because this widow keeps bothering me, I will grant her justice, so that she may not wear me out by continually coming.'" And the Lord said, "Listen to what the unjust judge says. And will not God grant justice to his chosen ones who cry to him day and night? Will he delay long in helping them? I tell you, he will quickly grant justice to them. And yet, when the Son of Man comes, will he find faith on earth?"

Luke 18:1-8

Faith Can Give Me a Different Prognosis–Julia Wright

I was epileptic until I was about six months old. My mom and dad were told that I would not make it one night when I had a grand mal seizure and had turned blue. My family had been praying for me: my grandfather (who was a pastor) and my grandmother. They always prayed for us. I came through, never had any seizures again, and never had to take any medication for epilepsy. I wouldn't have known that I ever had epilepsy, if my mother had not told me. I have never had any problems. Never—and I'm 49. So it was my grandmother's and grandfather's prayers. I always say that the "grandma prayers" came through. They were in South Carolina, and I was born and raised in Detroit, so they were not physically there. That is one thing I like about how God does things: you don't have to be there.

In 1982, the doctor diagnosed me as having cancer in my cervix. I said, "No, I don't." He said, "Yes, you do. You need to come in." I thought, "This man is just trying to get more money." He finally sent a registered letter saying that the carcinoma was in my blood stream, and I needed to come in right away. He said, "I'll tell you what, since you don't believe me, I'm going to send you for a second opinion." He was in one part of Michigan: Ypsilanti, which is about 45 miles from Detroit. He sent me to another suburban area of Detroit, about 25 miles away. When the doctor was so adamant about the cancer, I called my aunt and told her, "I don't want to tell anybody, but I have to go for a second opinion. They're saying that I have cancer." She said, "Don't say that." "I haven't claimed it. I don't have it as far as I'm concerned." She and I prayed on the phone that day before I went for the second opinion. I just dismissed it and said, "I do not have it." I am the type of person who will talk to God, and I will tell Him, "You said that You are my healer, and I trust You to prove Yourself."

It was a few weeks between the two appointments. So the second doctor came in, examined me, and said, "I don't have the right chart. I need to get your chart." He told the nurse, "I need this patient's chart," and they looked at the name. Finally, the nurse said, "What's your name?" I told them, "My name is Julia Wright." She said, "Doctor, this is her chart." He said, "It can't be because this is saying that she has cancerous polyps and malignant . . . There must be a mistake because there's nothing there."

Another time, in October 1986, I started not being able to walk and move normally. I couldn't straighten up my head, and it hurt to move my arm. I couldn't sleep. If I lay down, it hurt. If I sat up, it hurt. They finally diagnosed it clearly in January of 1987 as rheumatoid arthritis, the crippling type. I knew they weren't lying because my cousin had crippled badly before he was thirty-six years old. I have an aunt who is crippled; she doesn't like to move because of the pain. I said, "I will not allow this to happen to me." I prayed and told the Lord, "I'm not going to have it. You're going to have to fix this." I went home, took all of the painkillers and other things that they had given me, and flushed them down the toilet. I taught myself how to write again, so it wouldn't be noticeable and people wouldn't know that I was having pains in my neck when I had to turn my body. I bought some support shoes and taught myself to walk again. At the end of January, I went back to work, and June 5th of that year, I got married. After we had been married for about five years, I still couldn't lift my arm that much. Then one morning, I said, "Lord, this has gone on long enough. I'm tired of this. I am going to raise my arm with no pain in the Name of Jesus." Instantly, I was able to do it.

Medicine can give me a diagnosis, and faith can give me a different prognosis. I tell people, "Go to the doctor. If you find something wrong, or you feel something is wrong, don't worry about going to the doctor. When you find out what the diagnosis is, then you can specifically pray about it." I tell people, "God is the God of specificities. He deals with specifics." Sometimes God doesn't move immediately like we want Him to. But I am very specific when I talk with Him and let Him know. In March 1991, I miscarried as I was going into the second trimester, and the doctor had me come in. He did a pap smear and a DNC, and when he got the results, he called me back in. He said, "I'm showing carcinoma in the uterus," and I said, "You're wrong." He said, "I am not. Read the lab report for yourself." I said, "I don't care what this says; I'm telling you, I don't have it. Do another one." So he did it, and shortly thereafter, I had another appointment to hear the results. He said, "I am a deacon in a church, and my dad is an elder. We believe that God can heal, but I have never seen this happen. It was there. You read the report." I said, "But I told you that I didn't have it." The two tests were just a few weeks apart. I had no medication, no nothing. I have never had chemo. I have never had radiation. God just took it away.

One of the attributes of our God is that He is a healer, and His name is "Jehovah Rafa." When you learn how to appeal to a God that you have faith in, it is just like going to your dad. You can make Daddy do exactly what you want, depending on how you approach Him. That's what I do; I just remind Him that He said in His word, "By His stripes we were healed." I say, "At Calvary, I was healed. Everything was taken care of then. I expect You to prove Yourself, that You are my healer," and I remind Him, "I have done this for You; I have done that for You. Ever since I was a child, all I knew was You. I expect to see results." It's just like I am fussing. Then I ask Him, "If this is my time that You choose for me to leave this earth, I ask You to forgive me of all of my sins. I want You to hear me now."

He says He is faithful and just to forgive us, if we ask Him. If we call upon His name and pray to Him, He will answer our prayers, and He has proven it to me, over and over, throughout my life. A lot of times, people will ask God for things. I have found that rather than just asking Him, you thank Him for it: "I thank You in advance for my healing. I thank You in advance for meeting my financial needs. I thank You in advance." I don't know how He is going to bring it. But I thank Him for it.

I had eczema for ten years. My skin just went to pieces. They said nothing could be done. I had to use Cetaphil lotion instead of soap. I could not take hot baths. Nothing worked. I had to use a special shampoo and rub it on my skin like a lotion. That kept it from itching, but the flakiness would come back, and sometimes it would rub raw and bleed. The hair specialist said that if I wasn't careful, my hair could fall out. So I went to Israel, to the Dead Sea; because of all the minerals, it is believed to have healing powers. I dipped myself in the Dead Sea with the faith that I would be healed. After the first time I got in, I never had any more problems with the eczema. It went away. That was a real blessing.

My husband and I were in an accident in 1995. It had rained, and trucks had left the road ragged. The water settled on it, and the ice was there, but we didn't know it. I said, "Oh, Lord, we're on ice," and the truck spun around and then flipped. After it flipped, it turned back upright. The truck flipped twice, but the cab did not smash in. We weren't supposed to come out of there. The police said, "You flipped, and the cab didn't smash . . . ?" They had to cut my husband out. He came out with no broken bones and a little bit sore. I didn't have any broken bones. I had a cut because when the truck flipped, my head went forward on a mirror. God blessed us. No broken bones, just that cut. I didn't even let them do cosmetic surgery. I said, "Just leave it like that to remind the devil that he tried to kill me." That is what happens when you believe in a God who says He can heal and who can bless you. You have to have that faith.

In August 2000, I got sick all at once, with abdominal pain. They scheduled me for a sonogram. The sonogram showed that my ovary had burst, and I had to go to the hospital. Our pastor was already in the room when I got there. The hematologist came in, my husband and I were there, and Pastor asked the hematologist, "Will you leave and let us pray?" She said, "Oh, can I pray too?" and we said, "Sure," so we prayed. That night I just stayed awake and talked with God. If anybody had come in there, they would have thought I was nuts. The next morning they got me prepared to go for a CAT scan before surgery. I just told the Lord, "I thank You that I am healed." I just kept a positive confession at all times. When we did the CAT scan, it showed that the ovary had closed up. The doctor said, "I've never seen anything like this. You know how to read the sonogram. You saw the fluids." I said, "Yes I did; I saw them. That's okay. I know what happened." Once again God had healed me miraculously.

You are not going to stop me. That is how I have always been: having a faith where you don't doubt for a second that what you have been taught to believe in all these years can really happen. You will see a difference. God has proven it, not just in my health. For instance, one month into our marriage, my husband got caught between a wall and a forklift. It cut his leg up really bad. The doctor took him to the hospital, and the doctor said I would have to take care of the wound. He didn't know that I had medical training. I would clean the wound and wrap it, and as I did, I would pray, and my husband would pray with me. When we went back to the doctor, he couldn't take the stitches on the inside out because it had healed too quickly. He said, "Who changed your dressing and cleaned your wounds?" My husband said, "My wife did." And he said, "Then you had training." I said, "Yeah." He said, "But it healed too fast. We didn't get to take the stitches out." I said, "Well, it's okay. It will be all right."

I grew up in a Baptist church, not because anybody made me, but that was my choice.

Speaking in tongues was something that I wanted to do, and I asked my pastor about it. He said, "People who speak in tongues have a more disciplined prayer life," and I said, "That's what I want." Nobody laid hands on me. They didn't even know that I was asking the Lord for it, and one day, it happened. I was in my apartment, and I had been praying. A lot of times, God will give you the interpretation of it. Sometimes we have found that it is an actual language because I have found myself praying, and all of sudden, I might be praying in French or a dialect of an African language. I have found out that some of the words were Hebrew and I didn't know it until I started taking the Hebrew language. Then I was able to see what it was. Why did I want to speak in tongues? Because it is Biblical, for one thing, and because I like discipline. I like to have that balance in my life. I like that happy medium where things are balanced. I like my life where I am not scattered all over the place.

I have also seen miraculous things with non-believers. They couldn't explain it, and nobody else could. To give an example, my brother is not a believer. One time he was incarcerated; he was not supposed to get out until the year 2006. And he got out in 1995. He had called me and asked me to pray for him. I did; I prayed for him. We prayed, and they released him. The officer went to the house to check it out, to make sure it was okay for him to stay there with mom and dad. Mom called and said, "This man is mad. He doesn't know how this happened," and I thought to myself, "I do." I had sent my brother a Bible, and I underlined the Scripture that says, "With God, nothing is impossible to those who believe." God moved in that situation, and my brother is still out. God will answer your prayers.

Another fellow in prison did not believe in women preachers, but he started coming when I was there. I asked him, "When are you up for parole? You've been coming a long time."

"Oh, I've got five years before I go up for parole."

"Oh, yeah? Don't forget that Paul and Silas were in prison, and God caused their door to be opened. They were set free. If you can believe that God will do that, I'll pray with you now."

"I don't know if it will do any good, but okay."

I prayed for him, and the next week he came by and said, "Pastor Julia, Pastor Julia!" That was the first time he had ever called me "Pastor."

He said, "You won't believe this. I went up for parole, and I'm getting released."

"That quick? I thought you said it would take . . ."

"But you prayed for me, and God answered your prayer."

I said, "So what does this tell you?" He has been out since 1993. He calls me at least once a year. He and his wife got back together. He started teaching Sunday School. Then they started teaching the new believers' classes. So God has worked things out for non-believers also. I shouldn't say non-believers: they were people who were searching for something better.

How do you live? What is your life saying about your faith? I believe that your life is your best witness. How do I feel God's presence? It's a peace, a peacefulness. And then sometimes, He makes me laugh. It is a beautiful feeling of peacefulness and joy; with the Holy Spirit, you just have a peacefulness. People can see it in your skin tone. They can see it in your life, even the kids. The teachers don't understand the high school students who hear that "Ms. Wright is here today," and they come in and want hugs. I give them hugs, even the boys. It is something that God does for you. You just enjoy life.

Julia was interviewed by Puja Verma in June of 2002.
She is an African American woman in her 40's who attends a charismatic,
non-denominational congregation.

We Need Jesus as Our Healer
–Thomas Blondin

I had had headaches for years. They started when I was in sixth or seventh grade in school, and it was a continual, everyday thing. It was strange *not* to have a headache. I took something for a headache every day until I was around forty years old. I became a Christian in 1981, and I knew that the Lord was able to heal, but I never asked Him to remove these headaches. I needed to ask the Lord to heal me, but I wouldn't because . . . what if He doesn't? I feared that God was going to treat me the same way everybody else had, so I wouldn't ask Him. I was holding on to that. I believed He would heal everybody else and touch everybody all this time, but I never asked Him once to touch me and heal me.

You can tell me you believe that something will work and never try it, but then you are not really believing it. But if I believed that He would do this, then I should have had no problem asking. The only way we can get anything from the Lord is to ask, to say, "Lord, I need this." You will ask and then receive it because it is already paid for. Salvation was paid for 2,000 years ago at the cross, the same time my healing was paid for. When Jesus went to the cross, the stripes that He took and the blood that was shed was for us. We were bought back from Satan, all that Adam had sold out to Satan in the Garden. Jesus went and redeemed us from him. He bought us back, and all we had to do was accept it.

God called me to preach, and I answered. I had accepted the call and had already been preaching for about a year. I was studying a message on healing, and I reached inside my chair to get my pain medicine because my head was hurting, and I said, "Wait. No, I can't do this. God, if You can't heal me, I can't preach that You are a healer."

I put my Bible down, put the medicine back down, and got ready to go to church. I got in the truck and started to the church, and about halfway there I said, "Hey, wait a minute!" My head had quit hurting. Talk about faith rising up! So I went on and preached that message.

That was over eight years ago. I have not taken a thing at all for headache pain for over eight years. That was the first time I asked. He is real. The reason we don't have is because we won't ask and won't believe. That's it. I am no different than anybody else. God loves one just as much as He loves the other, and the only reason He did that is because I said, "God, I can't preach that You are a healer if You can't heal me. If You can't heal me, then You are not a healer." I knew He was a healer because I had already seen it work. We have prayed for people who had cancer, and they never go back to the doctor, never have an operation or chemotherapy, and are doing as well as ever. Only God can do it. The doctors can cut it out, but they can't heal. Only God can heal it.

He is a miracle worker, and He is alive today in us. He is in us doing the work through us, and the more I learn about Him and about the Word, the more I realize it has not got anything to do with me. All I have to do is say, "Lord, I'm willing." That's what I found out when He called me, and I began to preach. I could not do it, and I cried, "God, I can't do it!" And He said, "Good, I didn't want you do to it. I wanted you to be willing to do it." The thing that we have to do is to be a willing vessel. God will do the work. All you have to do is be willing. The only way we will ever receive anything from the Lord is to be willing to receive it. There is not a thing that I can do in this life to deserve anything from Him. It is what He has done through His mercy on my life—on our lives—and His grace.

My brother got hooked on the drugs that they give to cancer patients who are dying. It got to the point that he couldn't even talk anymore. I would ask him something, and the only thing he could do was to grunt. One night, I started to take him to the hospital, and he looked up and said, "Where are you going?" in a weak voice. He said, "No, I'm not going. Turn around." That evening when I left him, I had no idea in the world that he would be alive the next day. I thought that he would be dead because the life that was in him was gone. But God reached out that night. Two couples went to see him, and he asked them to pray for him, and they prayed. He had taken drugs, and he had taken so much, it was drying his blood and giving him all kinds of problems. The doctor said he could not make it, but God showed him wrong. He did make it, alive and here today. He was to the point of death, no more strength in him; he couldn't even talk. Just two couples that night came to visit and pray with him, and God worked a miracle there in his house. When I came to work the next morning, he was sitting there looking like there had never been a thing wrong with him a day of his life, so I knew something had taken place.

Whether you believe it or not, God is the Healer. The doctors can operate and cut off and take out and sew back, but they can't heal you. They can't cause you to mend. Only God can do this. I thank God for doctors because I broke my foot and my hand, and I sure needed somebody to do something. I was glad to see a doctor at that time, so he could get things set and put back together, but only God does the mending. We have to have doctors, but we need Jesus as our Healer. The church has gotten away from showing people Jesus because some think it is better to tell them the Lord Jesus loves you than to show you that love. We are in a society now that is, "Gimme, gimme, gimme; I get and take, and you can get it the best way you can." It's "Me and mine at the fore and no more." If you can't get it on your own, then you don't get it. But that is not showing Jesus.

He healed not only my headaches and my thoughts, but He healed some things from my childhood and my prejudices. God, He loves all of us. He has no respect of persons. I continue to remind Him, "Oh, Lord, you say you have no respect of persons. You did this for this one; then I know You are going to do it for me." And He does. He does it for me. The older we get in Him, the more that is required of us because now we have learned more. He is moving in our lives, every one of us. He is not dead. We may not see Him moving a great deal, but I can look back a year ago and see where God has moved me to. I can't tell you what He has done from yesterday to today, but I can look back a year ago and see where He has really done something. God is good. He is the Healer, and His Word is true, and I can believe that. When we believe something, He performs it.

It doesn't make any difference what it looks like, but faith causes mountains to move. Mark 11:20 says, "Have faith in God, and we begin to speak to the mountains." We can speak to the mountains in our faith and doubt not. We can see it happen: we can see the hand of God moving, not only in our life, but in our loved ones, our family, our church, our homes, our nations. It is up to us to pray and to seek God on every hand for everything in our life. First, we have to believe in God. We have to trust Him. It is not hard to serve a God who is a Healer, who loves us, who listens. We gather together, or we can pray at home and feel His presence come upon us and know we are not alone because they say, "Where two or three gather together, He will be in the midst." He wants us to share with the rest of the world.

Six years ago, my wife and I were in our living room praying, and the glory of the Lord came. He spoke revival to me about the church that I was going to that Sunday. I went to preach on Sunday night, and I told the pastor, "This is what God spoke to me: rather than pray for mission, He said revival." I went on that night and had a good service, and there was a woman in the church who said, "Lord, if I'm going up and going in a revival, then I need to be able to hear." She could hear some, but she had hearing aids. By the time she got to the back door to leave that night, her ears were open and clear, and she could hear. She called me the next day so excited; she said, "I can hear, I can hear!" So I have seen deaf ears in our church opened up.

The pastor told me, "Come on back," so I went back, and we had a four-month revival. From that, God worked mightily. Hers was the first miracle, even before it really got started. The first week they had one lady who was getting ready to go to the doctor for a tumor that had to be cut out of her, a knot of something that was in the side of her rib cage. That night, we were praying, and she said she felt something move, that it flew out of her. When she went to the doctor, it was gone. There was one man with hurting knees, and nobody prayed for it. The Lord spoke to him and said, "I am healing your knee," and he has never had the problem since. This revival brought in about thirty new people to the church, and it continued on for four months. God worked miracles the whole time.

We still live in a time of miracles, signs, and wonders that take place. The Word of God says signs and wonders are what follow the preaching of the Word. I have seen it; about every week somebody is touched by the Lord or healed. Jesus is on the right hand of the Father right now. He is not going to come back down here and do anything for me or you. He has already done it, but He is on the right hand of the Father, making intercession for me and you, praying for us that we will grab hold of it.

Thomas was interviewed by Georgianna Jackson in 2002;
he is a white man in his 40's serving in non-denominational ministry.

The Power of the Holy Spirit
–Patricia & Amber Dalton

Patricia begins . . .

The first time I remember a supernatural healing is when my leg grew out. I had one leg that was shorter than the other. I had to practice walking differently because one hip was higher than the other, and you don't walk right when one leg is shorter than the other. I had some back trouble from that. We started going to a little church, and my pastor there said, "God still heals people." I said, "I've heard that God heals people; I don't discount that." But at the time, I didn't know much about healing. He said, "Do you want us to pray for you?" We were over eating dinner with them after church and getting to know them better, and I said, "Yeah, I would love for you to pray for me," and he said, "We will." He prayed, and I could feel a warmth through my leg and hip area. It felt like warm oil being poured on the inside of my leg, and my leg grew out, right when he was praying in the Name of Jesus. That was the first time I had heard anybody pray. I was just sitting down, and his wife and he both were praying for me. They had their hands on my shoulder. I remember them getting oil, anointing oil, as symbolism.

That was new to me. I had never been prayed for by the anointing of oil and laying on of hands, but it definitely happened. My leg grew out, and I had to readjust and hem my pants to accommodate my new leg growth. I was thirty by then, and one leg had been an inch shorter my whole life. I saw it happen. I was watching, and it looked like it just grew out. All it felt like was warm oil from my hip down, all the way down my leg. I couldn't pinpoint exactly where it was growing, but I felt something was going on. It felt good. There was no fear or any hocus pocus. It felt very peaceful, a very natural thing, like sitting and talking.

I was elated. I was delighted because I was thinking, "Oh, boy, no more backache, no more trying to walk like I used to." Healing is such a good experience. You are almost glad that you had a problem to start with, so that it could be corrected, so that you could experience that sweet presence of the Lord and an inner feeling that God does care for you. God is . . . is God, and He is supposed to be able to correct anything that is wrong, since He designed us to start with. Why couldn't He fix what was not right in us? He can, and He does. I felt the presence of the Lord, and it was good. He does care about things that concern me. I have heard of people being healed of cancer, heart disease, and major diseases, and this doesn't compare with that type of miracle, but it is the fact that God loves you enough to be concerned about little things, like one of your legs being shorter than the other.

It made me want to know more about God. I wanted to pursue God. I wanted to find out more of His character. It is like love when something like that happens, like the personification of love. It is the substance of love. That whole period of our lives was a time when we were searching. We were looking, and we found out about the goodness of God. God was changing my children while He was changing me and giving me more insight on how to be a better parent. He helps you with every detail if you ask Him. I had not known that in such a personal way before. I knew the concept of a God and Jesus, but I never knew how personally He wanted to be with us.

People would ask me to pray for them, and I would, and God would do something. It was a step of faith. People would ask and say, "Would you pray for me? I have got so and so going on. Pray for me about this?" I don't know why, but people have been just drawn to me over the years, about all different kinds of things. You name it, whatever people have going on.

They would be friends, or sometimes people I had just met. So I would pray, and God would move. That same pastor talked so much about the Word, and He would say, "Well, be it according to your faith." You would hear him use that Scripture a lot of times. "Be it according to your faith. Do you believe God can do this? Do you believe that He is still the same? That He is the same today, yesterday, and forever—or don't you?" It really boils down to that. It has been at least thirty years that I would pray for things and see God move.

Once when my husband was working outside with a chisel, he accidentally hit it into part of his hand, the meaty part of the bottom of the thumb, and it slashed it open about an inch and a half. Ryan came in, and blood was running all over and dripping on the floor. He said, "I have just really cut my hand." I said, "Well, let's pray, and see what God does." This is right when we had found out about healing, hearing the word of healing and hearing the word of faith, and knowing that God still does that nowadays. I put my hand over it, and we prayed the Scripture that says, "If two agree as touching one thing and don't doubt in their heart . . ." if it's according to the will of God, then He will do it. We prayed in the Name of Jesus, the way that we had been hearing about, and when I moved my hand, his hand was healed. The gash was closed, and there is not even a scar except for a little wrinkle on his hand. We were really excited that God would do that. There was no bleeding, no anything. His skin just went back together. That was fun: that God would do that. We were delighted that God loved us enough to do that. We didn't have to go through the hassle of going to the emergency room, getting that stitched up, going through the antibiotics, doctoring it. God just—boom, miracle!—healed it up.

Another time, my son was in the hospital. He had flu-like symptoms and respiratory bronchitis and had been sick for several weeks. We took him to the hospital because I believe in medicine as well. I don't discount it. I am not one who would not use medicine if I thought that God was directing me in that way. Sometimes God does instantaneous miracles. Sometimes He heals over a period of time, but His will is to heal His people who believe. My son kept losing weight. He had lost about fifteen pounds and was really thin. He was in excruciating pain, and they couldn't find out what it was. They were getting ready to do a spinal tap. I thought that was bad news because that meant that they thought it was meningitis or something bad.

I called a woman who at the time was a pastor's wife in this area. I didn't know her that well, but I knew that she believed that God could heal. I said, "I have to pray with somebody who is going to agree with me in the Name of Jesus." So I called her and told her what the situation was by his bed in the hospital; I said, "Would you please agree with me that God will heal Rick? The doctors can't determine what is wrong with him, and he is really sick," and she said, "Sure, I'll pray with you." She started praying and said, "I loose angels into that room to minister healing to him." I heard this sound, and I started looking around to see what in the world was going on there. I felt a presence, the presence of the Lord, and that something really good was going on in that room.

When I hung up, Rick opened his eyes and said, "My head feels much better." One of the worse symptoms of the whole thing was excruciating head pain; it had been going on for days. They had him on pain-killing medication, but at that point, he woke up and said, "I am feeling much better. My head hardly even hurts now," and up until that point, all the medicine they had given had not touched it. After the prayer, his fever dropped immediately, just like that. He got color back in his face, and the doctor came in and said, "Well, I don't know what has happened here, but we are not going to do that spinal tap. It looks like we don't need to at this point. We will see in the morning what we need to do." They continued giving him glucose all through the night, and then by the next morning, he was good to go, sitting up eating his breakfast and laughing with his friends who came to see him. So they let him go, and he was well.

When I pray, I say, "In the Name of Jesus," and sometimes I quote Scripture. I know I don't do anything; it is only through the power of the Holy Spirit and Jesus working through me that anything happens. I just call on Him to help us and do what He says He will do in the Word—and He does it. There are so many healing Scriptures in the Bible, from Isaiah all the way through the New Testament. One of His names is Healer. That is one of the things that He does, and He has done it for us. You know that it is the truth in your life when you have seen it happen so many times. You get to know Jesus as a healer. You get to know Him, His personality, and His characteristics, who He is and what He does.

I always thank Him for what He has done. It is so wonderful to know that He cares enough to do that for you; it makes Him very real to you. You can sense His presence. The Word says that faith is the evidence of things hoped for, the substance of things not seen. When you get to see things God does, it builds your faith. Jesus said, "Blessed are those who see and believe, but more blessed are those who do not see and yet believe." You are blessed when you don't see anything and you believe that He is who He says He is because it changes your life. You become different, and you can see an improvement in the real you, in your spiritual self. It changes all of you. But when you see things, it's a blessing too, and it builds faith.

It is key to get quiet before God because there is just so much noise going on all the time. You have to be quiet and get before God and listen. He will tell me things about my children: about situations that they might be getting into, that I need to pray about. When my daughter, Heather, was about sixteen, she was going through a rebellion. God would tell me specific things that I would need to pray. When she would tell me that she was going to a certain place, I would know where she was going instead. The Lord would speak to my heart and tell me where she was going—and it would be people I wouldn't even know. One time, I had to go and get her because she was about to get in trouble, and the Lord showed me where. I didn't even know where that person's house was, but I found her.

I used to listen to Black Sabbath, Pink Floyd, Grand Funk Railroad, Deep Purple, Leon Russell, and the Who, but the Lord told me to get rid of some of my records after I got saved, after I got baptized in the Spirit. I had been listening to all that and was still into it. He spoke to me and said, "You need to get that stuff out of your house." I didn't know why. I didn't know anything about that, so I burned them because I didn't want to take them down to the dumpster, and I didn't want to chop them up. When I burned them, these yells came out. It was a very strange thing. It was like yelling, and it wasn't on any turntable. It was just yells. There are supernatural things in our world; not just your natural things going on. There is a war going on in the spirit realm. A lot of people are firm believers that there is nothing else beyond what we can see. But once you realize, "Hey, there is more going on than we can see with our eyes," it opens up a lot to you.

I first spoke in tongues when I was 23. Friends of ours were telling us, "That's a gift that's for today. That will help you. It will help the Scripture be more alive to you." When you get the baptism of the Holy Spirit, it illuminates the Word, and you are more sensitive to spiritual things. One day, I was reading this Scripture that you should get into your prayer closet and make your requests known, and I literally got in the closet. I started praying and said, "Lord, I see in Your Word that it is Your will to baptize people in the Holy Spirit. I see in Acts here, all these people went and got baptized in the Holy Spirit. I am asking in Jesus' Name for You to baptize me in the Holy Spirit," and I said, "I don't think I'm going to come out of this closet until I have the baptism of the Holy Spirit." Sure enough, I just started praising the Lord. I had my hands up, and I said, "Lord, I praise You. And I thank You for baptizing me in the Holy Spirit."

That was the turning point. When I studied the Bible, it became very real to me. It was more real, whereas it used to be, "I'm going to make myself study this Bible." It wasn't fun. I didn't enjoy it. It was like academia, but after that, I loved it. I wanted to get every translation there was of the

Bible. Now I have fifteen different translations. I could not pass a Bible up without wanting to read it. The Word becomes a part of you. It comes alive. At that point, I was going through a period of discontentment. But when I got baptized into the Spirit, life started making more sense; I got a joy that I didn't have before. When I found out the Good News and the hope that God can give you, and when I was baptized in the Spirit, everything started making sense to me for the first time. There is a purpose here; there is a plan for our lives. If people knew how much fun it is being a Christian, everybody would want to be a Christian. I think that religion has made it look like it is not fun and taken all the joy out of it. But it is fun!

Her daughter, Amber, shares her story . . .

When I was about eight or nine, I had an ear infection. We had gone to the doctor, and I had taken antibiotics, and nothing seemed to be happening. We were watching Benny Hinn, and I was sitting on the couch. I was lying there, and my ears felt like they were really hot. I said, "Mom, something is going on with my ear," and it was burning up. She felt my ear, and it was so hot. Then Benny Hinn said, "Somebody's ear is being healed right now," on the TV and just started praying for me, and my ear got really hot, and the whole side of my arm got hot, my whole left side. It was just burning up, and then it went away. I felt this tingling all over me, and then he said, "Somebody's ear is being healed right now; they just received it." Mom and I were praying, and it went away. My ear was healed.

Then we went to a revival in Pensacola, Florida, and we got slain in the spirit. Wow, it was so great. I was supersensitive; the pastor walked by me and touched my shoulder, and I went wham—just fell on my face. I was out for five minutes; I didn't even know what was going on. When he touched my shoulder it got really warm, and then I closed my eyes and felt like I was floating. It was awesome. It was the biggest sense of peace I have ever had in my life. All I could think about was the presence of God, being at His feet and worshipping Him. It was great. It was like nobody else was there. I couldn't feel anything, and then I started to wake up.

Another time, I heard mom speaking in tongues, and I said, "Mom, what are you doing?" I thought, "That's really cool." She said, "I'm praying in tongues," and I said, "Well, what is that? I want to do it." She told me it is a gift that God gives you; you can receive it if it is God's will to give it to you. I thought, "I want it." So we prayed, and I got the tingling thing again, and it just came out. I didn't want to have the language and not know what it meant. Mom said, "Ask God to translate it for you." You don't want to pray in tongues and not have the translation for what you are saying, so I prayed and said, "God, please tell me what this means, so I can share it with other people." Then it popped in my head, and I wrote it down. He told me what it meant, and it was praise. It was about animals, about God loving His children, and the lion and the lamb being able to get along with each other. That was really cool.

Now I speak in tongues as much as I can. I love doing it. I have heard of people losing it if they don't practice it. From then on, I just did it, whenever I was in a hard situation, felt uneasy about anything, or felt like praising God. During a test at school, that sometimes helps me. I will pray in tongues silently and say, "God, please give me wisdom, so I can remember what I've read." It really comes through sometimes. It's amazing.

One time my best friend, Amy, and I were praying at a concert. She had never really known what it was like to have a relationship with God; she just went to church on Sunday. But she really got intimate with God that weekend, and I put my hand on her back and started praying for her. She said, "Your hand is burning up on my back." I said, "Really?" and she said, "Yeah," and she was crying. It was really cool. I could feel the heat coming out of my hand on her back. She said, "This is so weird." For me, it was cool.

I always have dreams, and sometimes they fulfill things. The day before my friend, Erin, got in a car accident, I dreamed that she was in a bad wreck. I was at a funeral in my dream, and I was crying, and I woke up crying. I rebuked the devil and said, "I bind you, Satan, from over my friend, and I put the blood of Jesus over her." I said, "I bind death from over her in Jesus' Name." The next day she did get in a wreck, but she didn't die. Erin is a miracle in herself. They had the wreck, she woke up, and the seat where her little sister had been was empty. She started screaming, and she was wondering why people weren't trying to get her out of the car. It is because they had taken her pulse, and she didn't have one. They thought, "She's dead." There was blood everywhere. She did not have a pulse for three or four minutes, but she had no brain damage from that. They were just attending to her little sister because they thought Erin was dead. The helicopter paramedics came to pick them up and take them to the hospital. They had called the mortician to come get Erin and had told the helicopter to go, but then Erin started screaming. They turned the helicopter around to come back and get her. Her leg was broken in three places. She is on crutches; her femur bone was shattered, but she is walking. She will be going back to school when it starts up again after the holidays.

God just spared her. She was in a little white Ford Contour, and it was wrapped around a tree like an accordion. The man who got Erin out of the car said that he had never seen a wreck that bad that anybody survived. Erin was stuck in it; it was around the tree, and they had to cut her out. Somehow I was forewarned about it, and we believe that God spared her life supernaturally. There is something that she is destined to do, and it hadn't been carried out at fifteen years old. She told me that she is really excited about how strong her testimony is going to be now. Her dad had been a non-believer, and she told me, "Amber, my daddy is praying for me; he is praying for me!" She said, "I would do it all over again, if it meant my daddy would pray. Now that I have gotten in this wreck, He has to look to God."

Patricia is in her 40's, and Amber is in her teens; they were interviewed by Andrew Cousins in the spring of 2002. Both are white and members of a non-denominational congregation.

Healing is a Spiritual Matter
–Colin and Cathy Winn

Colin begins his story . . .

I was involved in an automobile accident on my way home from work on a Friday afternoon. I was rear-ended by the car behind me at about sixty miles an hour. I was driving a pickup truck at the time, and even though I had my seatbelt on, my head went through the back window. I got bounced around, and at first, after everything stopped, I just felt very dazed and rattled from everything. It was a pretty violent crash; both vehicles were totaled. When I started to get up out of the truck, one of the other men who was there said, "Oh, my God, he's bleeding," and I was. My head was cut up, and I was trying to get out of the truck. My wife, Cathy, had to come get me. EMS was there, and they went ahead and let Cathy take me to the emergency room. I was very sore and having little glitches of head problems, but as each day went by, I got worse and worse. I tried to go to work on Monday; I was only there for a very brief period. I couldn't remember how to turn my computer on, let alone operate it.

At the emergency room, I had been listed as having a severe whiplash and a mild concussion. They just wanted us to check with our family doctor. The earliest appointment we could get was the Thursday following the accident. On Monday, when I came home from work, I was very disoriented: having trouble trying to understand and process. Progressively, it was getting worse and worse. Wednesday morning I tried to go to work again, and that's when it really got bad. I was having stroke-like symptoms; my speech was becoming incredibly slurred. I lost the use of my left side. My foot was turned and dragging, so I called to tell my wife, "I'm coming home; call the doctor. I'm coming now, and if they can't see us, we are going to the emergency room." We went to the doctor, and she couldn't figure out what was wrong either. I explained to her what had happened, and she immediately called a neurologist and scheduled for him to see me that day. We went over there, and he was pretty concerned.

They started scheduling all kinds of tests at the hospital and said, "You're not going back to work; don't even think about that." We went through the tests with the MRI. Nothing showed up. Then we had the EEG; nothing showed up, doing all the different tests. The doctor came back and told us that it appeared that I had a closed head traumatic brain injury. After the testing, they immediately wanted to admit me for therapy. The tests came back that I was considerably below average. Everything was slow: my speech was slow, my thinking was slow, my reasoning was slow. Being able to understand my environment had slowed. I couldn't go out in public without having anxiety attacks because I couldn't understand what was going on. I was losing the ability to communicate with people.

They determined later that instead of just having the one injury to the back of my head when I went backward, I also went up into the cab of the truck and had impact with the top, and then I went forward, and either the rearview mirror came down and hit me in the forehead, or I went into it. I had three separate impacts to my skull. The damage in the brain was so scattered that it was causing all kinds of problems, like motor skills, endurance, speech, vision, and understanding—as far as comprehension of things, being able to reason, to calculate. I was losing my math skills. What used to be regarded as daily functions, I had lost. I would forget to brush my teeth, things that you know automatically. My wife would have to say, "You need to go get a shower." I wouldn't think of it; I was in this dazed state.

I started different therapies: physical therapy, speech therapy, occupational therapy. At this point, I was told by the neurologist that there is nothing we can do medically or surgically. What you are now is who you will be. The best thing to do is forget about the other person. He is gone. He is not going to be there. I found out later that they took my wife aside and asked her if she had good insurance, and if she had ever thought about going back into the workforce because the husband she had was gone forever. Then they set up another EEG and did an arteriogram, trying to see if anything was starting to show up through the different tests. Everything kept coming back negative. They were saying that there is so much separation of all the fibers in the brain where all the messages are transferred that the brain is not able to function. It was misfiring on everything. They tried to teach me how to cheat my brain. In other words, this is your condition, but you can get around some of the problems and become functional to a certain extent. I resisted a lot of it because I didn't want to accept it. But gradually, over time, you start powering down; you start accepting that this is the way you are going to be. You don't like it, but you are getting constant reinforcement of "You can't, you can't." After about six months, I was getting really down. I saw that everything that I had worked for, everything I had in life, was over. It was gone. I was at a crossroads, and I knew that if I didn't hurry up and get back to work, I was going to be replaced. They had already gracefully tried to keep the position open for six months.

I still had memory; I had memories of me. I knew me before. This new me I didn't know; I was a stranger to myself. I didn't like it. At the same time that I knew what I was able to do before and had understanding of it, holes were also created in my old memory, and I couldn't remember certain things. If you were to come by during an evening, by the time I went to bed, I might not remember anything we said. I wouldn't be able to retain that memory. Having so much information to manage at work, there was no way I would be able to do my job. All this was going to be gone. My wife had to drop me off over at rehab because I couldn't even drive a vehicle.

There was one particular day when I was really down and depressed. It was on a Friday, and I had just failed a driver's evaluation with the hospital. They gave me a test to see if I could qualify to go for a test for driving. I didn't make it halfway through, and the lady said, "Let's just stop." I failed that miserably, just trying to see if I could get a shot trying to get my license. My wife said, "What's wrong with you today? You really seem depressed." I said, "I'm losing everything." She said, "Come on, we're going home, and we're going to pray." I said, "We've been praying. We've got people everywhere praying. I'm on prayer chains. I'm on prayer walls. I'm getting tired; we're praying coast-to-coast, and nothing's happened yet." She said, "Today is going to be different."

Colin's wife, Cathy, continues their story . . .

We had a conflict: the conflict was that my husband was being programmed to look at things logically, while I was using my faith in God and what I perceived God was still going to do. From the very beginning, when I would pray, I felt as if the Lord was saying that this was all for a testimony. I didn't know the big picture, but I believed that my husband would be back. Then Colin would come in telling me, "The old Colin is dead and gone. Don't look for me." I would get frustrated; I didn't want to come against everything they were saying, but I didn't want him to give up. Before the accident he and I both had very strong faith, but after the accident, that part of his brain did not work anymore. It was gone, and he would tell me, "I still believe in God, and I believe everything, but you have to pray for me now."

We had people all over the United States praying. We were getting letters from Florida, Georgia, Utah, just everywhere. His life was touching people. We were getting well-wishers sending prayers. However, he was about to lose his job because he couldn't come back. He had had a very demanding position at a very large company. It is a significant operation, and his position is key to the equipment sales. He handles a lot of information, as well as seeing that it gets to the appropriate people. All of a sudden he can't even do things in the kitchen or brush his teeth. How is he going to handle this information? If he was instructed to do something, he could follow through. But he could not initiate on his own. He was very complacent. If you said, "Colin, go do this," Colin would do it. But for him to sit there and think, "I should probably do this," that didn't work. If you asked him a question, he would respond back. But if you talked to him in conversation, he would not engage.

When I took him to therapy that Friday, I knew he was really bad. At times, he had regressed to where I had a four- or five-year-old child again. I felt like I had lost my husband, and I had this small child, yet he was a forty-year-old man. It was very trying to keep a balance and respect him as my husband, but treat him like my son. He was really down that Friday, so when I took him to therapy that morning, I made up my mind. He is going to be over there for several hours. When I get back home, I am hitting the knees, and it is going to be prayer time. This time I am going to get some answers.

All along the way we had been having all kinds of different prayers: alone, together, with churches, with other people. But there is always a time and a place for everything, a time for something to begin and a time for it to end. That day, he had done about all he could do; we had been through all of our ups and downs, and I said, "I'm tired of it too, Lord. I want Your will to be done, but please, let's get on with it." That day was it; I just knew it. Everything was clicking. I knew after I let Colin out that I had to go home and I had to pray. I was going to pray until something was accomplished.

So I came home. I started praying, and I went out in this spiritual thing, and when I "woke up," it was several hours later. I don't know exactly what was said, what I prayed, what I saw or did not see, or what was going on. But when I came back to myself, I knew that today something was changing, that this was it. On the way over to get Colin, I kept hearing this thing in my head, and it kept saying, "Time's up. This has been for a certain time, and time is up," and I knew that was spiritually sound. My spiritual self knew this. I picked Colin up, and he was worse than he had been. I thought to myself, "I will not believe this." This is not what I was getting from my Lord a little bit ago. Something is changing today.

I can't tell you how I felt when he came dragging out for me to pick him up. I thought, "Where is it? Time's up!" It wasn't, and that infuriated my spirit. I drove home mad. I didn't feel like God had failed me. I felt like somewhere between me and God and the healing, Satan had interfered. I won't even say Satan; let's say some kind of block got in the way. I felt, "I know what I know, and this is not going to hinder it. It is nothing I can do. It is a promise; it is something I know from God, and it is going to be. I am upset. I am mad at this now. When we get home, we are going into prayer again." When I know what I know, I know it isn't just me. It is not a confidence I have in myself, but a higher power—and then you can get out of my way! Nobody is going to tell me different; I have felt that way my whole life. There is not only healing; God makes provision for us in every aspect of our lives, and that is what we have to learn to do: to trust Him in everything. Whether my husband was healed or not wasn't the biggest issue. The biggest issue was that I had confidence in God, and no matter what happened, He was in control of it. Nobody else and nothing else could change that.

We get home, and our son who still lives with us came in from work too. I told them, "We are going to pray as a family." We got into soul-searching, gut-wrenching, down-and-dirty prayer as far as really baring our souls. I looked at Colin when we had finished praying, and his eyes were still foggy; they had been foggy ever since his brain injury. You couldn't get the clear sparkle, the "You see me, I see you; we understand" look. It was never there. The Bible says that your eyes are the windows to your soul, and I looked at him, and there was no change, and that infuriated my spirit. I said, "Hold it; we're going to pray again." So we joined hands, and we all started praying. This time, when we opened our eyes and I looked at Colin, there was a little bit of light starting to come into his eyes. I could see the difference. Colin felt somewhat better, so my son and I got together. I told him, "Watch your dad; something's happening." I could see it, and I wanted him to see it too because our son also is a good Christian. As the day went on, my husband was feeling a little better. His face had some tone showing, and he was smiling more, and he started using his hand. He wasn't aware of it, but we were watching him. We were going to watch him all weekend to see what would happen.

Colin continues . . .

We went through the evening and around the house like we normally do and ended up going to bed that evening. But the big thing was Saturday morning, waking up. When I woke up Saturday morning and laid there on the bed and opened my eyes, I could tell right then it was different, genuinely different. Things were faster for me, as far as being able to understand. I could tell a change had happened. I didn't say anything at first; I didn't want to. I wanted Cathy to be able to take it in and recognize. She did right away.

Saturday was a very active day for me. I was not back all the way at that point, but you could tell something was happening. On Sunday, I was making phone calls and telling people. Also on Sunday, I started to get this weird sensation in my head. It wasn't constant. It just came and went. It was like something was moving. Nothing was crawling around in my head, but something was moving, and it would come for a while and then it would leave. Each time it would leave, I was faster and sharper. I understood better, and then it would level off, and I would level off. Hours later, it might start again; it would happen two or three times during the day. It went on like that for about two weeks, and each time it would happen, I would be a little bit sharper or a little bit clearer. I was starting to be able to get back into what felt like me again.

When I went back to rehab the following week, my speech therapist—I remember this very well—said, "You're going to have to tell me what happened. You left here Friday one way, and you come in today a completely different man. What has happened? We don't see this." Everybody at rehab, all the therapists who were working with me, were making different comments through the course of the week. They were trying to find out what happened, and I told them about what went on Friday as far as the prayer, and how I woke up Saturday, and I literally woke up! My brain was awake; I had come out of that sleepy-daze state. I was telling this story, and one occupational therapist responded, "Isn't it wonderful what you have when you give the person the right motivation?" I said, "What motivation? I couldn't do this. If it had been that easy for me to turn it around, I would have done it months ago. It wasn't in me to be able to do it." We had some heated discussions because I was introducing God into an environment where they try to keep it capped. It got a little bit heated, but I didn't care; I was too excited. One of the good things was that I was smiling. Everybody was talking about it: "You never smiled. Now you're smiling." I said, "I have reasons to smile." It wasn't that I frowned all the time, but my facial muscles didn't want to work.

Motor skills and muscular responses hadn't been there, and all of a sudden, they were coming back. I had Cathy take me by the office, and I talked to them. At that point, it was very early on with the healing taking place, and some of them were trying to be pleasant and cordial. They told me later that they didn't believe it because I was still stumbling. My speech was still off, and I was having trouble. I was getting very winded. But they didn't know how bad I had become; only one person had come by the house. "I'm coming back," I said. They thought, "He won't be able to do his job," and I found out that they were in the process of replacing me. That made me all the more determined to get back. I started going in to work before my time at therapy. I spent an hour here and there, starting to get things around my desk updated, trying to show them I am coming back. I found out later that that was the only thing that kept me from being replaced. He is showing an interest. He is making an attempt. Let's see what he can do. Let's give him a little bit more time.

Because the turnaround for me was so dramatic at rehab, they went ahead and called to see about getting me scheduled for another driver's exam. The lady at the hospital said, "It's just been a little over two weeks. He failed it. I don't think he is going to be ready." They just said, "Let him try because you will be impressed." We got started doing the same test, and the lady said, "I can't believe this." She said, "You're doing so well. Do you have time to go for a driver's test right now? I have an opening in my schedule, if you have the time. Let's put you on the road and see what you do." I drove her all over, and she said, "You are perfect." At that point, she cleared me for driving, whereas a little over two weeks earlier I had failed miserably.

The healing has been ongoing. I don't have that little feeling in my head anymore. It only lasted a little over two weeks, but each time I was better. At times, there is doubt, and I have problems, and other times it comes back, and I do better. But those times of being down are less. Times of being improved, of getting more like me, are more frequent. I am well on my way back. At work, I am doing 100% of what I used to do. It was decided that my performance would determine if they would keep me, and they did. I have been instrumental in a lot of the changes that have been taking place around there and taking on a lot of responsibility to make it happen. A year ago people wouldn't give me a chance.

Long before the accident, early on in our marriage, both of us were very devout as far as our beliefs. We were very dedicated. It is not just in a church setting but something that we live and participate in and practice. For Cathy to come home when she is overwhelmed by something and go before the Lord with it is a common thing. It was part of our life. If there were issues between the two of us, we would pray. If it was something about somebody else, we would pray. Healing is a spiritual matter; a lot of people want to look at it as physical because the symptoms are physical. But healing is spiritual. All the time we are trying to work in a physical sense with physical remedies, and we leave out the most important element of all.

Colin and Cathy were interviewed by Sue Heiney in July of 2002. Both are white, in their 40's, and members of a non-denominational congregation.

Made in the USA
Lexington, KY
13 December 2011